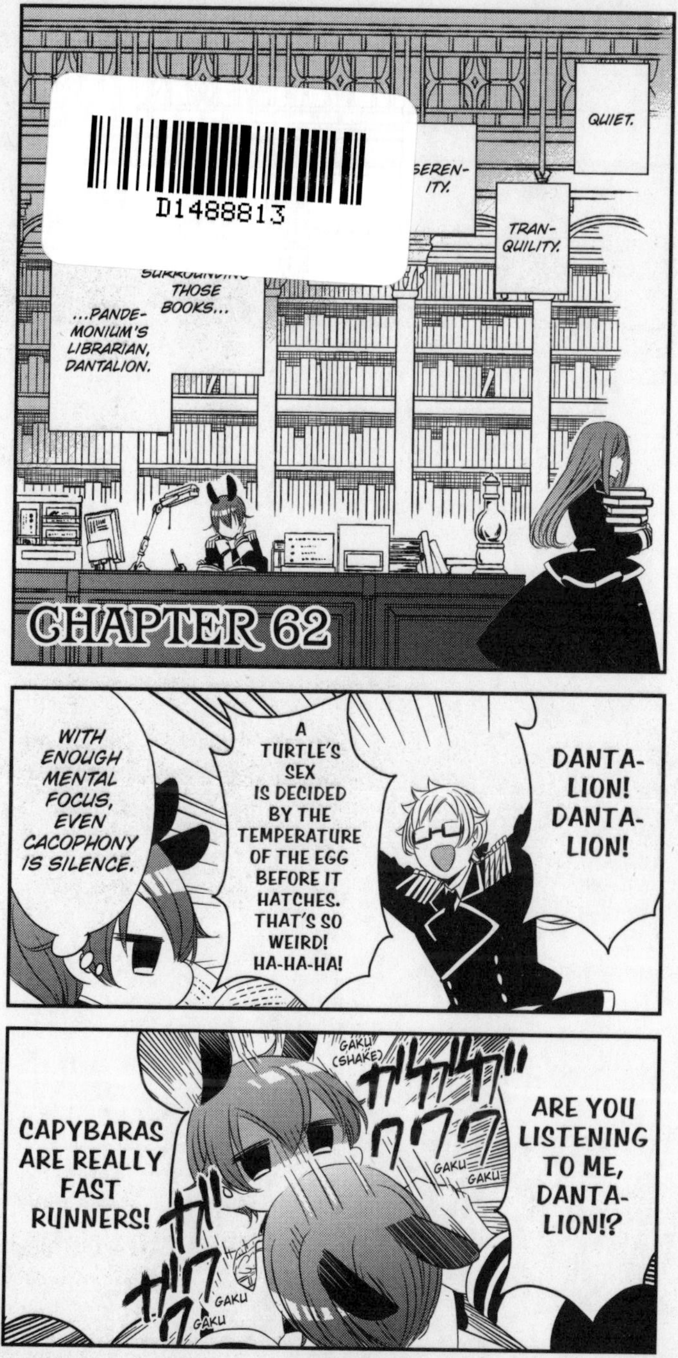
QUIET.
SEREN-ITY.
TRAN-QUILITY.
THOSE BOOKS...
...PANDE-MONIUM'S LIBRARIAN, DANTALION.
CHAPTER 62
DANTA-LION! DANTA-LION!
A TURTLE'S SEX IS DECIDED BY THE TEMPERATURE OF THE EGG BEFORE IT HATCHES. THAT'S SO WEIRD! HA-HA-HA!
WITH ENOUGH MENTAL FOCUS, EVEN CACOPHONY IS SILENCE.
ARE YOU LISTENING TO ME, DANTA-LION!?
GAKU (SHAKE)
GAKU GAKU
CAPYBARAS ARE REALLY FAST RUNNERS!
GAKU GAKU

(PHYSICAL) CACOPHONY

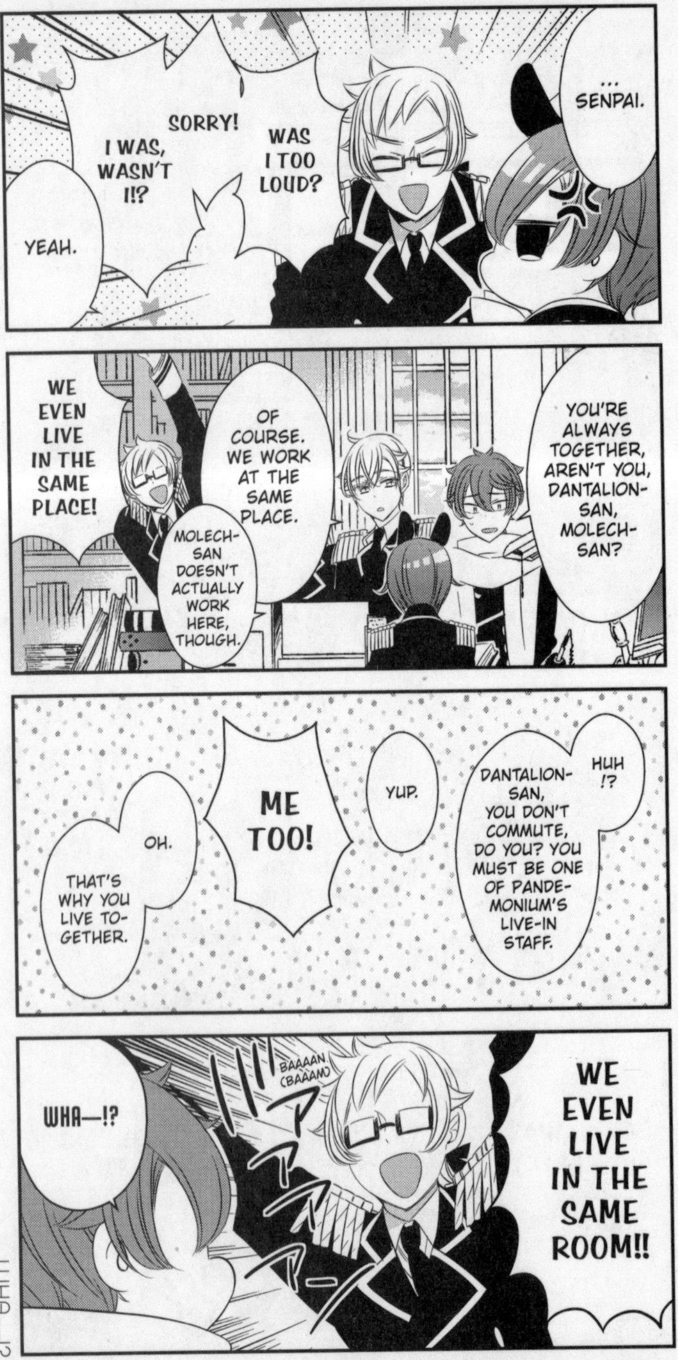
...SENPAI.
SORRY! WAS I TOO LOUD?
I WAS, WASN'T I!?
YEAH.
YOU'RE ALWAYS TOGETHER, AREN'T YOU, DANTALION-SAN, MOLECH-SAN?
OF COURSE. WE WORK AT THE SAME PLACE.
MOLECH-SAN DOESN'T ACTUALLY WORK HERE, THOUGH.
WE EVEN LIVE IN THE SAME PLACE!
HUH!?
DANTALION-SAN, YOU DON'T COMMUTE, DO YOU? YOU MUST BE ONE OF PANDEMONIUM'S LIVE-IN STAFF.
YUP.
ME TOO!
OH.
THAT'S WHY YOU LIVE TOGETHER.
WE EVEN LIVE IN THE SAME ROOM!!
BAAAAN (BAAAN)
WHA—!?

WHA—!?

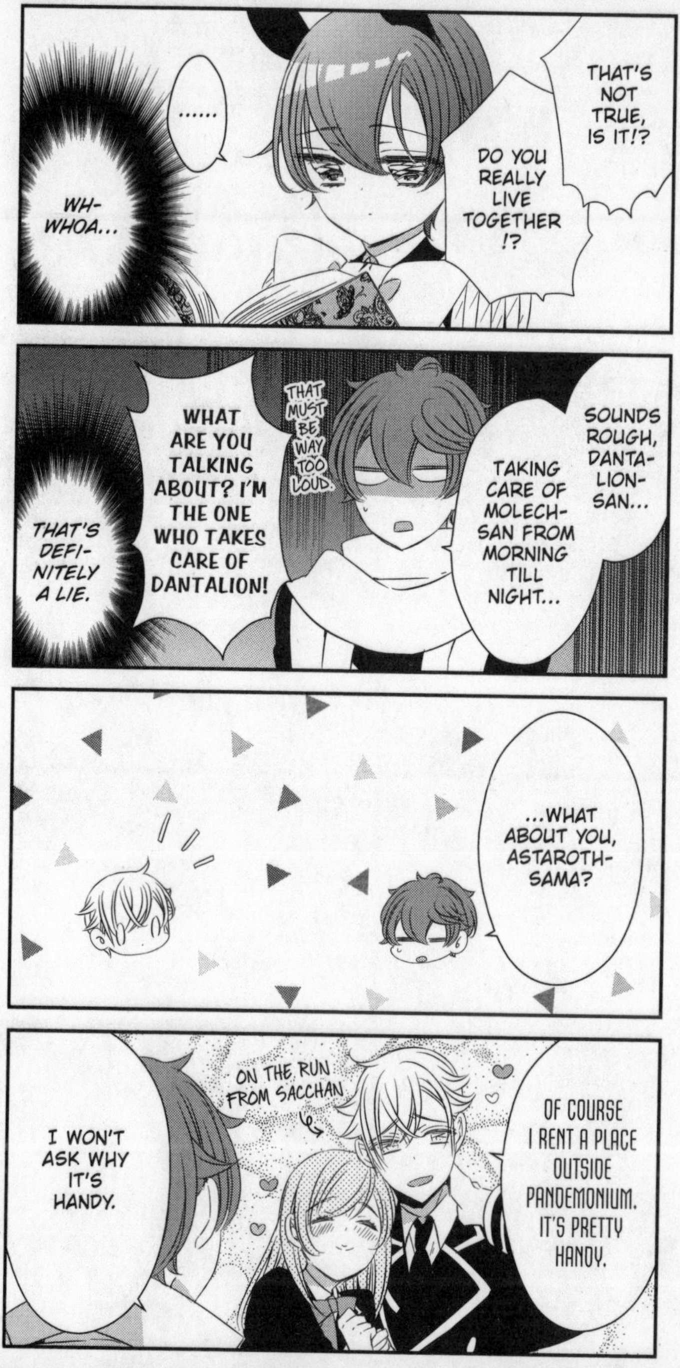
THAT'S NOT TRUE, IS IT!?
DO YOU REALLY LIVE TOGETHER !?
......
WH- WHOA...
SOUNDS ROUGH, DANTA-LION-SAN...
TAKING CARE OF MOLECH-SAN FROM MORNING TILL NIGHT...
THAT MUST BE WAY TOO LOUD.
WHAT ARE YOU TALKING ABOUT? I'M THE ONE WHO TAKES CARE OF DANTALION!
THAT'S DEFI-NITELY A LIE.
...WHAT ABOUT YOU, ASTAROTH-SAMA?
OF COURSE I RENT A PLACE OUTSIDE PANDEMONIUM. IT'S PRETTY HANDY.
ON THE RUN FROM SACCHAN
I WON'T ASK WHY IT'S HANDY.

I'LL PRETEND I DIDN'T HEAR THAT

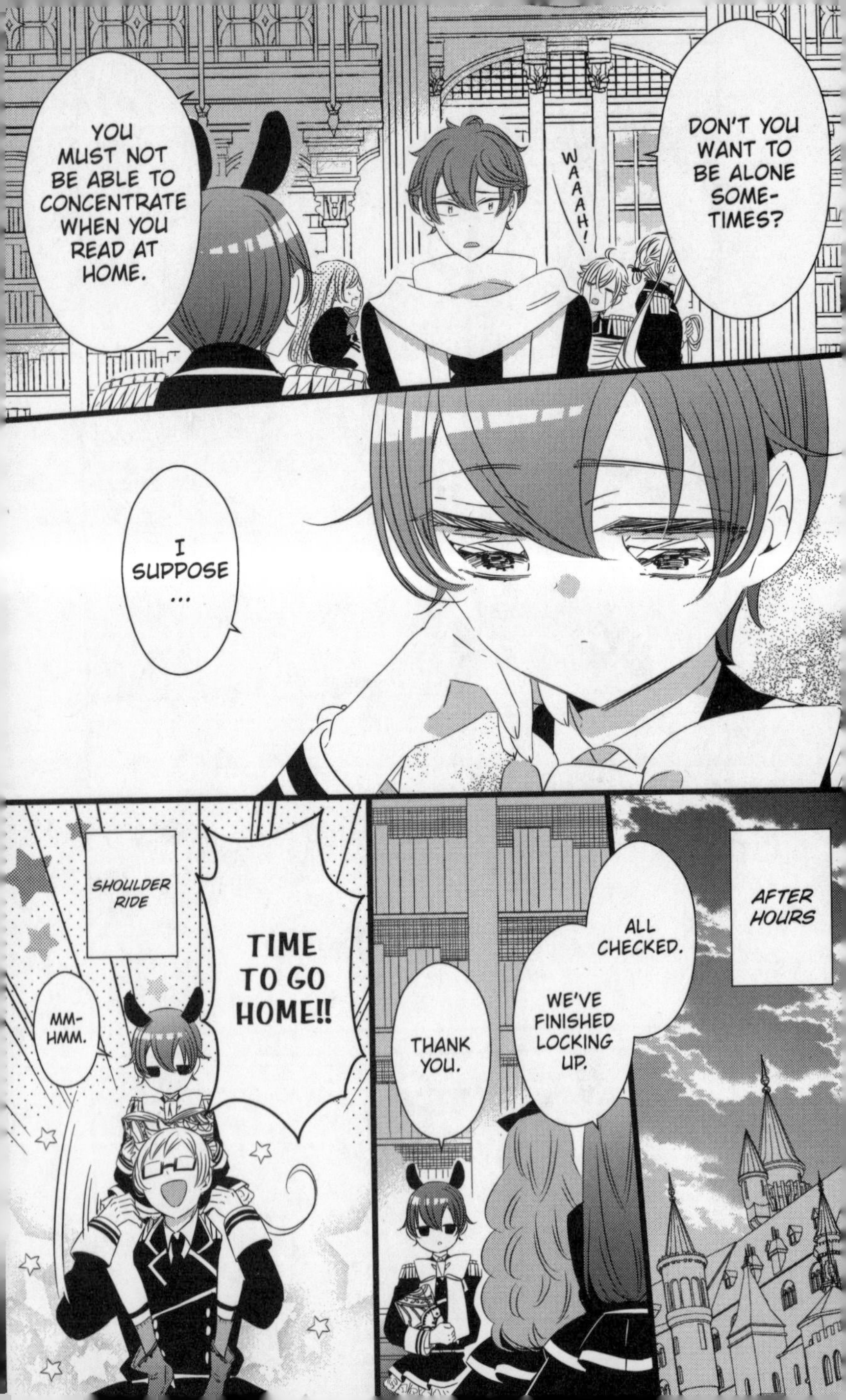
DON'T YOU WANT TO BE ALONE SOME-TIMES?
WAAAAH!
YOU MUST NOT BE ABLE TO CONCENTRATE WHEN YOU READ AT HOME.
I SUPPOSE ...
AFTER HOURS
ALL CHECKED.
WE'VE FINISHED LOCKING UP.
THANK YOU.
TIME TO GO HOME!!
SHOULDER RIDE
MM-HMM.

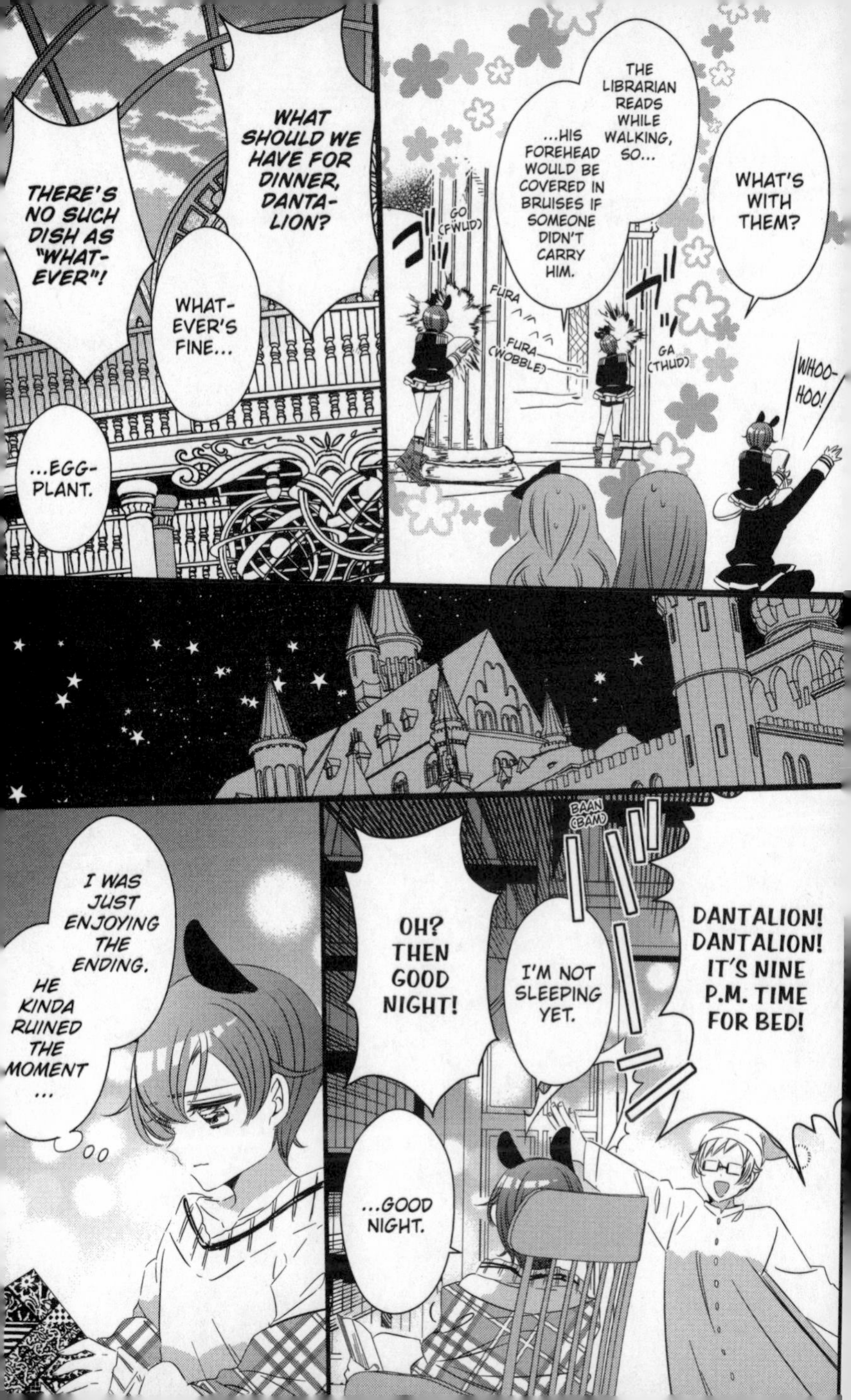
WHAT'S WITH THEM?
THE LIBRARIAN READS WHILE WALKING, SO...
...HIS FOREHEAD WOULD BE COVERED IN BRUISES IF SOMEONE DIDN'T CARRY HIM.
GA (THUD)
GO (FWUD)
FURA
FURA (WOBBLE)
WHOO-HOO!
WHAT SHOULD WE HAVE FOR DINNER, DANTALION?
WHATEVER'S FINE...
THERE'S NO SUCH DISH AS "WHATEVER"!
...EGGPLANT.
BAAN (BAM)
DANTALION! DANTALION! IT'S NINE P.M. TIME FOR BED!
I'M NOT SLEEPING YET.
OH? THEN GOOD NIGHT!
...GOOD NIGHT.
I WAS JUST ENJOYING THE ENDING.
HE KINDA RUINED THE MOMENT...

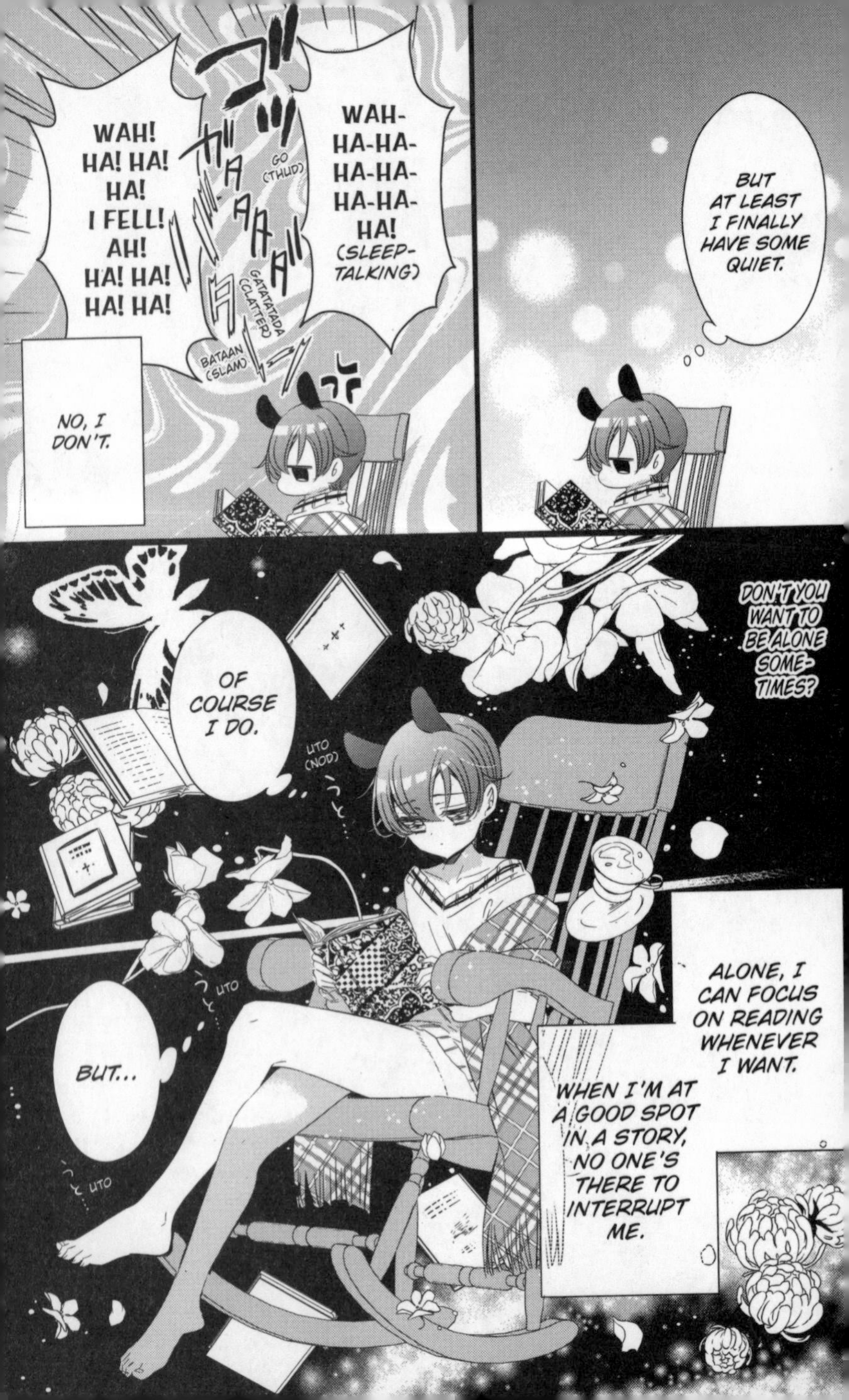
BUT AT LEAST I FINALLY HAVE SOME QUIET.
WAH-HA-HA-HA-HA-HA-HA-HA! (SLEEP-TALKING)
GO (THUD)
GATATATADA (CLATTER)
WAH! HA! HA! HA! I FELL! AH! HA! HA! HA! HA!
BATAAN (SLAM)
NO, I DON'T.
DON'T YOU WANT TO BE ALONE SOME-TIMES?
OF COURSE I DO.
UTO (NOD)
ALONE, I CAN FOCUS ON READING WHENEVER I WANT.
WHEN I'M AT A GOOD SPOT IN A STORY, NO ONE'S THERE TO INTERRUPT ME.
UTO
BUT...
UTO

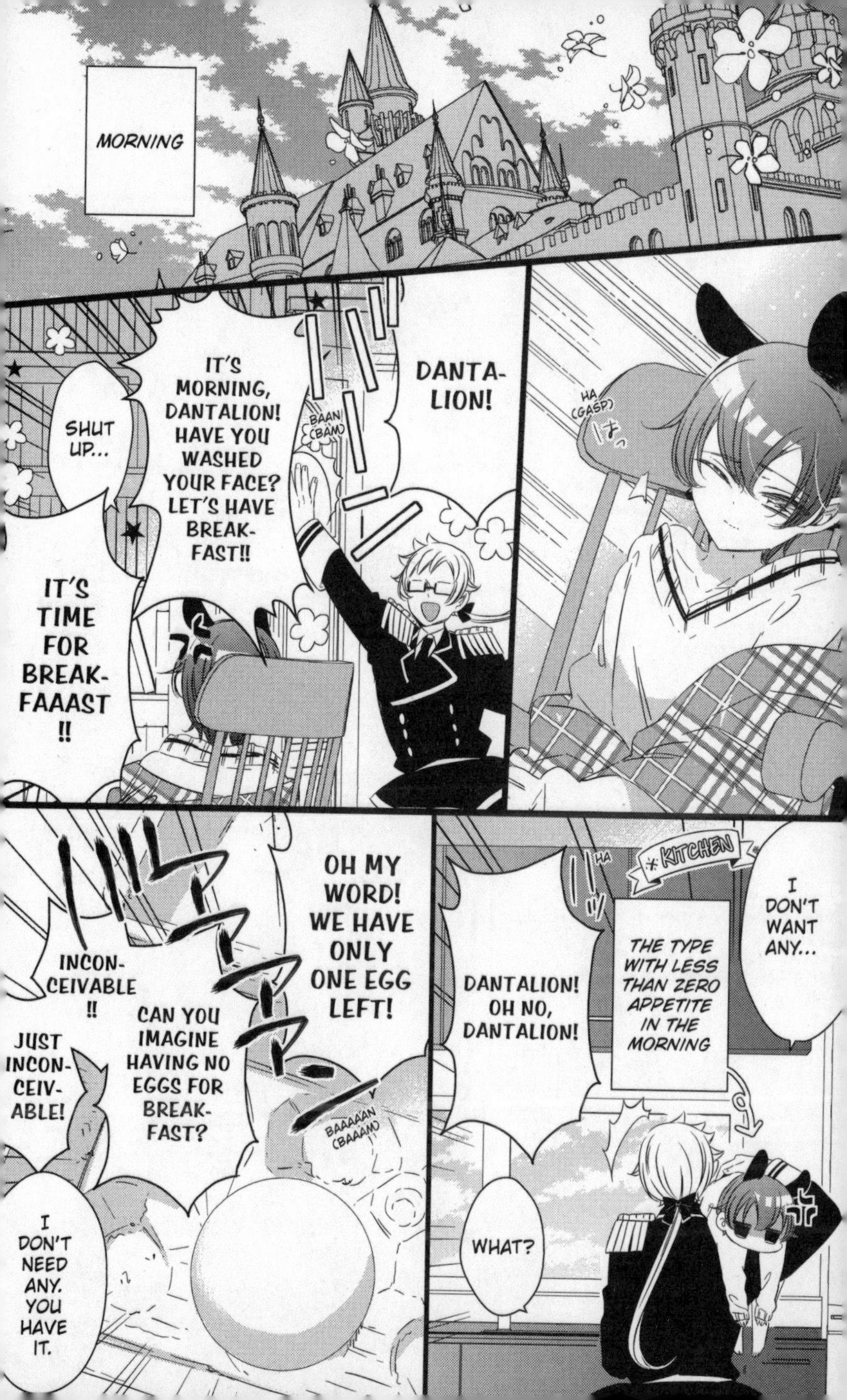
MORNING
HA (GASP)
DANTALION!
BAAN (BAM)
IT'S MORNING, DANTALION! HAVE YOU WASHED YOUR FACE? LET'S HAVE BREAKFAST!!
SHUT UP...
IT'S TIME FOR BREAKFAAAST!!
KITCHEN
I DON'T WANT ANY...
HA
THE TYPE WITH LESS THAN ZERO APPETITE IN THE MORNING
DANTALION! OH NO, DANTALION!
WHAT?
OH MY WORD! WE HAVE ONLY ONE EGG LEFT!
INCONCEIVABLE!!
CAN YOU IMAGINE HAVING NO EGGS FOR BREAKFAST?
JUST INCONCEIVABLE!
BAAAAAN (BAAAM)
I DON'T NEED ANY. YOU HAVE IT.

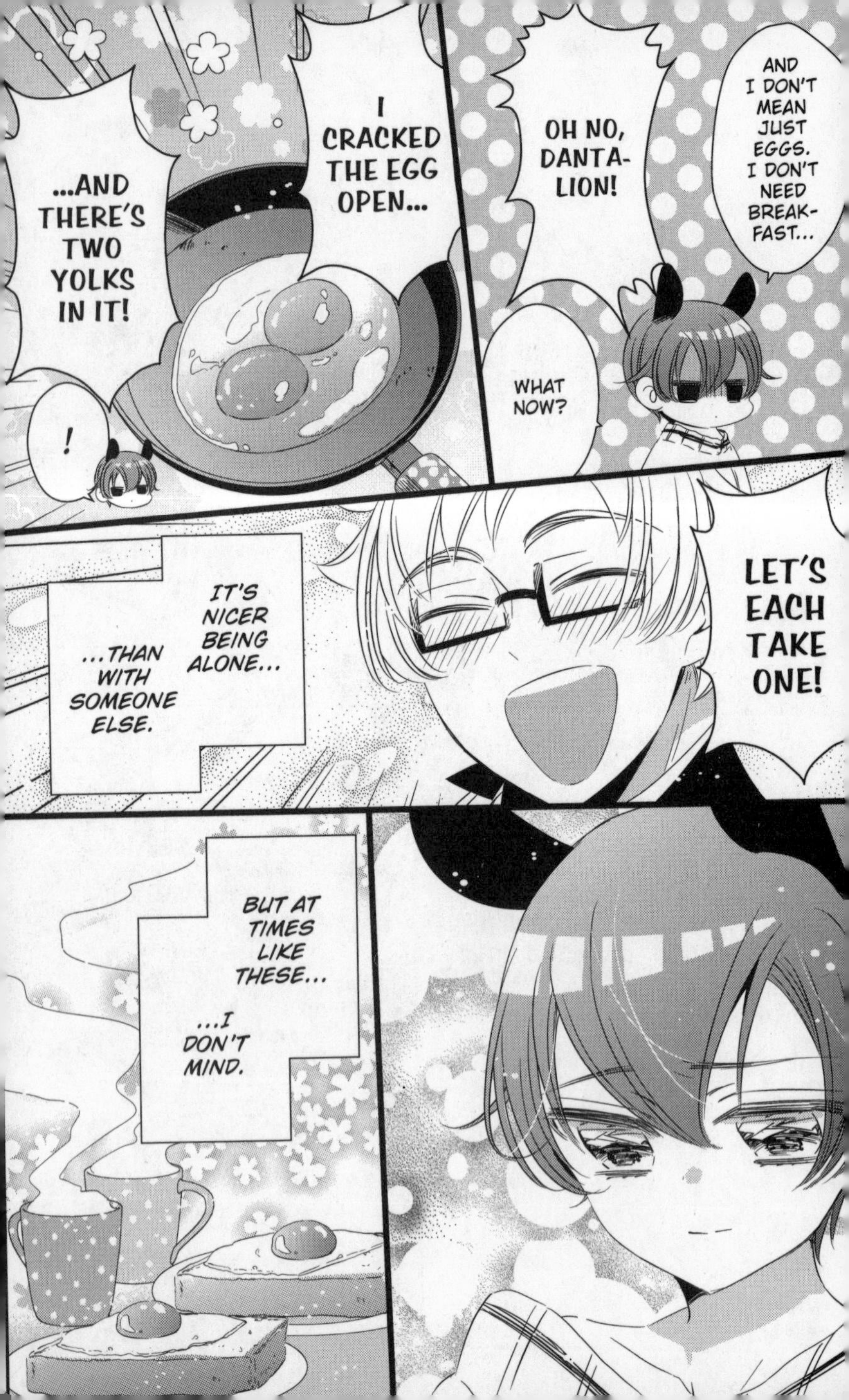
AND I DON'T MEAN JUST EGGS. I DON'T NEED BREAK-FAST...
OH NO, DANTA-LION!
WHAT NOW?
I CRACKED THE EGG OPEN...
...AND THERE'S TWO YOLKS IN IT!
!
LET'S EACH TAKE ONE!
IT'S NICER BEING ALONE...
...THAN WITH SOMEONE ELSE.
BUT AT TIMES LIKE THESE...
...I DON'T MIND.

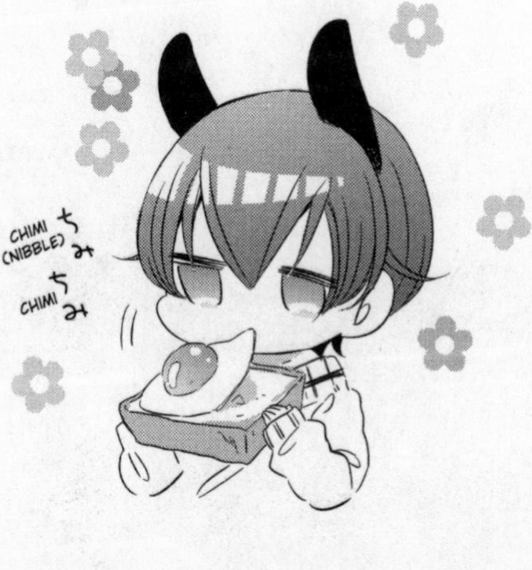
CHIMI (NIBBLE) ちみ
CHIMI ちみ

As Miss Beelzebub Likes

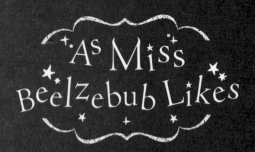

CHAPTER 63

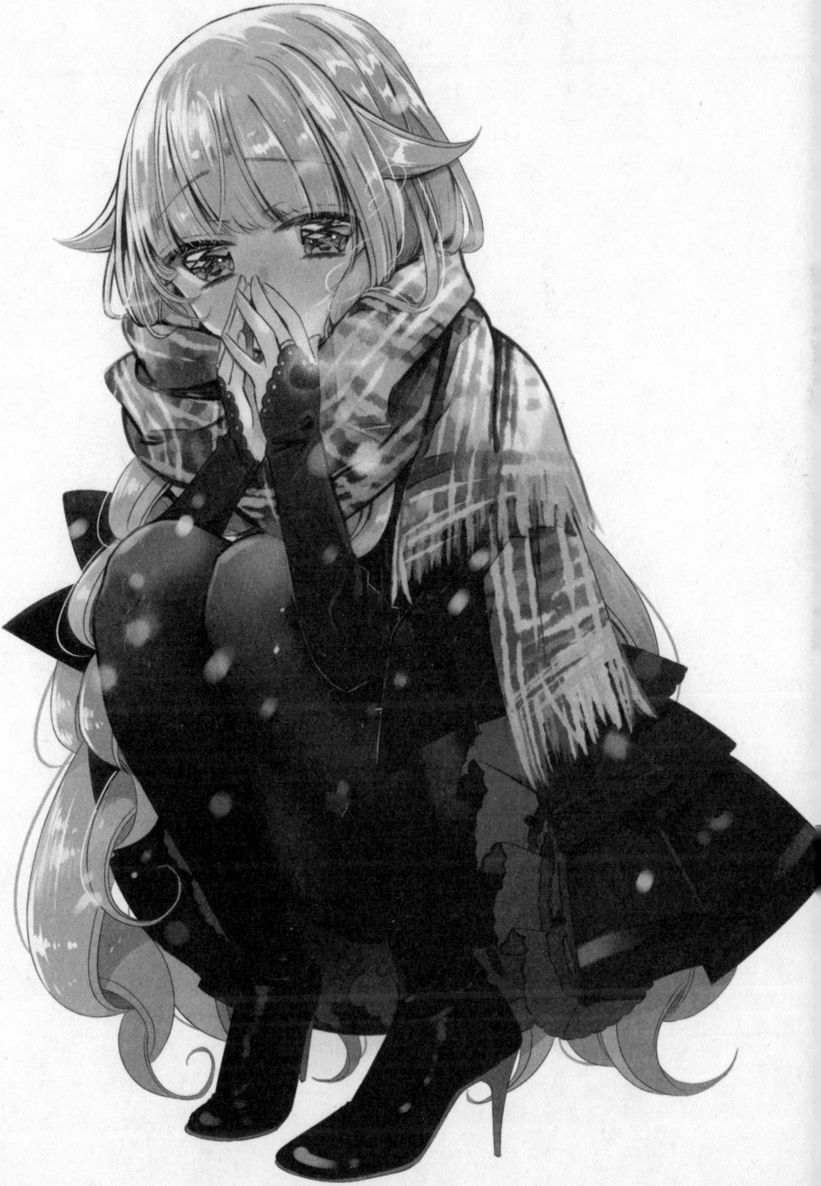

As Miss Beelzebub Likes

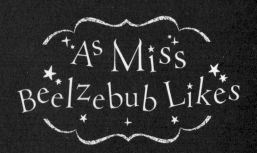

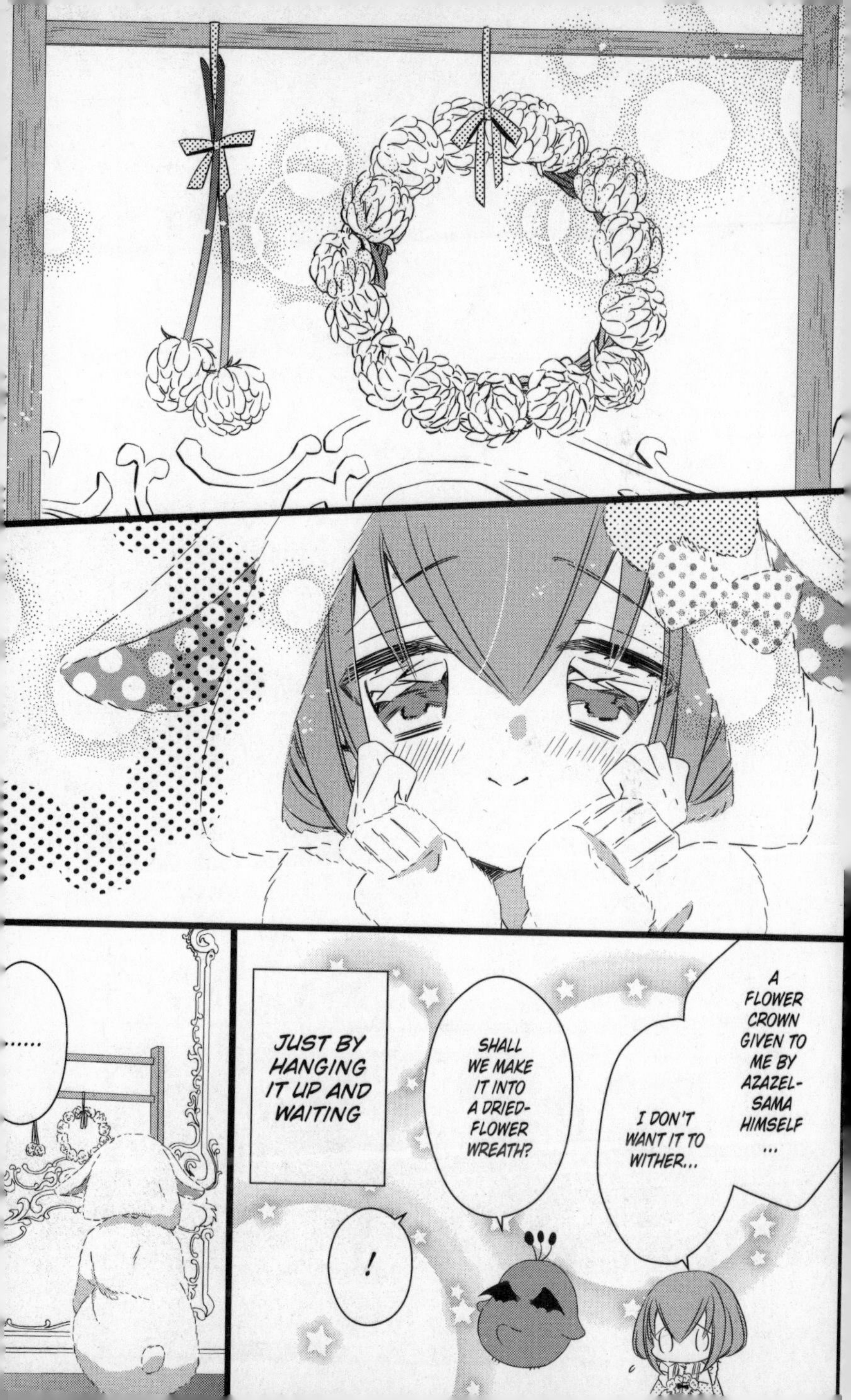
A FLOWER CROWN GIVEN TO ME BY AZAZEL-SAMA HIMSELF ...
I DON'T WANT IT TO WITHER...
SHALL WE MAKE IT INTO A DRIED-FLOWER WREATH?
JUST BY HANGING IT UP AND WAITING
!
......

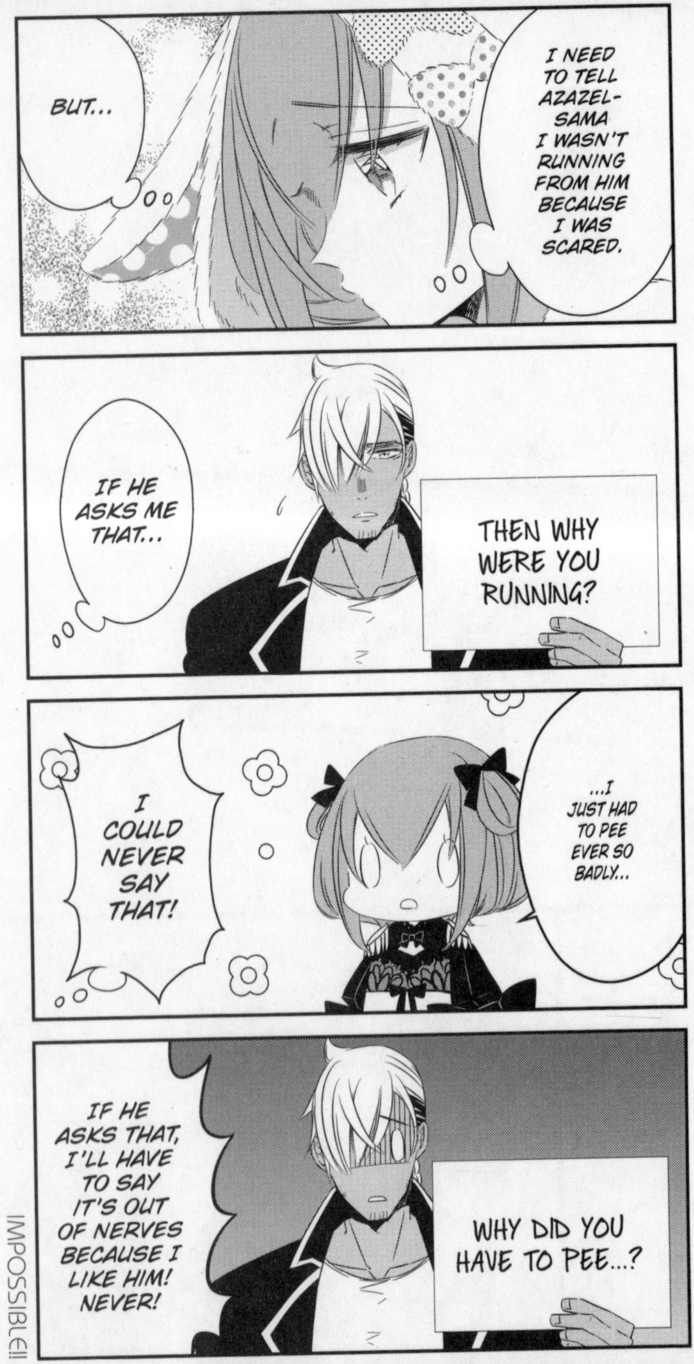
I NEED TO TELL AZAZEL-SAMA I WASN'T RUNNING FROM HIM BECAUSE I WAS SCARED.
BUT...
THEN WHY WERE YOU RUNNING?
IF HE ASKS ME THAT...
...I JUST HAD TO PEE EVER SO BADLY...
I COULD NEVER SAY THAT!
WHY DID YOU HAVE TO PEE...?
IF HE ASKS THAT, I'LL HAVE TO SAY IT'S OUT OF NERVES BECAUSE I LIKE HIM! NEVER!
IMPOSSIBLE!!

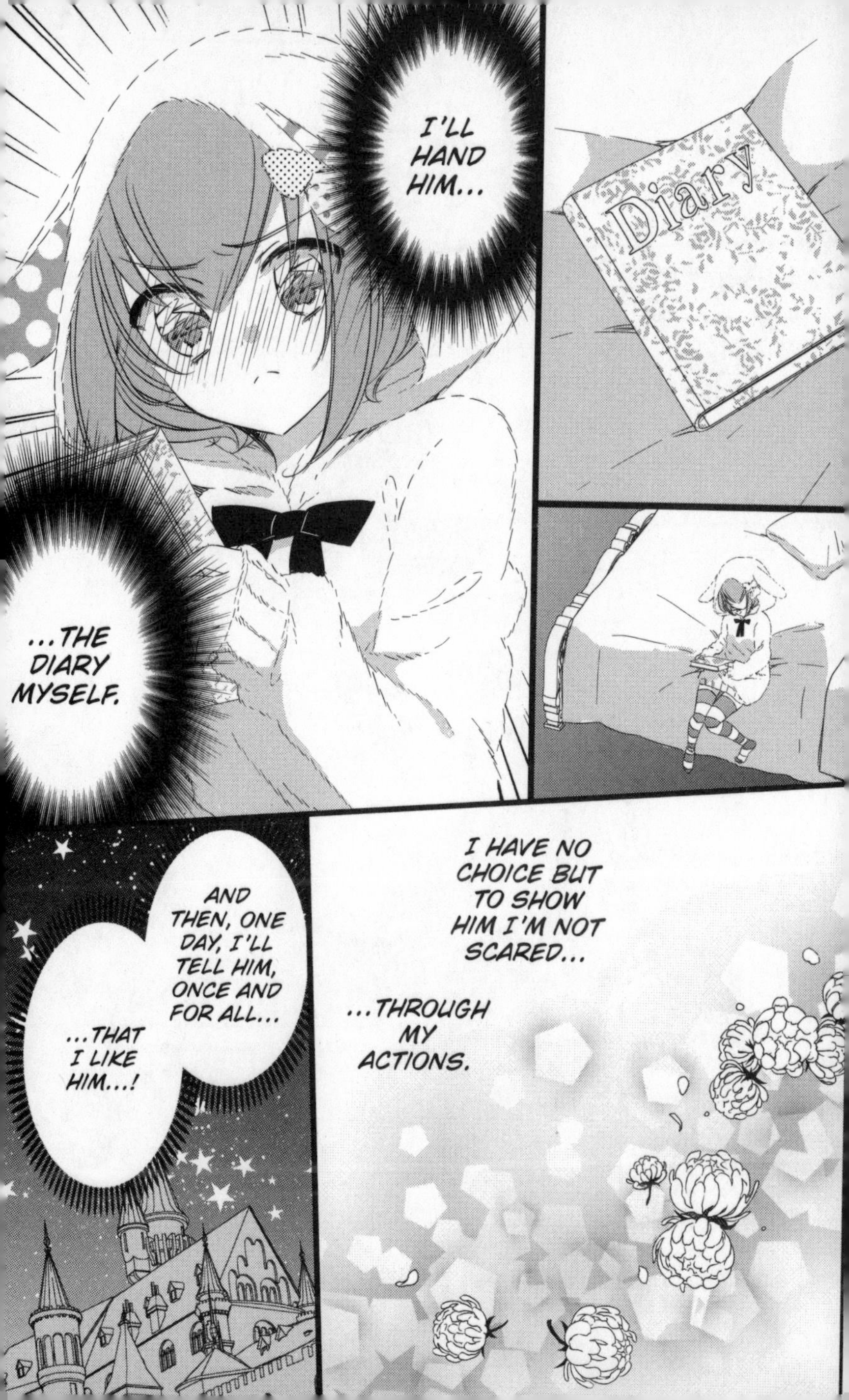
Diary
I'LL HAND HIM...
...THE DIARY MYSELF.
I HAVE NO CHOICE BUT TO SHOW HIM I'M NOT SCARED...
...THROUGH MY ACTIONS.
AND THEN, ONE DAY, I'LL TELL HIM, ONCE AND FOR ALL...
...THAT I LIKE HIM...!

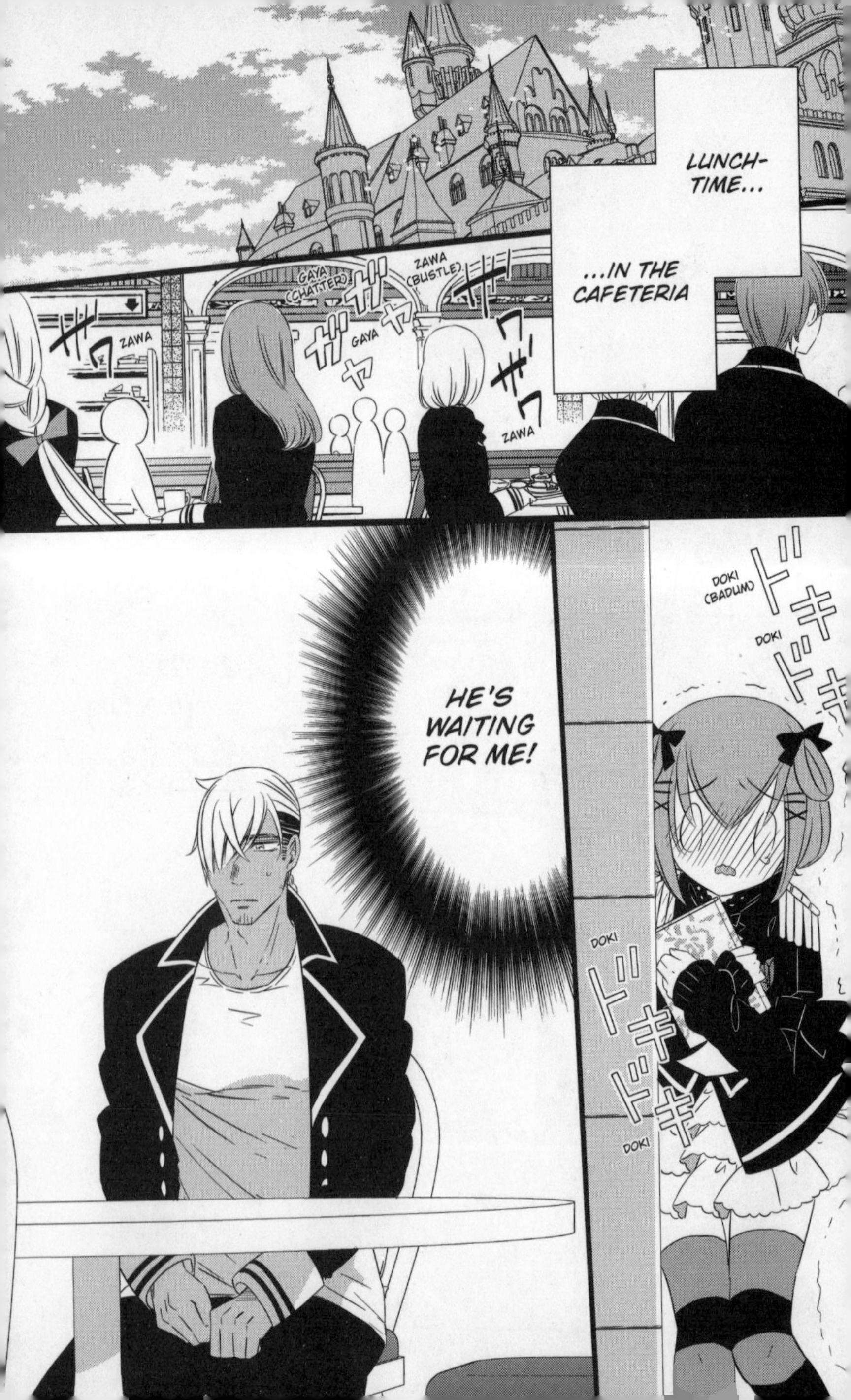
LUNCH-TIME...
...IN THE CAFETERIA
ZAWA (BUSTLE)
GAYA (CHATTER)
ZAWA
GAYA
ZAWA
DOKI (BADUM)
DOKI
DOKI
DOKI
HE'S WAITING FOR ME!

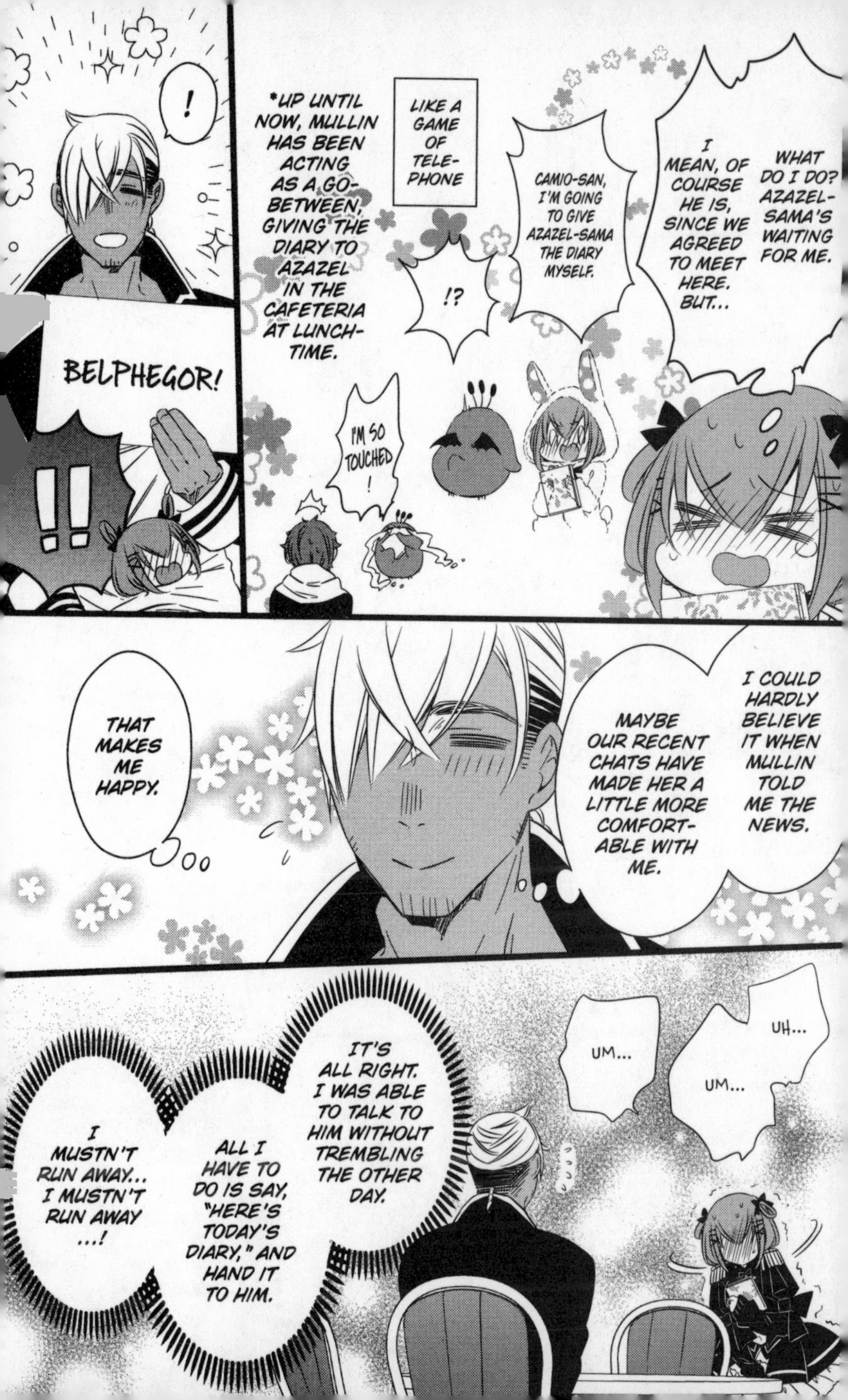
WHAT DO I DO? AZAZEL-SAMA'S WAITING FOR ME.
I MEAN, OF COURSE HE IS, SINCE WE AGREED TO MEET HERE. BUT...
CAMIO-SAN, I'M GOING TO GIVE AZAZEL-SAMA THE DIARY MYSELF.
!?
LIKE A GAME OF TELE-PHONE
*UP UNTIL NOW, MULLIN HAS BEEN ACTING AS A GO-BETWEEN, GIVING THE DIARY TO AZAZEL IN THE CAFETERIA AT LUNCH-TIME.
I'M SO TOUCHED!
!
BELPHEGOR!
!!
I COULD HARDLY BELIEVE IT WHEN MULLIN TOLD ME THE NEWS.
MAYBE OUR RECENT CHATS HAVE MADE HER A LITTLE MORE COMFORT-ABLE WITH ME.
THAT MAKES ME HAPPY.
UH...
UM...
UM...
IT'S ALL RIGHT. I WAS ABLE TO TALK TO HIM WITHOUT TREMBLING THE OTHER DAY.
ALL I HAVE TO DO IS SAY, "HERE'S TODAY'S DIARY," AND HAND IT TO HIM.
I MUSTN'T RUN AWAY... I MUSTN'T RUN AWAY ...!

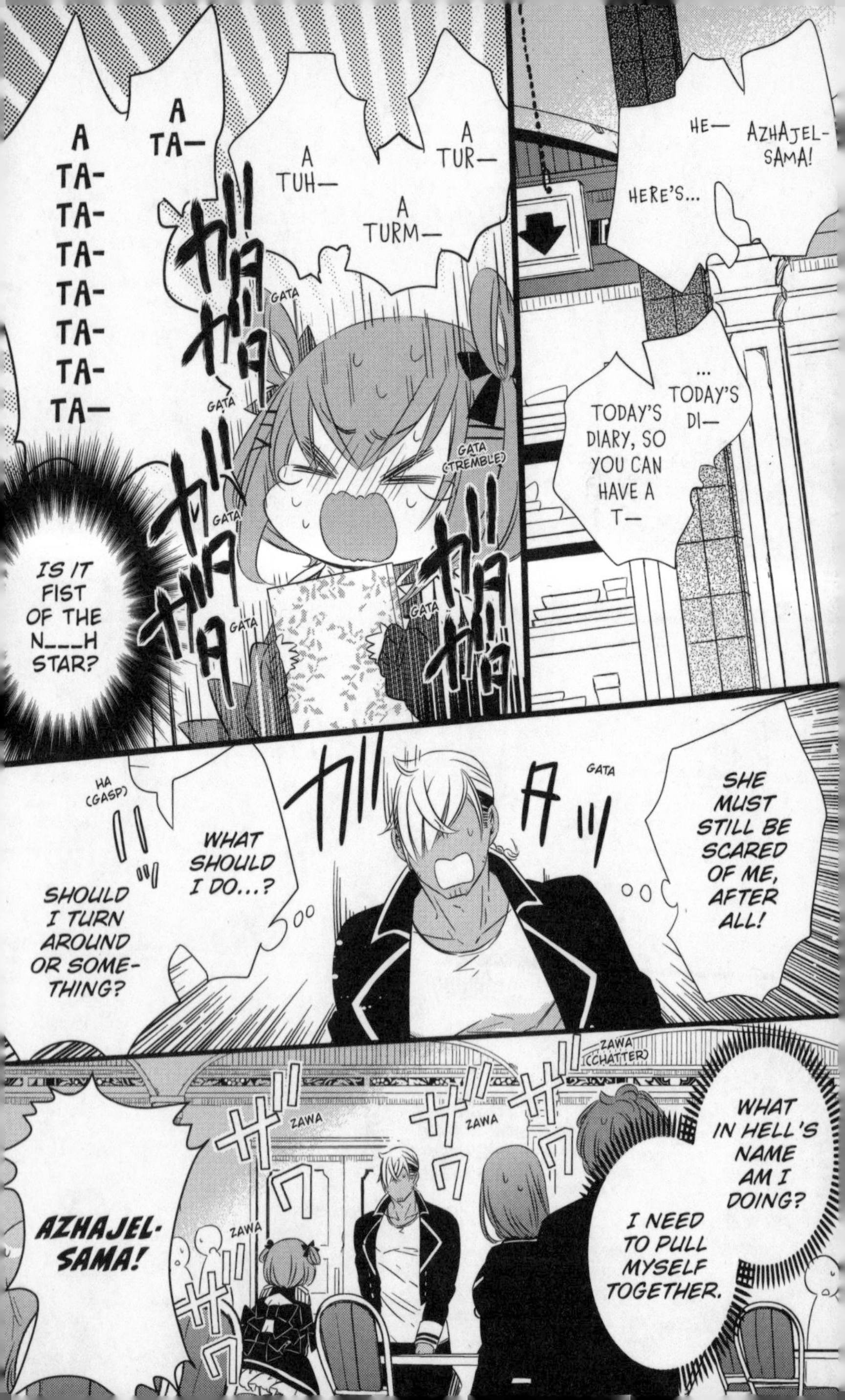
HE— AZHAJEL-SAMA!
HERE'S...
... TODAY'S DI—
TODAY'S DIARY, SO YOU CAN HAVE A T—
A TUR—
A TUH—
A TURM—
A TA—
A TA-TA-TA-TA-TA-TA-TA-TA—
GATA
GATA
GATA (TREMBLE)
GATA
GATA
GATA
IS IT FIST OF THE N___H STAR?
SHE MUST STILL BE SCARED OF ME, AFTER ALL!
GATA
WHAT SHOULD I DO...?
HA (GASP)
SHOULD I TURN AROUND OR SOMETHING?
WHAT IN HELL'S NAME AM I DOING?
I NEED TO PULL MYSELF TOGETHER.
ZAWA (CHATTER)
ZAWA
ZAWA
ZAWA
AZHAJEL-SAMA!

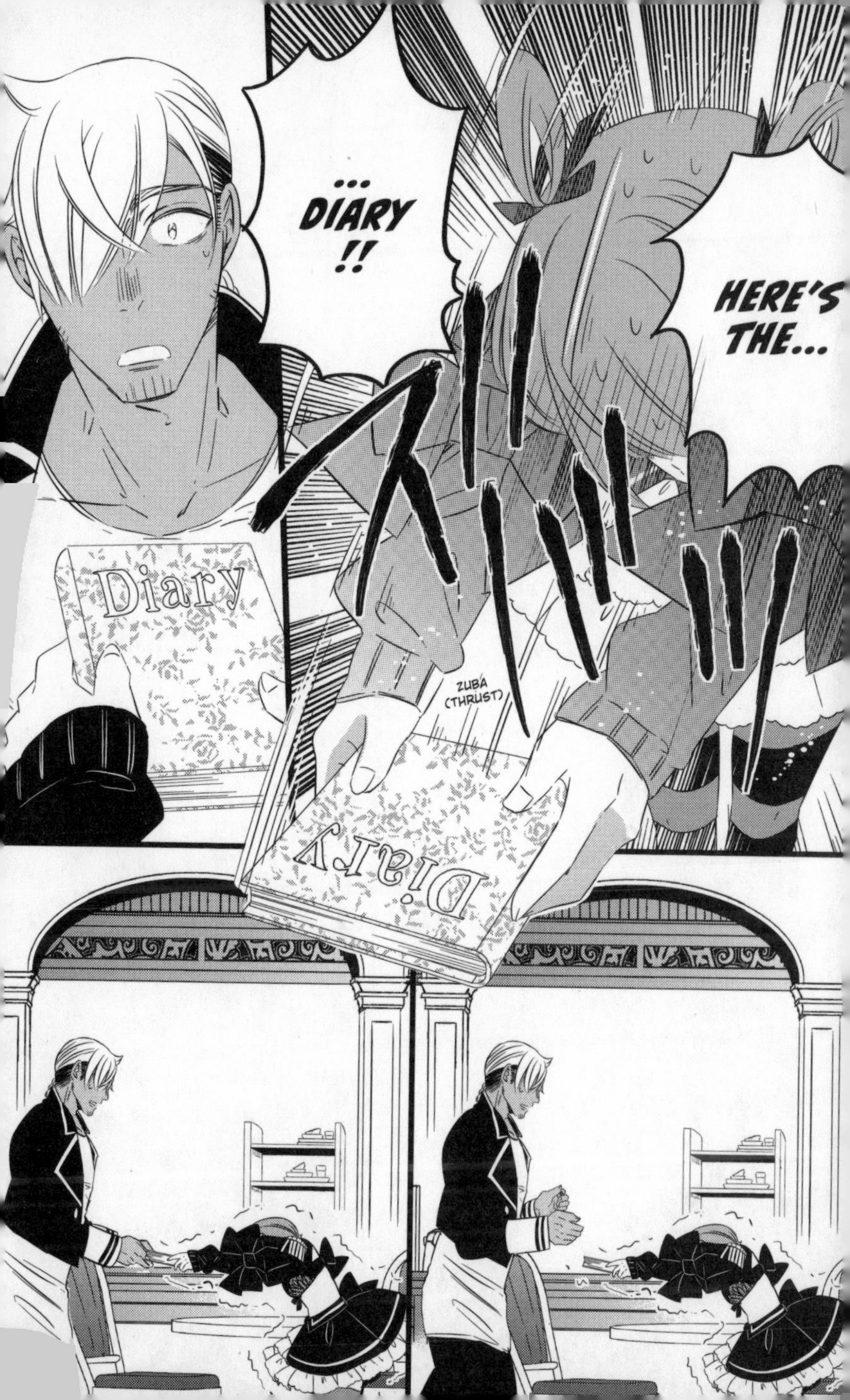
HERE'S THE...
...DIARY!!
ZUBA (THRUST)
Diary

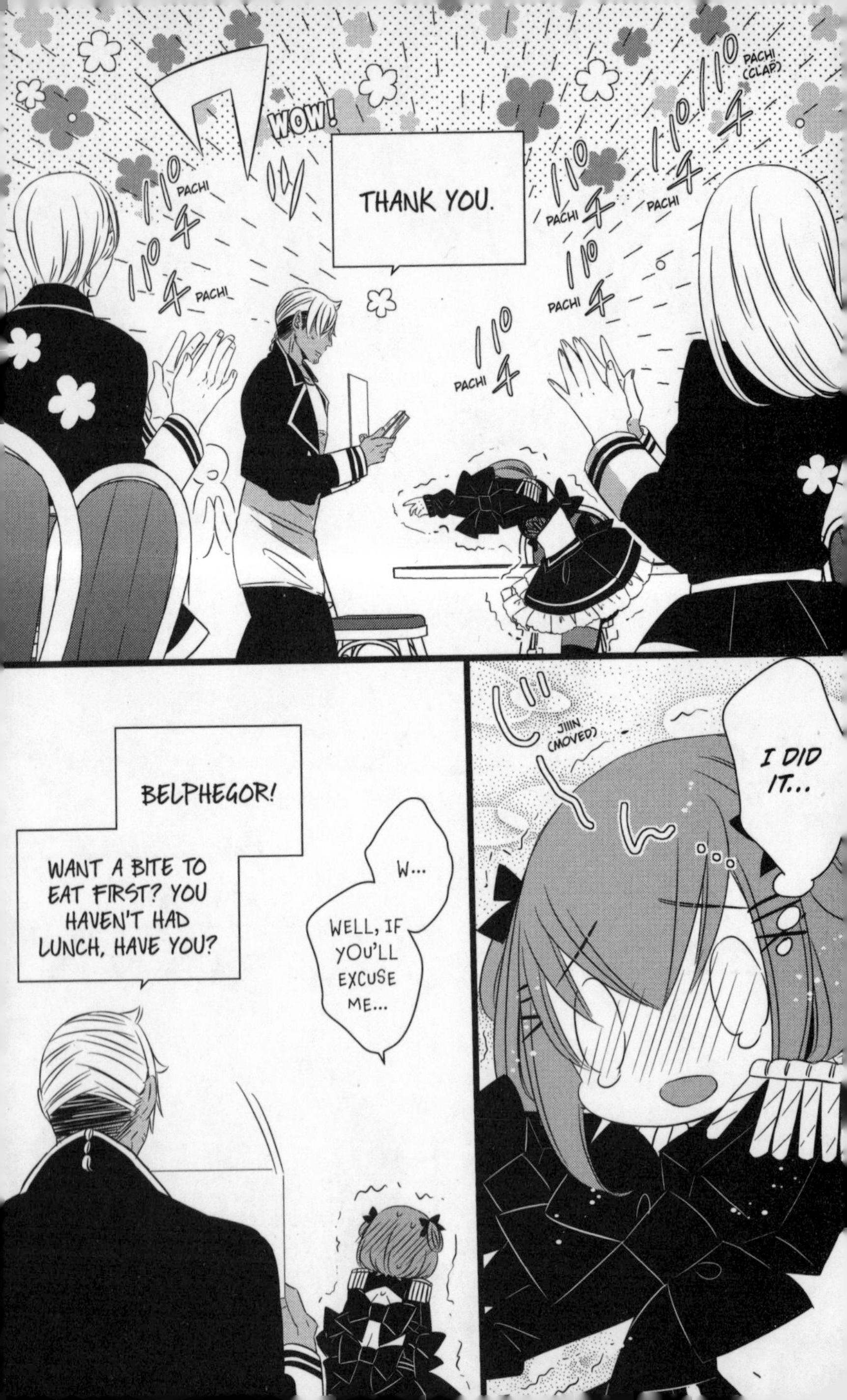
PACHI (CLAP)
WOW!
THANK YOU.
PACHI
PACHI
PACHI
PACHI
PACHI
PACHI
JIIIN (MOVED)
I DID IT...
BELPHEGOR!
WANT A BITE TO EAT FIRST? YOU HAVEN'T HAD LUNCH, HAVE YOU?
W...
WELL, IF YOU'LL EXCUSE ME...

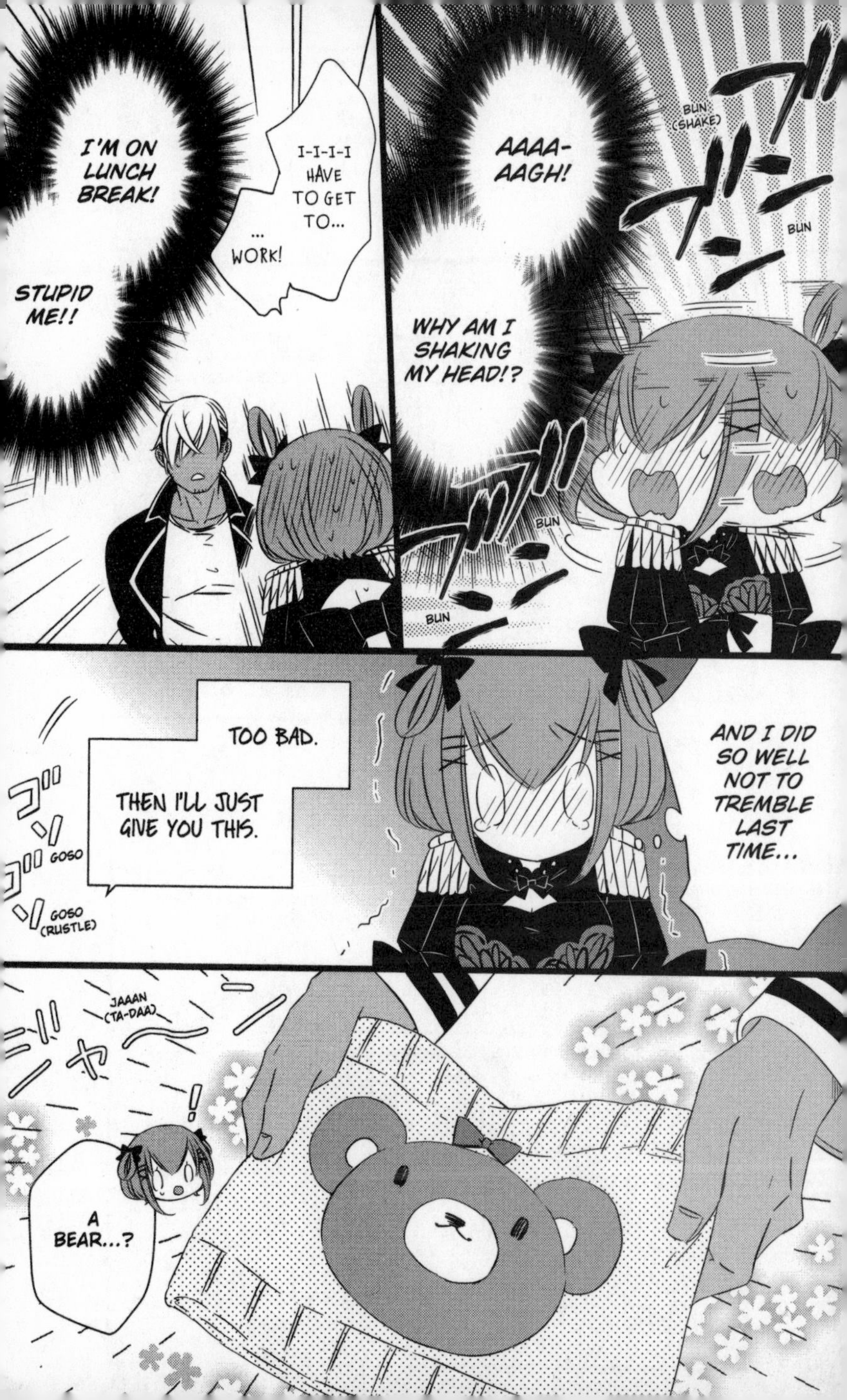
AAAA-AAGH!
BUN (SHAKE)
BUN
WHY AM I SHAKING MY HEAD!?
BUN
BUN
I-I-I-I HAVE TO GET TO...
... WORK!
I'M ON LUNCH BREAK!
STUPID ME!!
AND I DID SO WELL NOT TO TREMBLE LAST TIME...
TOO BAD.
THEN I'LL JUST GIVE YOU THIS.
GOSO
GOSO (RUSTLE)
JAAAN (TA-DAA)
A BEAR...?

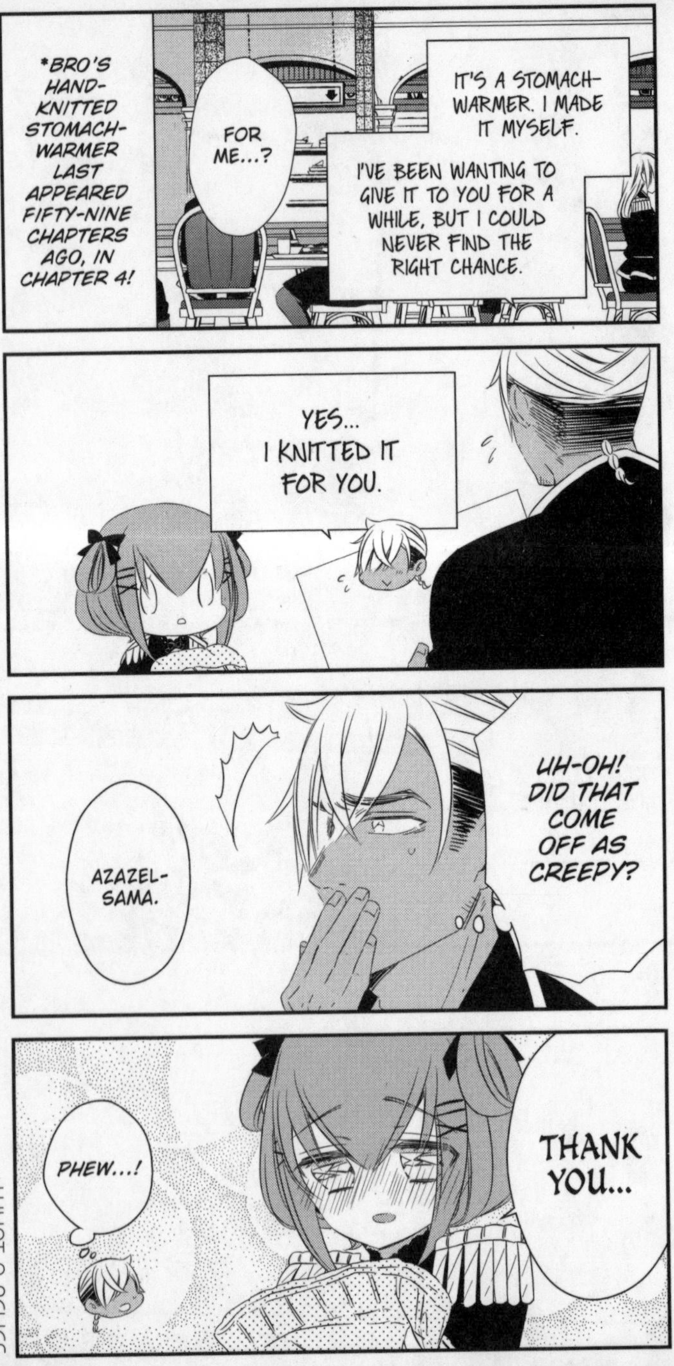
IT'S A STOMACH-WARMER. I MADE IT MYSELF.
I'VE BEEN WANTING TO GIVE IT TO YOU FOR A WHILE, BUT I COULD NEVER FIND THE RIGHT CHANCE.
FOR ME...?
*BRO'S HAND-KNITTED STOMACH-WARMER LAST APPEARED FIFTY-NINE CHAPTERS AGO, IN CHAPTER 4!
YES... I KNITTED IT FOR YOU.
UH-OH! DID THAT COME OFF AS CREEPY?
AZAZEL-SAMA.
THANK YOU...
PHEW...!

WHAT A RELIEF

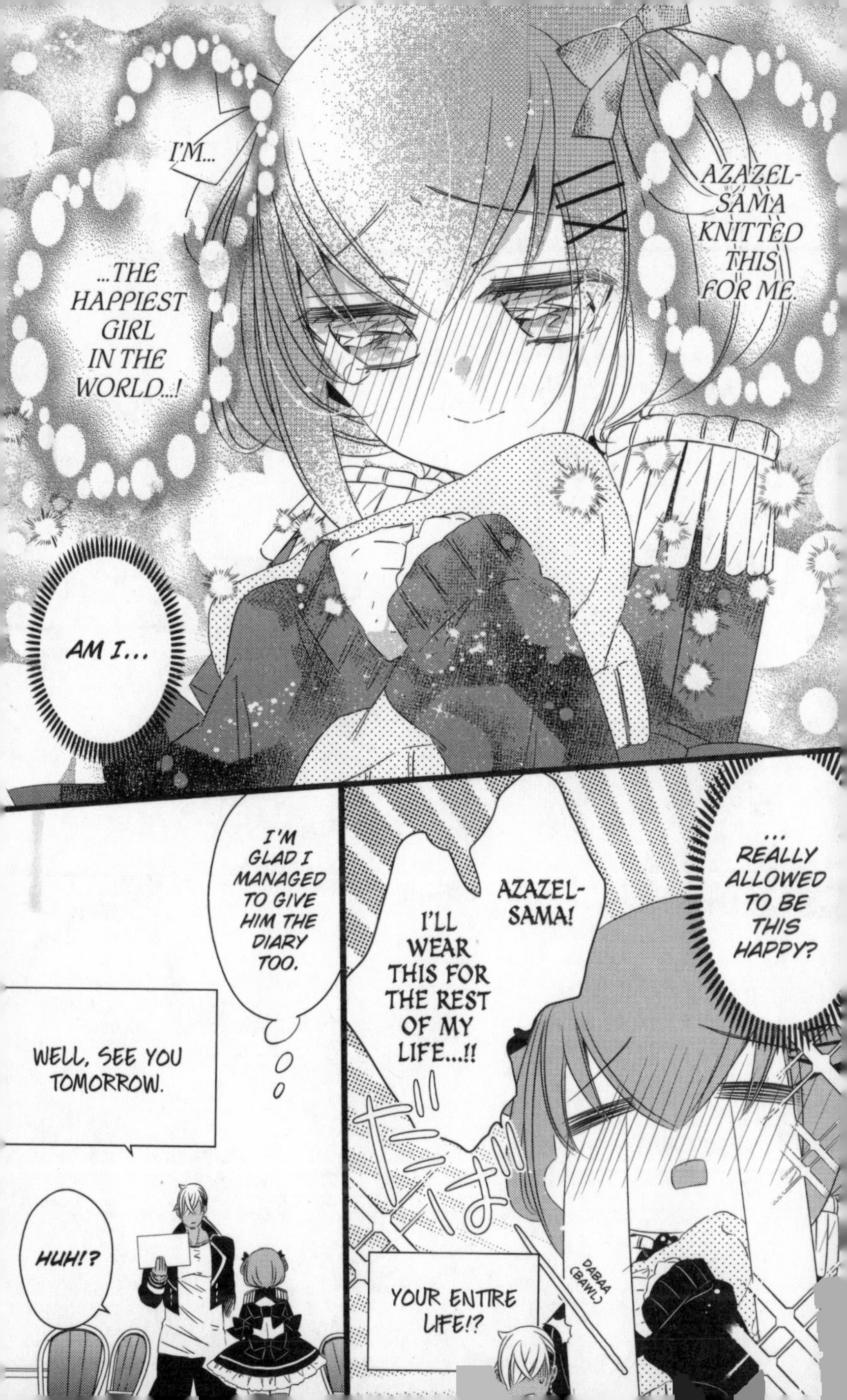
AZAZEL-SAMA KNITTED THIS FOR ME.
I'M...
...THE HAPPIEST GIRL IN THE WORLD...!
AM I...
...REALLY ALLOWED TO BE THIS HAPPY?
AZAZEL-SAMA!
I'LL WEAR THIS FOR THE REST OF MY LIFE...!!
DABAA (BAWL)
YOUR ENTIRE LIFE!?
I'M GLAD I MANAGED TO GIVE HIM THE DIARY TOO.
WELL, SEE YOU TOMORROW.
HUH!?

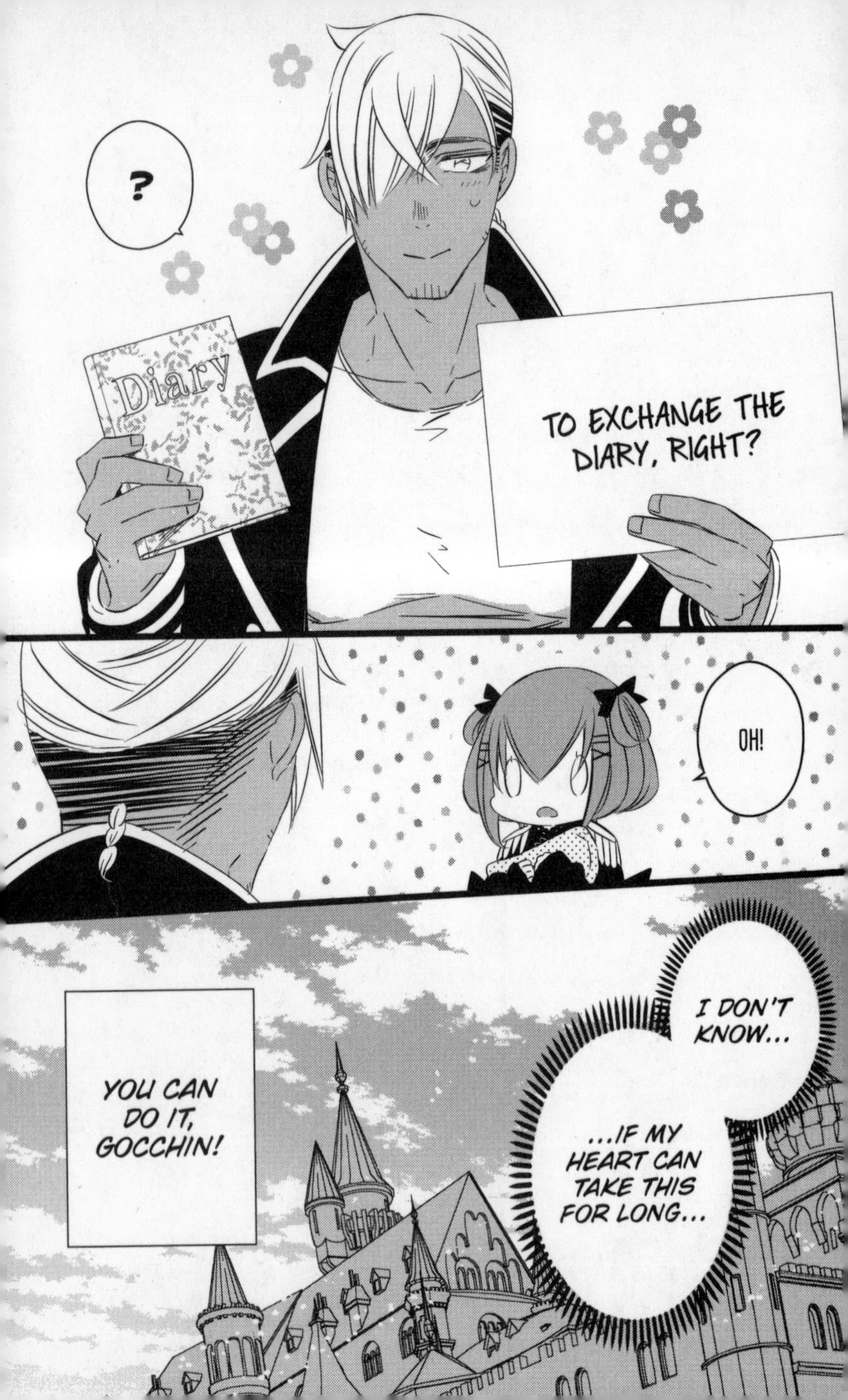
?
Diary
TO EXCHANGE THE DIARY, RIGHT?
OH!
I DON'T KNOW...
...IF MY HEART CAN TAKE THIS FOR LONG...
YOU CAN DO IT, GOCCHIN!

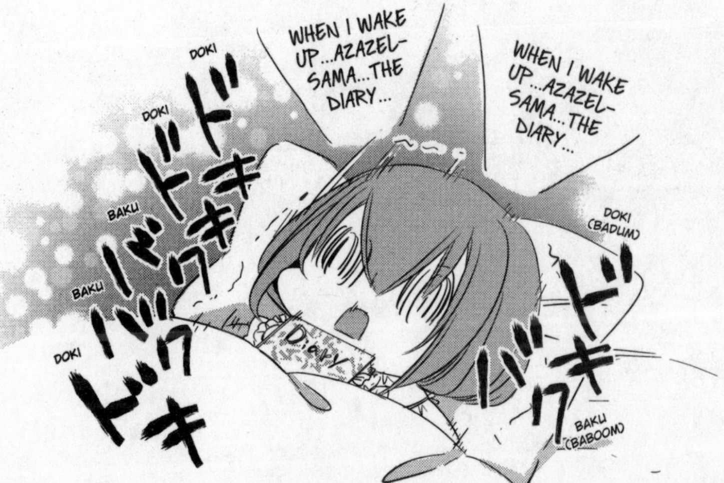
WHEN I WAKE UP...AZAZEL-SAMA...THE DIARY...
DOKI (BADUM)
BAKU (BABOOM)
WHEN I WAKE UP...AZAZEL-SAMA...THE DIARY...
Diary
DOKI
DOKI
BAKU
BAKU
DOKI

As Miss Beelzebub Likes

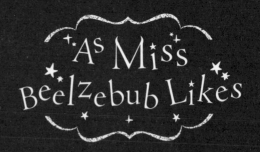

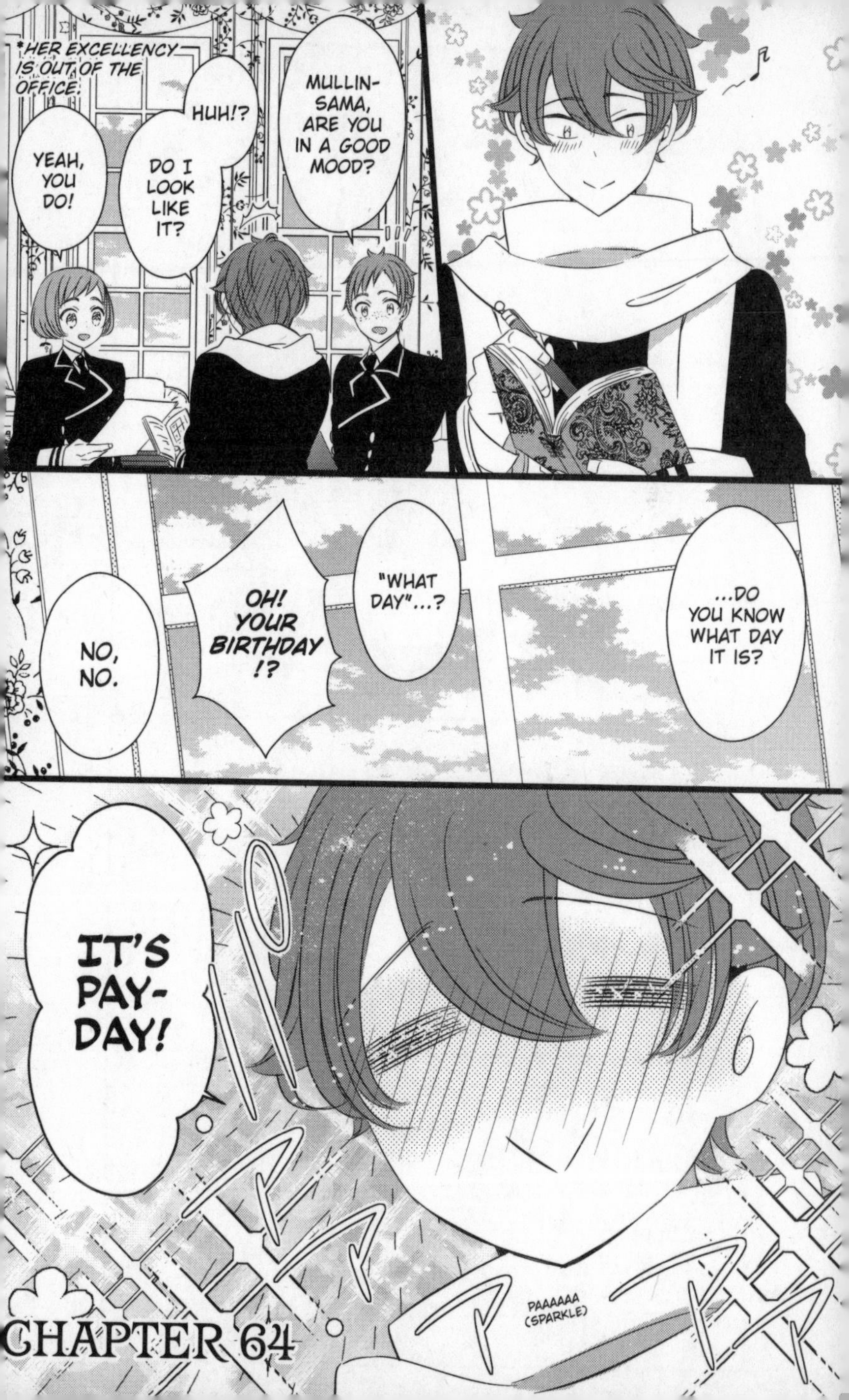
MULLIN-SAMA, ARE YOU IN A GOOD MOOD?
HUH!?
DO I LOOK LIKE IT?
YEAH, YOU DO!
*HER EXCELLENCY IS OUT OF THE OFFICE.
...DO YOU KNOW WHAT DAY IT IS?
"WHAT DAY"...?
OH! YOUR BIRTHDAY!?
NO, NO.
IT'S PAY-DAY!
PAAAAAA (SPARKLE)

CHAPTER 64

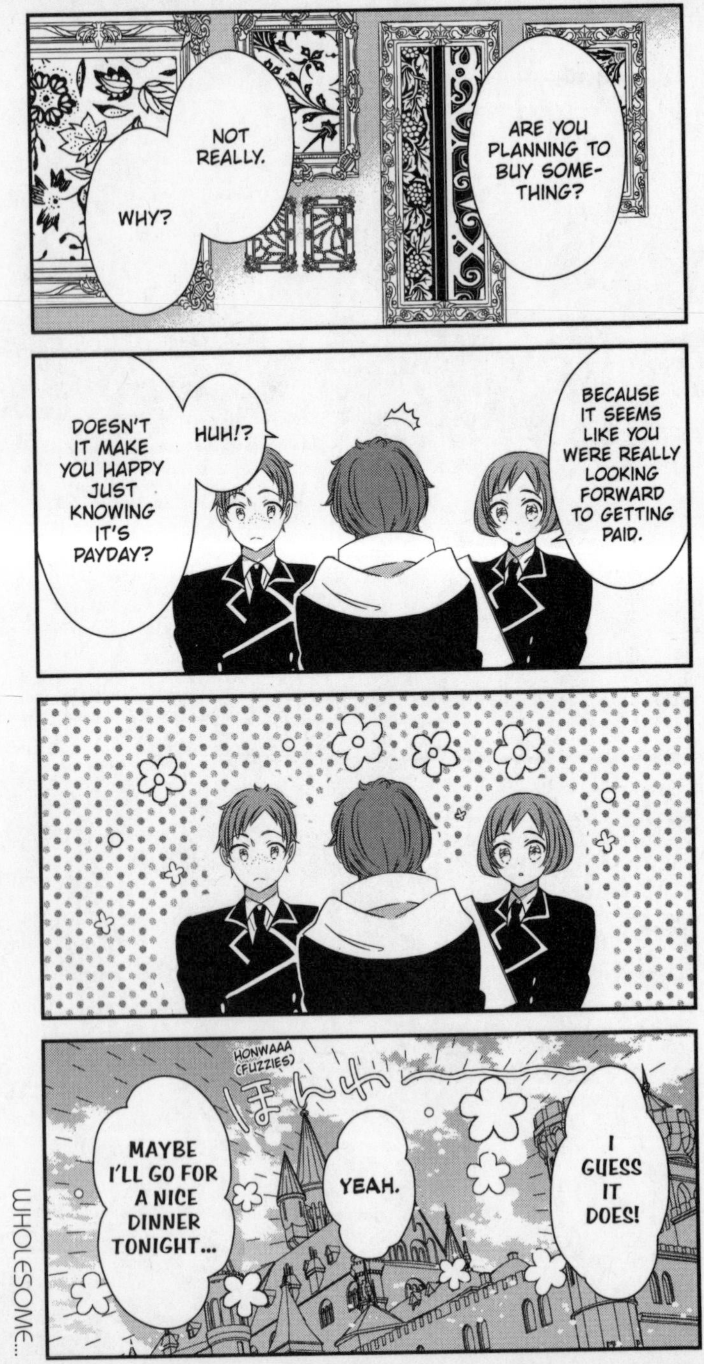
ARE YOU PLANNING TO BUY SOME-THING?
NOT REALLY.
WHY?
BECAUSE IT SEEMS LIKE YOU WERE REALLY LOOKING FORWARD TO GETTING PAID.
HUH!?
DOESN'T IT MAKE YOU HAPPY JUST KNOWING IT'S PAYDAY?
I GUESS IT DOES!
HONWAAA (FUZZIES)
ほんわ
YEAH.
MAYBE I'LL GO FOR A NICE DINNER TONIGHT...
WHOLESOME...

HAPPY THOUGHTS

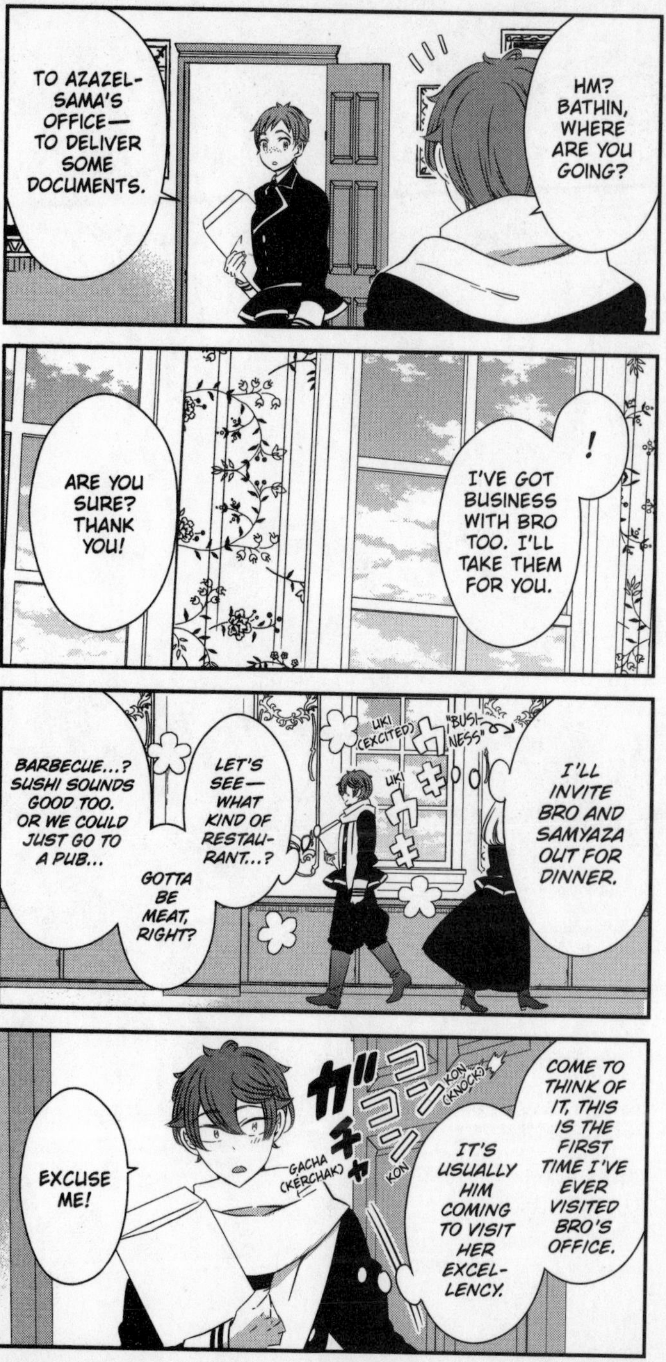
HM? BATHIN, WHERE ARE YOU GOING?
TO AZAZEL-SAMA'S OFFICE—TO DELIVER SOME DOCUMENTS.
!
I'VE GOT BUSINESS WITH BRO TOO. I'LL TAKE THEM FOR YOU.
ARE YOU SURE? THANK YOU!
I'LL INVITE BRO AND SAMYAZA OUT FOR DINNER.
"BUSINESS"
ウキ
UKI (EXCITED)
ウキ
UKI
LET'S SEE—WHAT KIND OF RESTAURANT...?
GOTTA BE MEAT, RIGHT?
BARBECUE...? SUSHI SOUNDS GOOD TOO. OR WE COULD JUST GO TO A PUB...
COME TO THINK OF IT, THIS IS THE FIRST TIME I'VE EVER VISITED BRO'S OFFICE.
IT'S USUALLY HIM COMING TO VISIT HER EXCELLENCY.
コン
KON (KNOCK)
コン
KON
ガチャ
GACHA (KERCHAK)
EXCUSE ME!

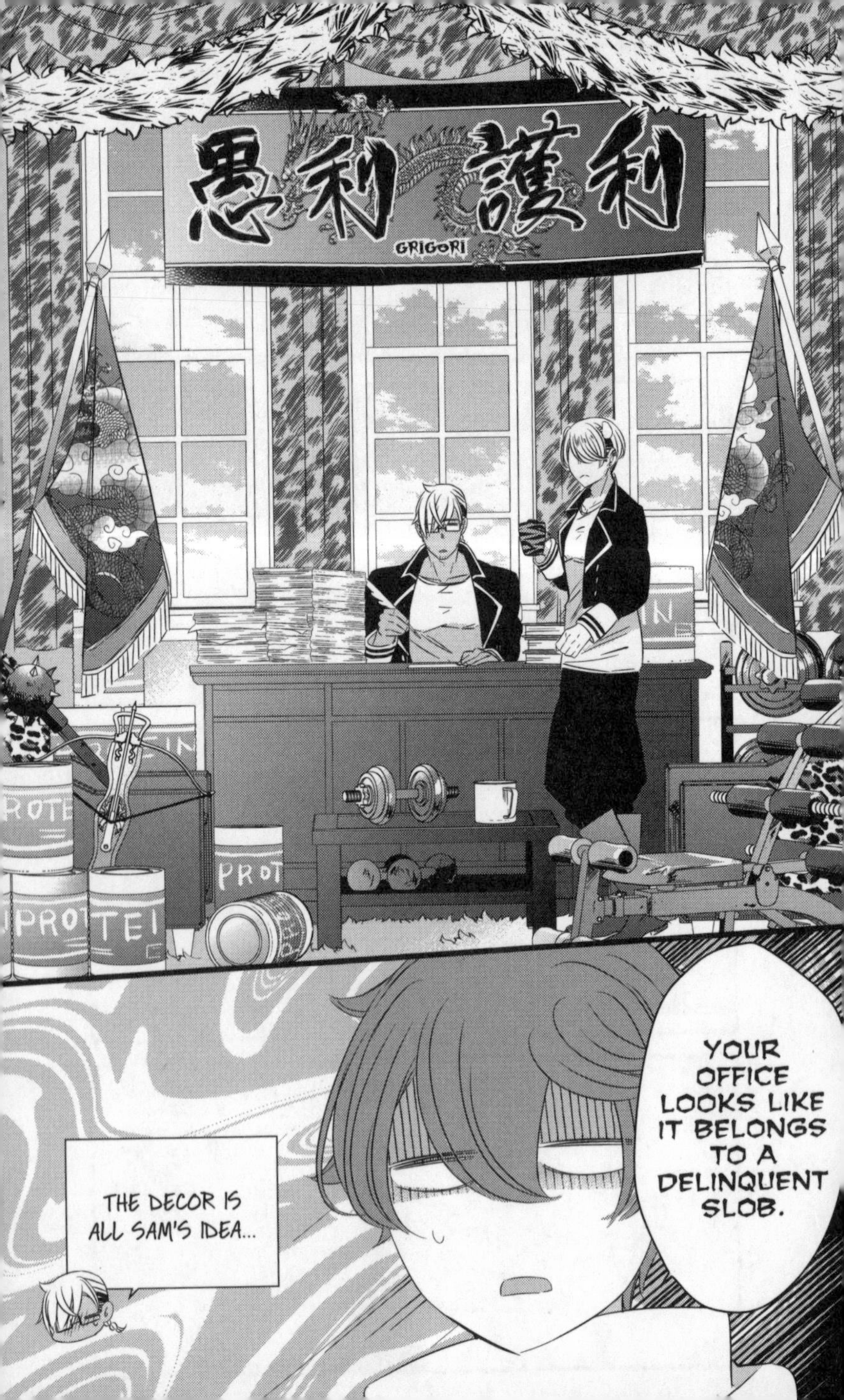
愚利護利
GRIGORI
YOUR OFFICE LOOKS LIKE IT BELONGS TO A DELINQUENT SLOB.
THE DECOR IS ALL SAM'S IDEA...

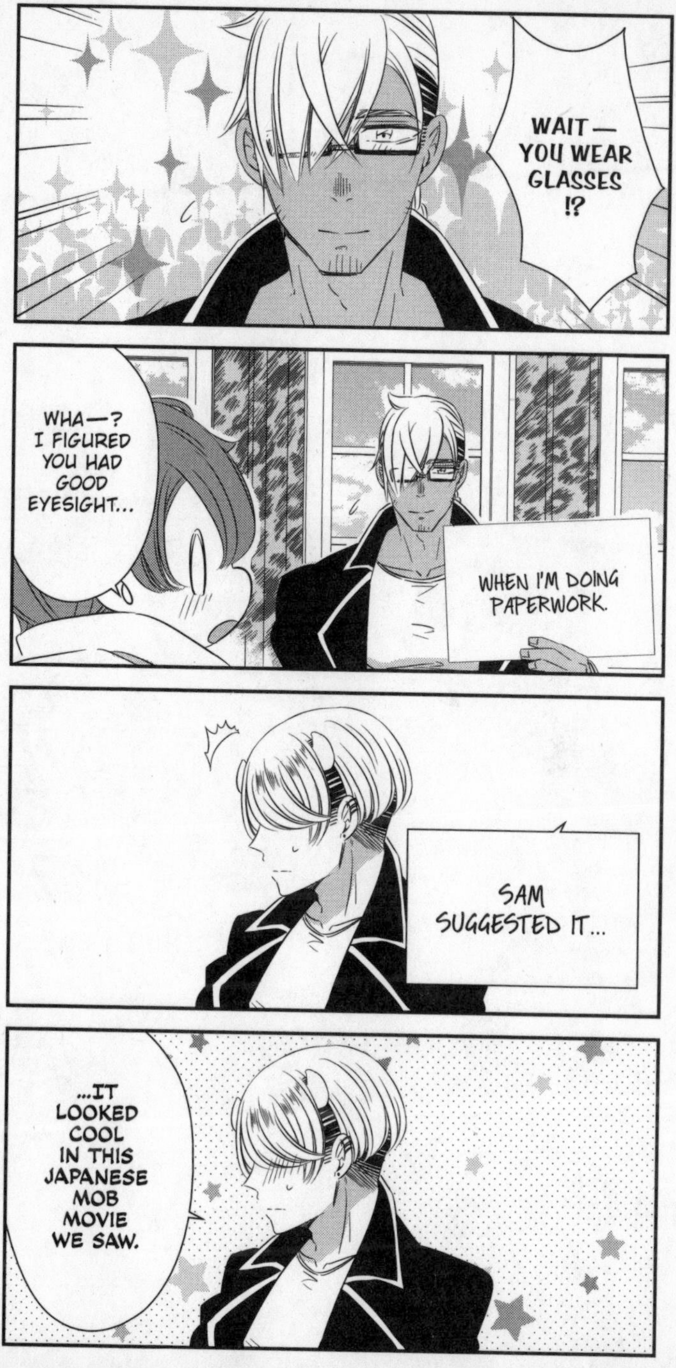
WAIT— YOU WEAR GLASSES !?
WHA—? I FIGURED YOU HAD GOOD EYESIGHT...
WHEN I'M DOING PAPERWORK.
SAM SUGGESTED IT...
...IT LOOKED COOL IN THIS JAPANESE MOB MOVIE WE SAW.

INTELLECTUAL YA_UZA?

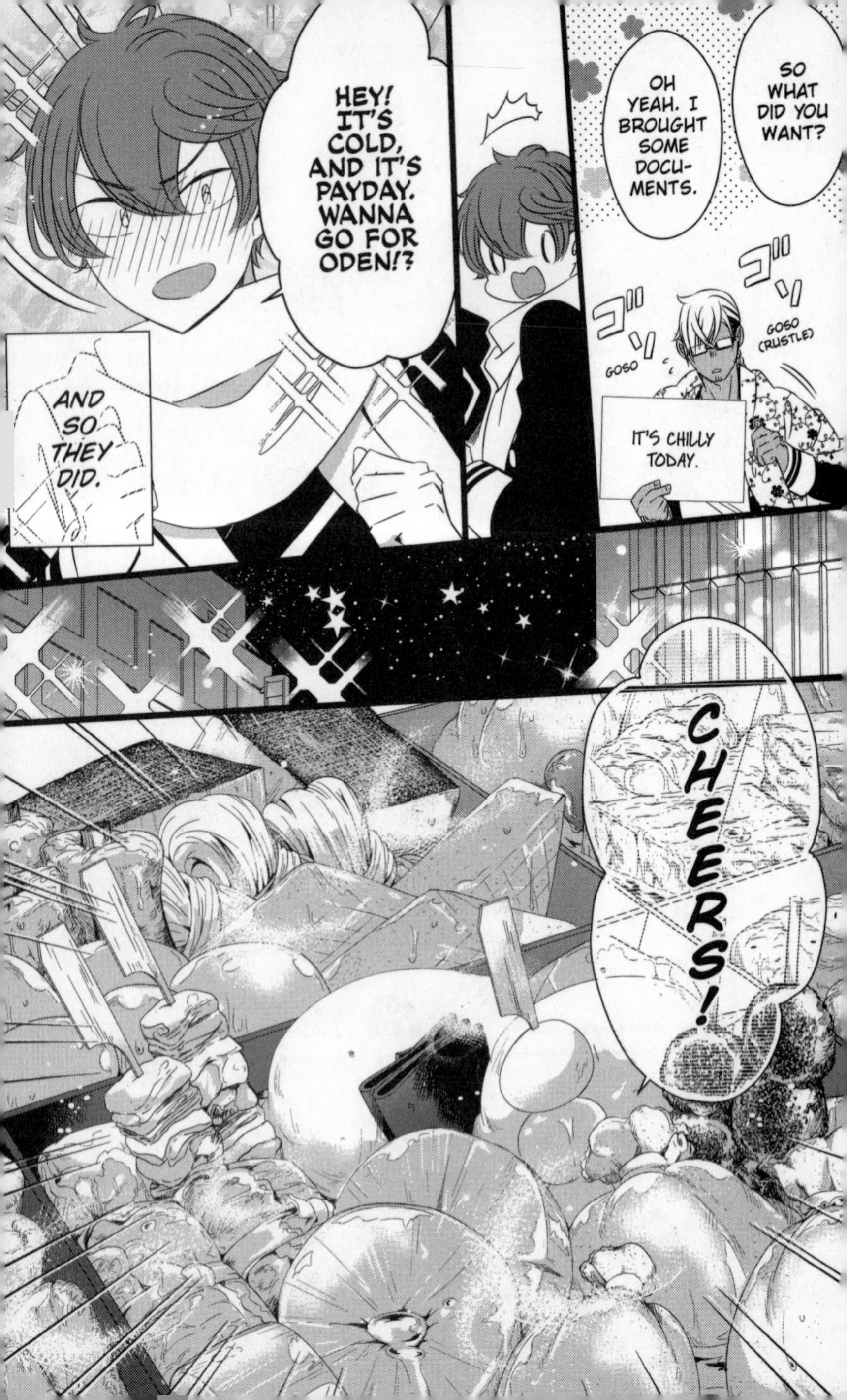
SO WHAT DID YOU WANT?
OH YEAH. I BROUGHT SOME DOCU-MENTS.
GOSO (RUSTLE)
GOSO
IT'S CHILLY TODAY.
HEY! IT'S COLD, AND IT'S PAYDAY. WANNA GO FOR ODEN!?
AND SO THEY DID.
CHEERS!

WHAT A NICE SON

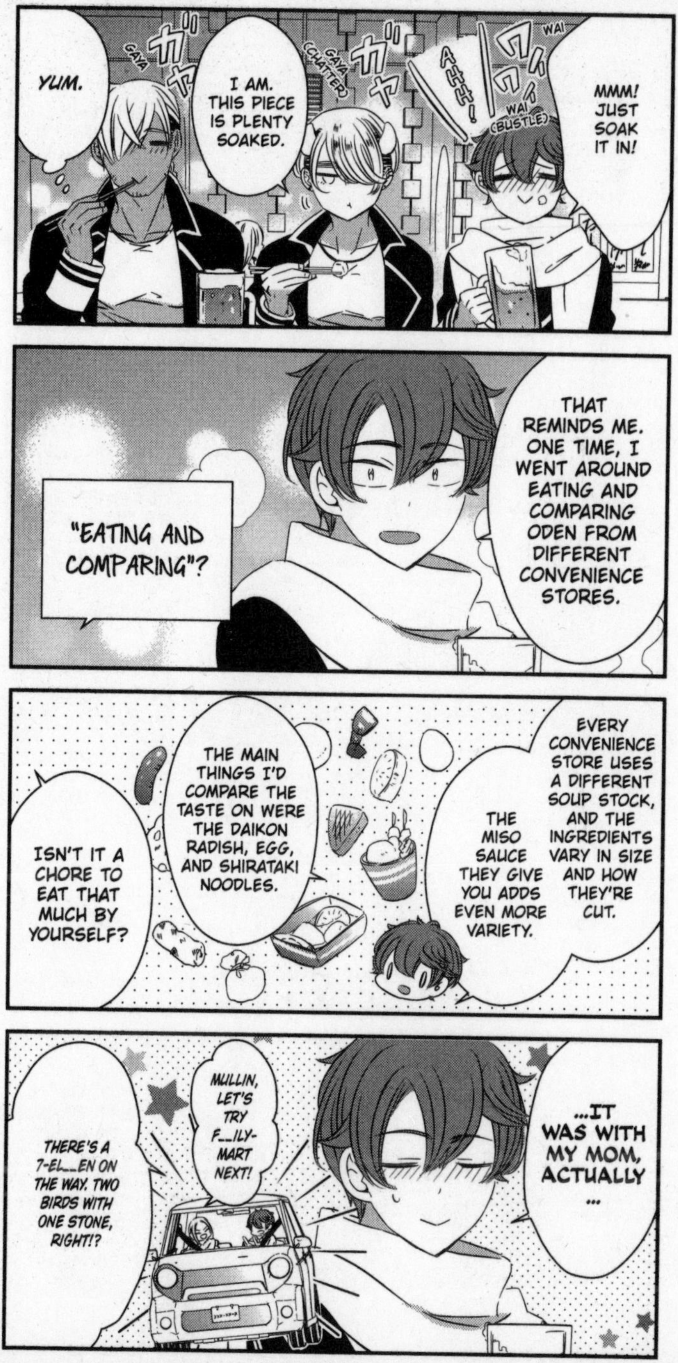
WAI
AHH!
WAI (BUSTLE)
MMM! JUST SOAK IT IN!
GAYA (CHATTER)
I AM. THIS PIECE IS PLENTY SOAKED.
GAYA
YUM.
THAT REMINDS ME. ONE TIME, I WENT AROUND EATING AND COMPARING ODEN FROM DIFFERENT CONVENIENCE STORES.
"EATING AND COMPARING"?
EVERY CONVENIENCE STORE USES A DIFFERENT SOUP STOCK, AND THE INGREDIENTS VARY IN SIZE AND HOW THEY'RE CUT.
THE MISO SAUCE THEY GIVE YOU ADDS EVEN MORE VARIETY.
THE MAIN THINGS I'D COMPARE THE TASTE ON WERE THE DAIKON RADISH, EGG, AND SHIRATAKI NOODLES.
ISN'T IT A CHORE TO EAT THAT MUCH BY YOURSELF?
...IT WAS WITH MY MOM, ACTUALLY...
MULLIN, LET'S TRY F__ILY-MART NEXT!
THERE'S A 7-EL__EN ON THE WAY. TWO BIRDS WITH ONE STONE, RIGHT!?

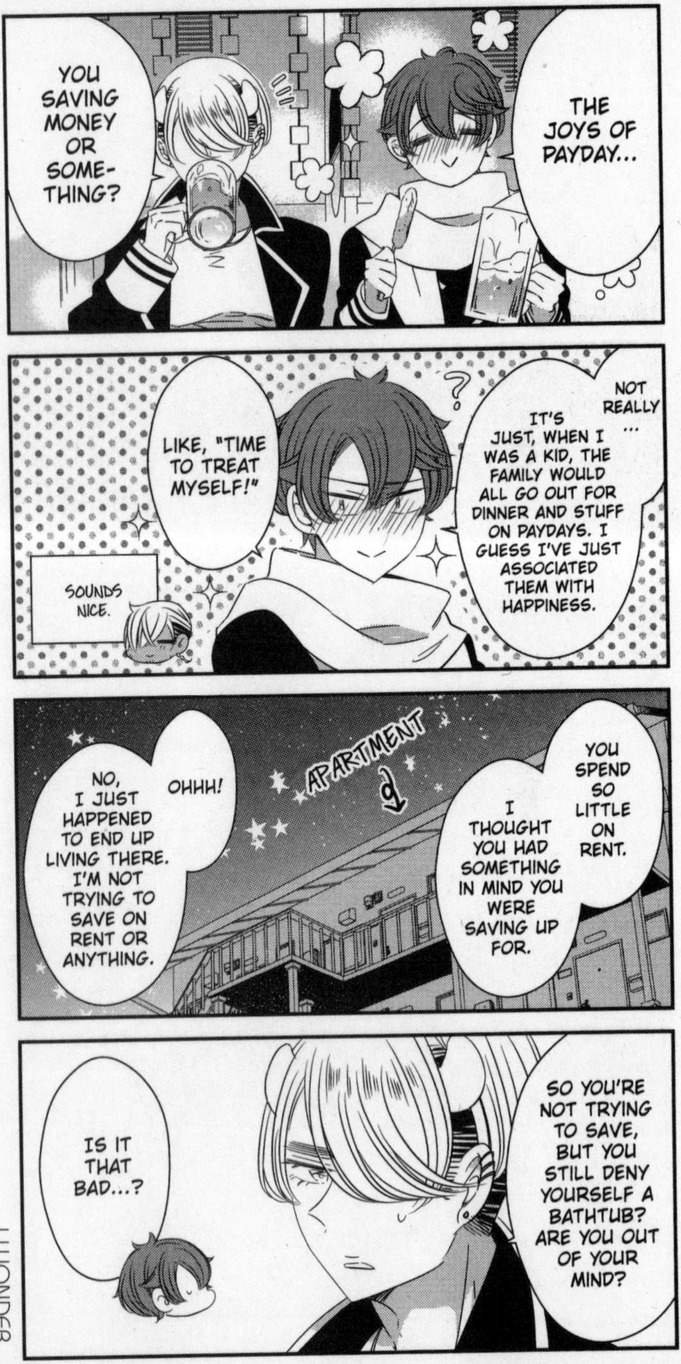
THE JOYS OF PAYDAY...
YOU SAVING MONEY OR SOMETHING?
NOT REALLY...
IT'S JUST, WHEN I WAS A KID, THE FAMILY WOULD ALL GO OUT FOR DINNER AND STUFF ON PAYDAYS. I GUESS I'VE JUST ASSOCIATED THEM WITH HAPPINESS.
LIKE, "TIME TO TREAT MYSELF!"
SOUNDS NICE.
YOU SPEND SO LITTLE ON RENT.
I THOUGHT YOU HAD SOMETHING IN MIND YOU WERE SAVING UP FOR.
APARTMENT
OHHH!
NO, I JUST HAPPENED TO END UP LIVING THERE. I'M NOT TRYING TO SAVE ON RENT OR ANYTHING.
SO YOU'RE NOT TRYING TO SAVE, BUT YOU STILL DENY YOURSELF A BATHTUB? ARE YOU OUT OF YOUR MIND?
IS IT THAT BAD...?

I WONDER...

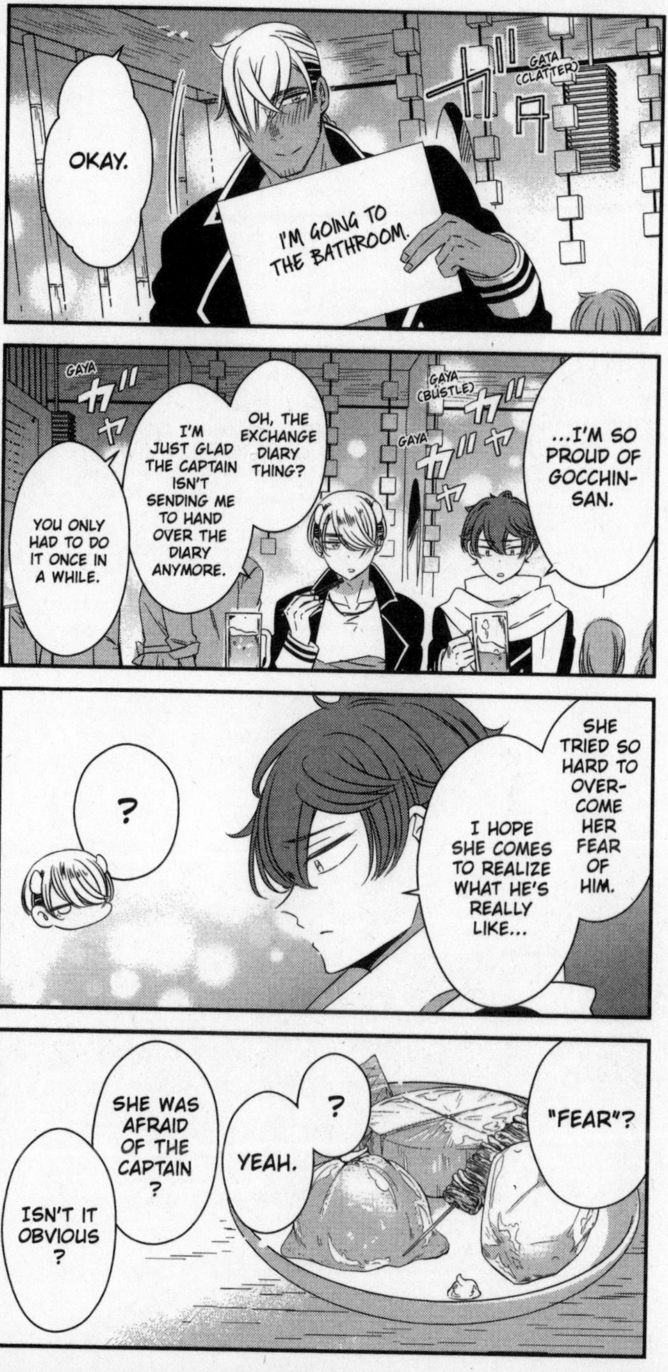

GATA (CLATTER)
I'M GOING TO THE BATHROOM.
OKAY.
...I'M SO PROUD OF GOCCHIN-SAN.
GAYA (BUSTLE)
GAYA
OH, THE EXCHANGE DIARY THING?
I'M JUST GLAD THE CAPTAIN ISN'T SENDING ME TO HAND OVER THE DIARY ANYMORE.
GAYA
YOU ONLY HAD TO DO IT ONCE IN A WHILE.
SHE TRIED SO HARD TO OVER-COME HER FEAR OF HIM.
I HOPE SHE COMES TO REALIZE WHAT HE'S REALLY LIKE...
?
"FEAR"?
?
YEAH.
SHE WAS AFRAID OF THE CAPTAIN?
ISN'T IT OBVIOUS?

UNDERSTANDING A YOUNG GIRL'S HEART

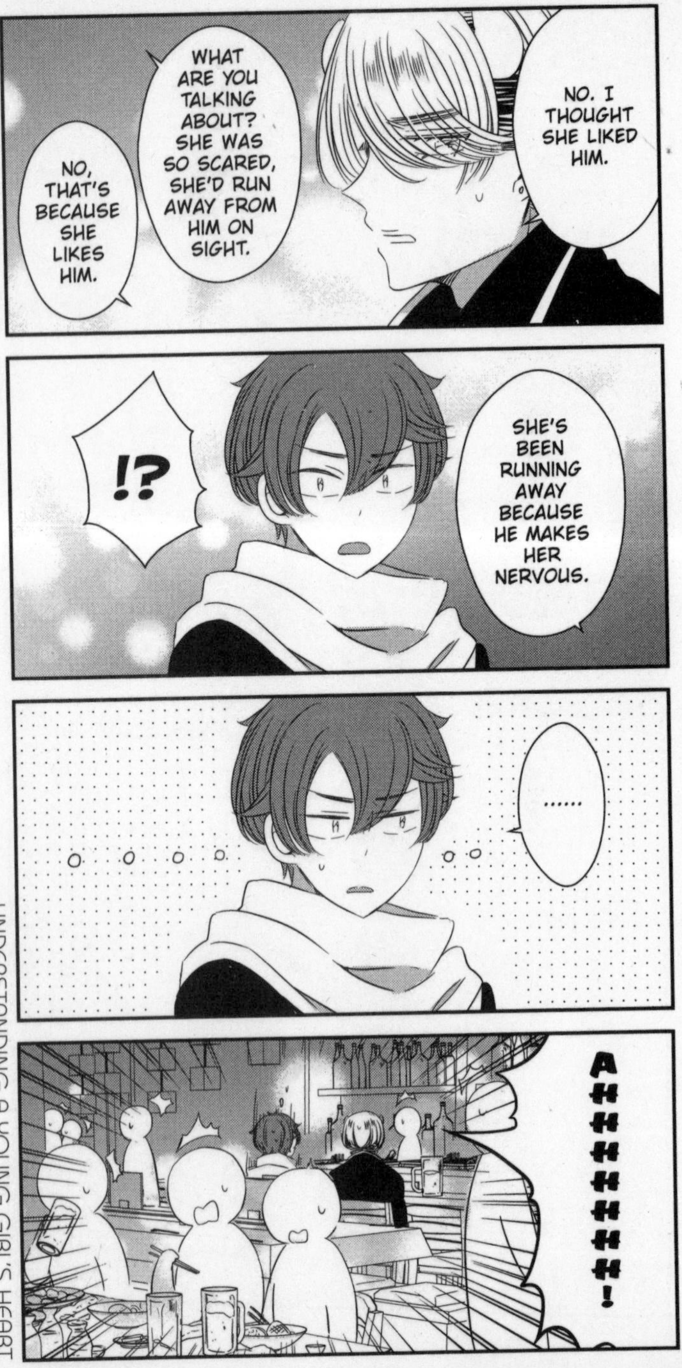
NO. I THOUGHT SHE LIKED HIM.
WHAT ARE YOU TALKING ABOUT? SHE WAS SO SCARED, SHE'D RUN AWAY FROM HIM ON SIGHT.
NO, THAT'S BECAUSE SHE LIKES HIM.
SHE'S BEEN RUNNING AWAY BECAUSE HE MAKES HER NERVOUS.
!?
......
AHHHHHHHHH!

NO BIG DEAL...

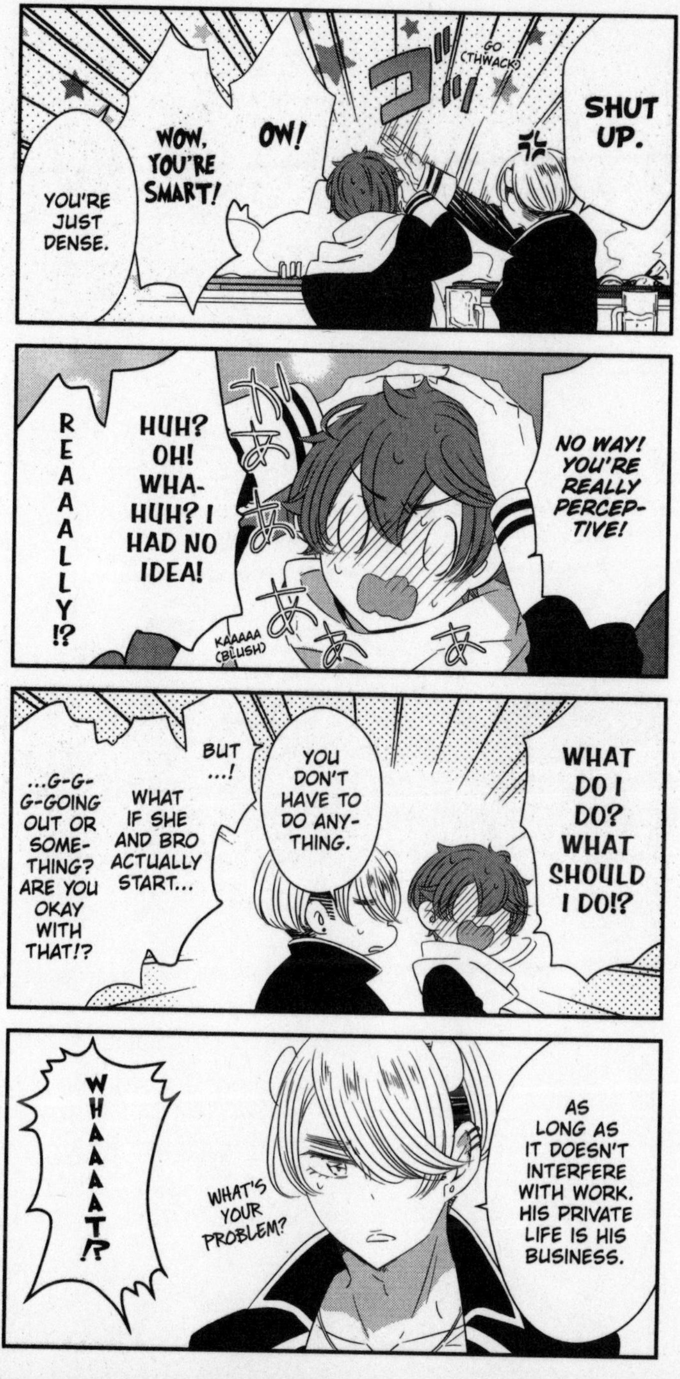
SHUT UP.
GO (THWACK)
OW!
WOW, YOU'RE SMART!
YOU'RE JUST DENSE.
NO WAY! YOU'RE REALLY PERCEPTIVE!
KAAAAA (BLUSH)
HUH? OH! WHA-HUH? I HAD NO IDEA!
REAAAALLY!?
WHAT DO I DO? WHAT SHOULD I DO!?
YOU DON'T HAVE TO DO ANYTHING.
BUT...!
WHAT IF SHE AND BRO ACTUALLY START...
...G-G-G-GOING OUT OR SOMETHING? ARE YOU OKAY WITH THAT!?
AS LONG AS IT DOESN'T INTERFERE WITH WORK. HIS PRIVATE LIFE IS HIS BUSINESS.
WHAT'S YOUR PROBLEM?
WHAAAAAT!?

CALM DOWN ALREADY

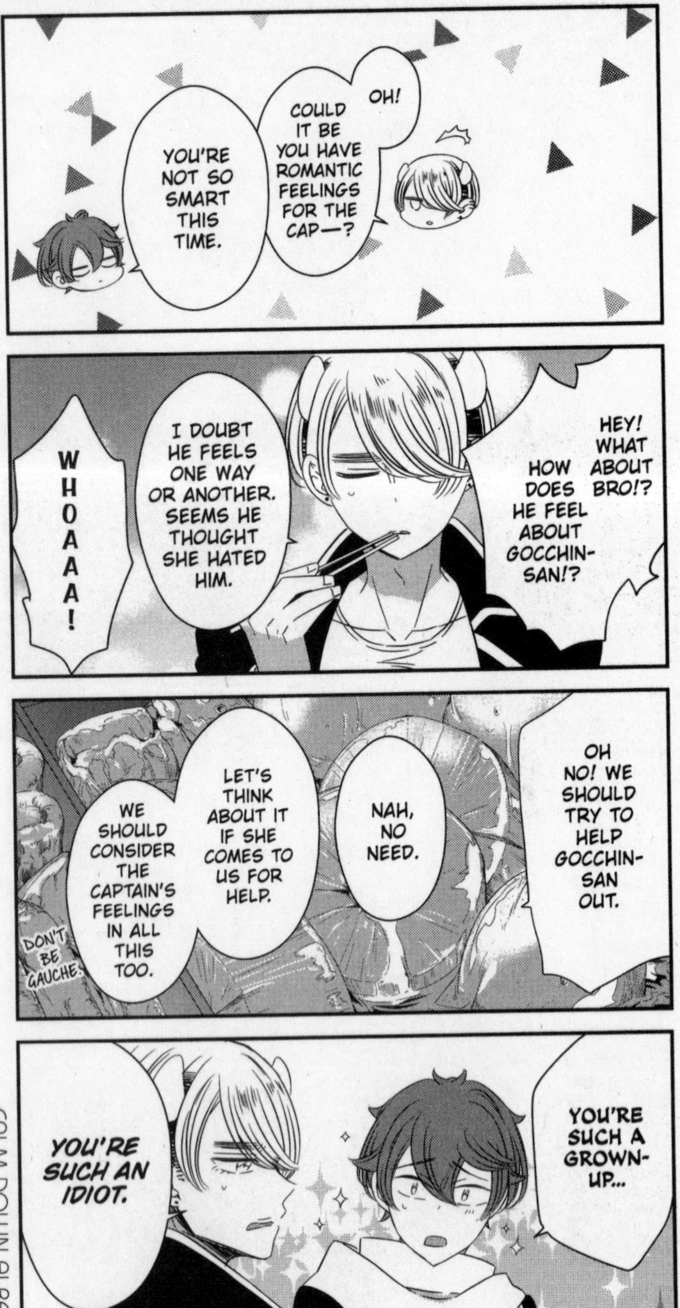

OH!
COULD IT BE YOU HAVE ROMANTIC FEELINGS FOR THE CAP—?
YOU'RE NOT SO SMART THIS TIME.
HEY! WHAT ABOUT BRO!?
HOW DOES HE FEEL ABOUT GOCCHIN-SAN!?
I DOUBT HE FEELS ONE WAY OR ANOTHER. SEEMS HE THOUGHT SHE HATED HIM.
WHOAAAA!
OH NO! WE SHOULD TRY TO HELP GOCCHIN-SAN OUT.
NAH, NO NEED.
LET'S THINK ABOUT IT IF SHE COMES TO US FOR HELP.
WE SHOULD CONSIDER THE CAPTAIN'S FEELINGS IN ALL THIS TOO.
DON'T BE GAUCHE.
YOU'RE SUCH A GROWN-UP...
YOU'RE SUCH AN IDIOT.

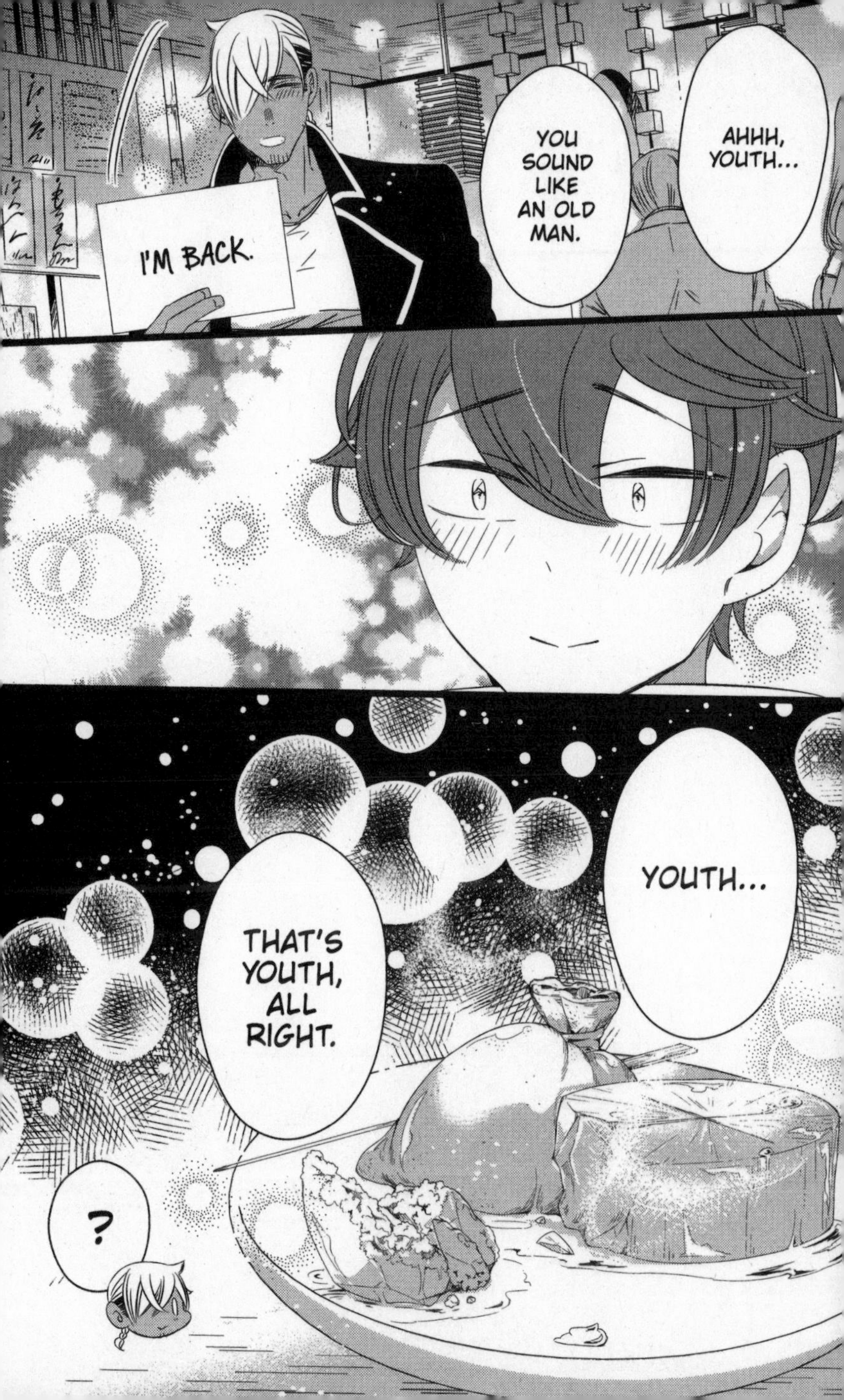
AHHH, YOUTH...
YOU SOUND LIKE AN OLD MAN.
I'M BACK.
YOUTH...
THAT'S YOUTH, ALL RIGHT.
?

As Miss Beelzebub Likes

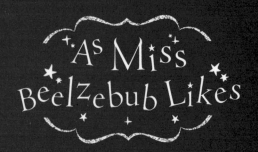

LET'S MAKE A FLUFFY PHONE STRAP

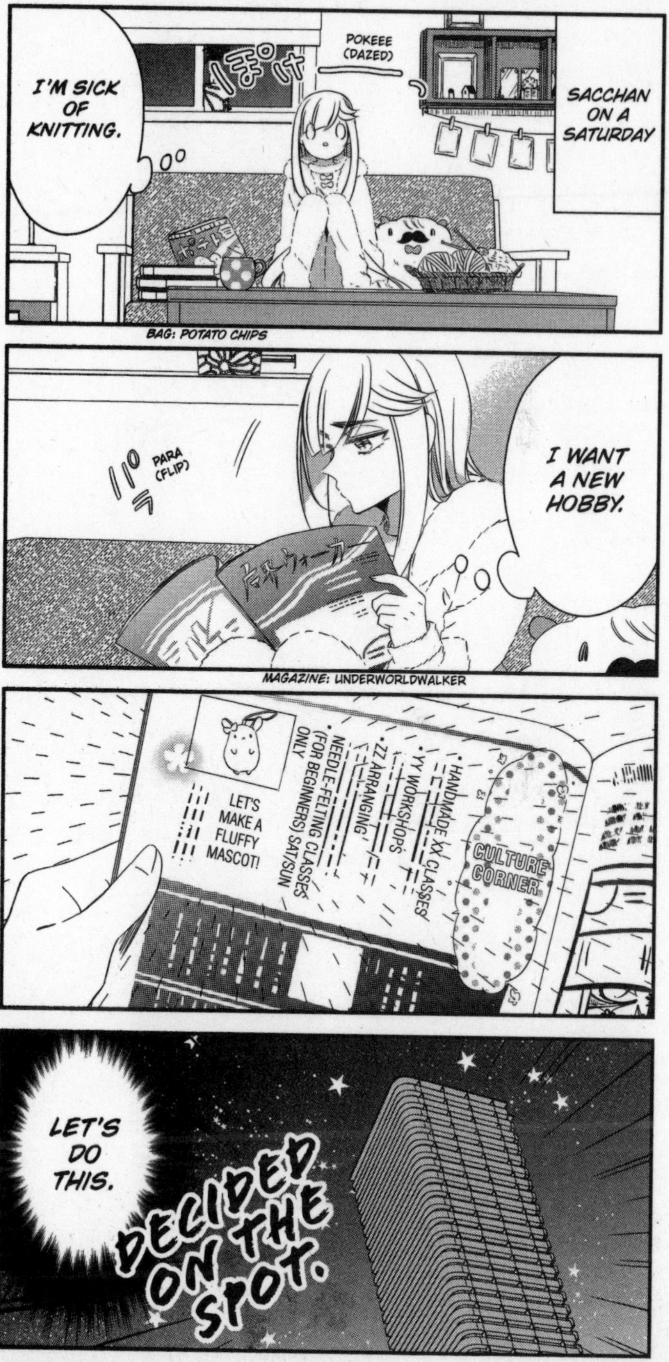
SACCHAN ON A SATURDAY
POKEEE (DAZED)
I'M SICK OF KNITTING.
BAG: POTATO CHIPS
I WANT A NEW HOBBY.
PARA (FLIP)
MAGAZINE: UNDERWORLDWALKER
CULTURE CORNER
•HANDMADE XX CLASSES
•YY WORKSHOPS
•ZZ ARRANGING
•NEEDLE-FELTING CLASSES (FOR BEGINNERS) SAT/SUN ONLY
LET'S MAKE A FLUFFY MASCOT!
LET'S DO THIS.
DECIDED ON THE SPOT.

CHAPTER 65

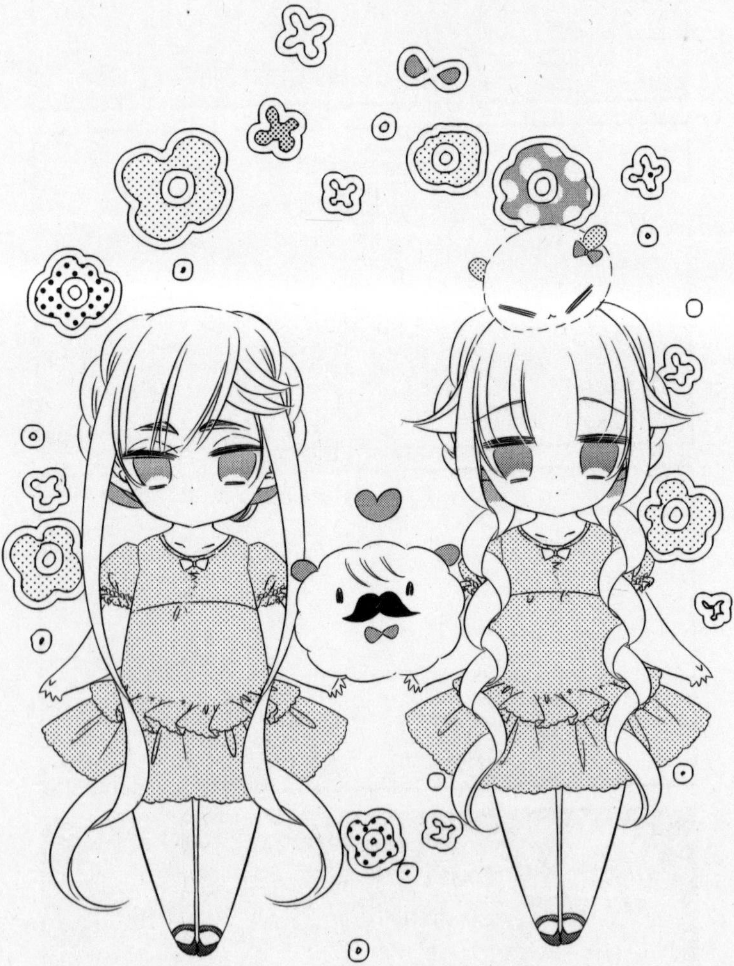

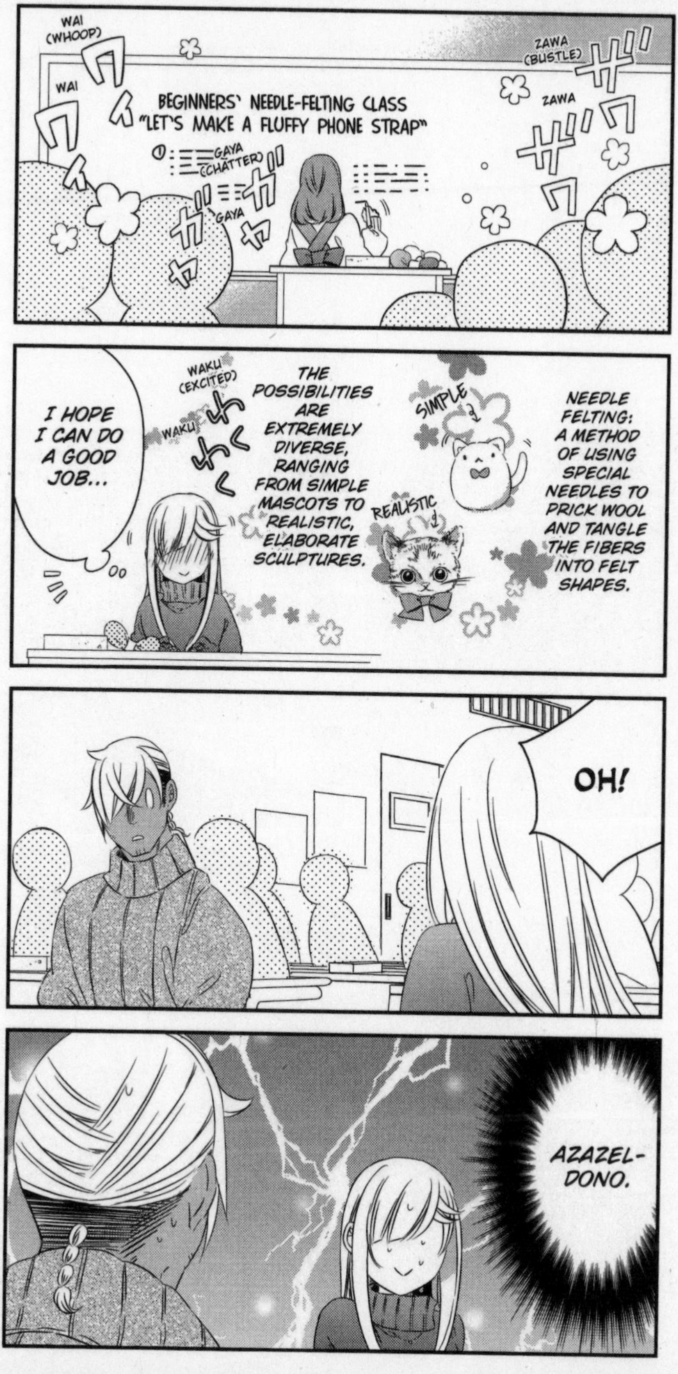
ZAWA (BUSTLE)
ZAWA
BEGINNERS' NEEDLE-FELTING CLASS "LET'S MAKE A FLUFFY PHONE STRAP"
GAYA (CHATTER)
GAYA
WAI (WHOOP)
WAI
NEEDLE FELTING: A METHOD OF USING SPECIAL NEEDLES TO PRICK WOOL AND TANGLE THE FIBERS INTO FELT SHAPES.
SIMPLE
REALISTIC
THE POSSIBILITIES ARE EXTREMELY DIVERSE, RANGING FROM SIMPLE MASCOTS TO REALISTIC, ELABORATE SCULPTURES.
WAKU (EXCITED)
WAKU
I HOPE I CAN DO A GOOD JOB...
OH!
AZAZEL-DONO.

HE'S HERE!

SILENTLY WISHING EACH OTHER LUCK

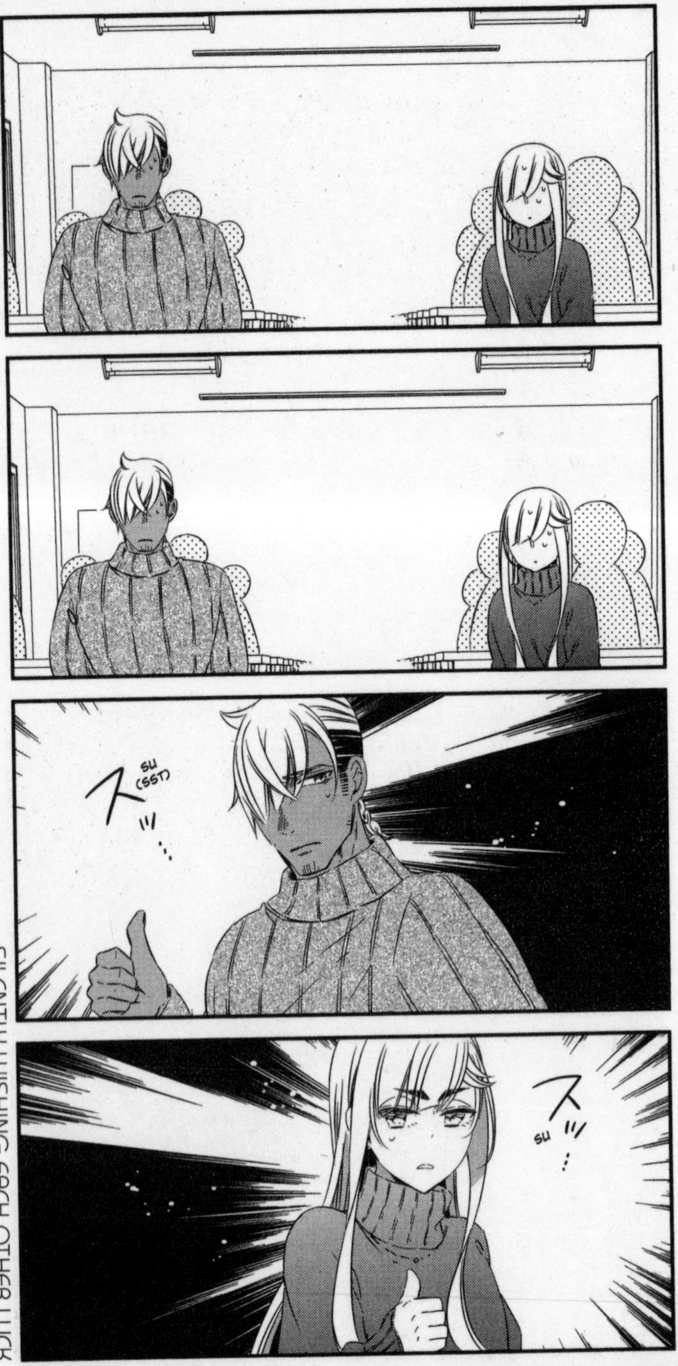
スッ…
SU (SST)
スッ…
SU

THE HELL IS THIS?

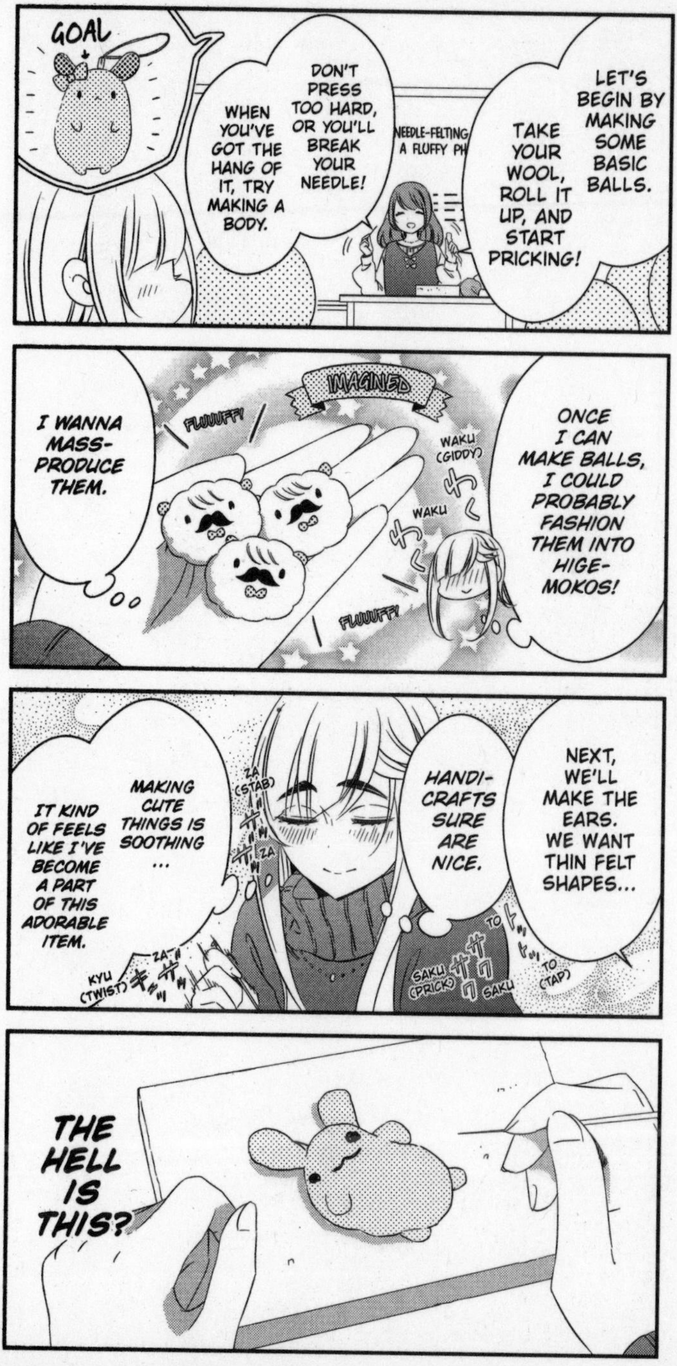
LET'S BEGIN BY MAKING SOME BASIC BALLS.
TAKE YOUR WOOL, ROLL IT UP, AND START PRICKING!
NEEDLE-FELTING A FLUFFY PH
DON'T PRESS TOO HARD, OR YOU'LL BREAK YOUR NEEDLE!
WHEN YOU'VE GOT THE HANG OF IT, TRY MAKING A BODY.
GOAL
IMAGINED
ONCE I CAN MAKE BALLS, I COULD PROBABLY FASHION THEM INTO HIGE-MOKOS!
WAKU (GIDDY) WAKU
FLUUUFF!
FLUUUFF!
I WANNA MASS-PRODUCE THEM.
NEXT, WE'LL MAKE THE EARS. WE WANT THIN FELT SHAPES...
TO TO (TAP)
SAKU (PRICK) SAKU
HANDI-CRAFTS SURE ARE NICE.
ZA (STAB) ZA
MAKING CUTE THINGS IS SOOTHING...
IT KIND OF FEELS LIKE I'VE BECOME A PART OF THIS ADORABLE ITEM.
ZA
KYU (TWIST)
THE HELL IS THIS?

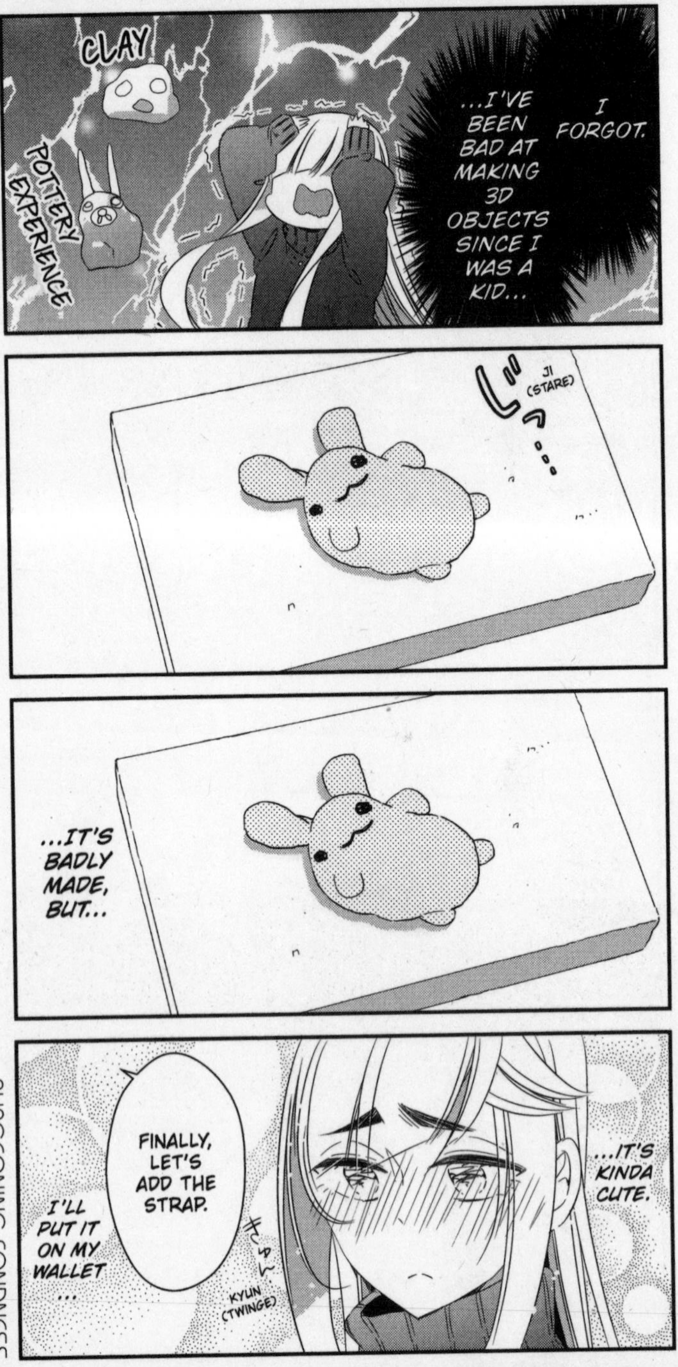
I FORGOT.
...I'VE BEEN BAD AT MAKING 3D OBJECTS SINCE I WAS A KID...
CLAY
POTTERY EXPERIENCE
JI (STARE)
...IT'S BADLY MADE, BUT...
...IT'S KINDA CUTE.
KYUN (TWINGE)
FINALLY, LET'S ADD THE STRAP.
I'LL PUT IT ON MY WALLET...

BURGEONING FONDNESS

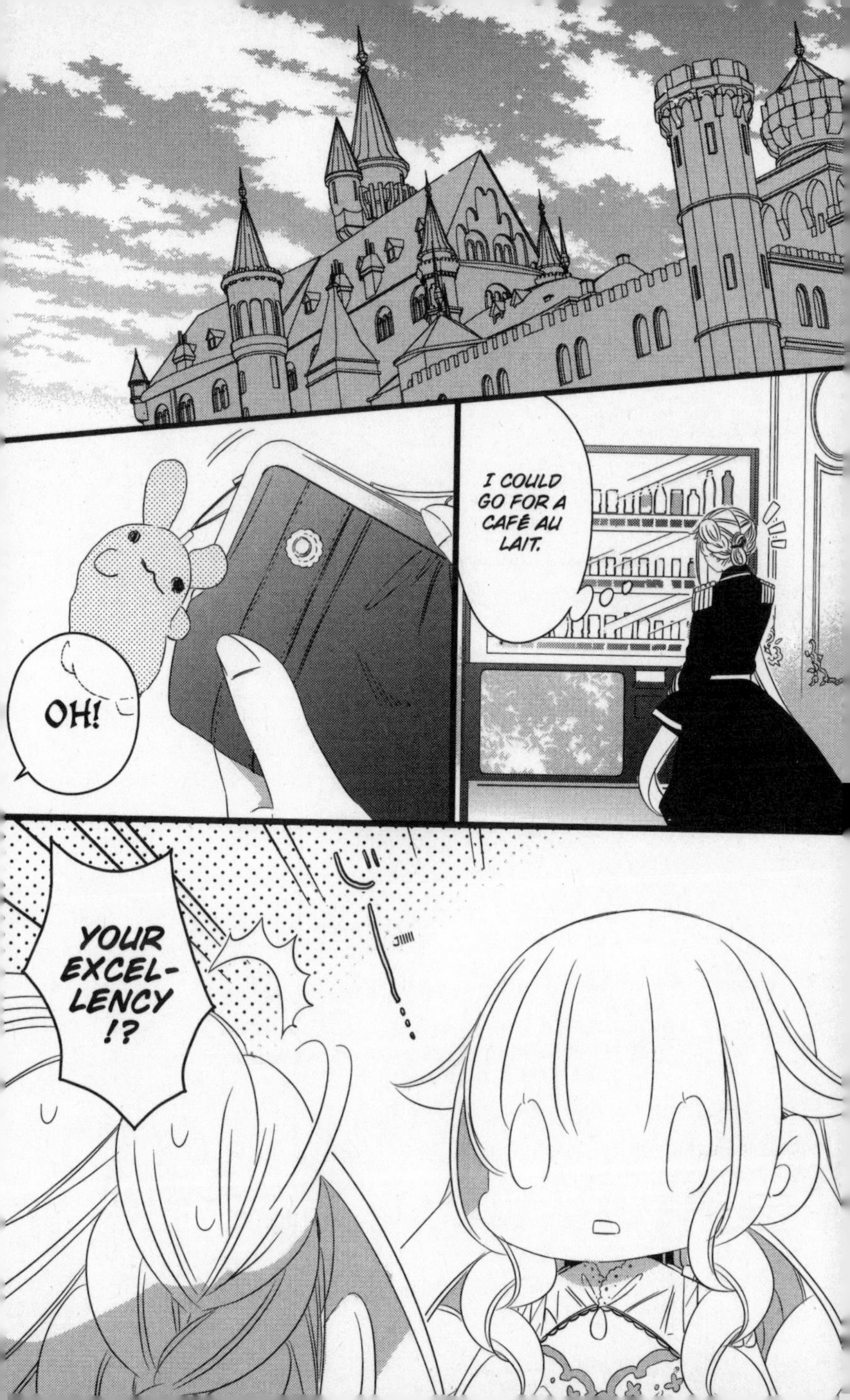
I COULD GO FOR A CAFÉ AU LAIT.
OH!
JIIII
YOUR EXCEL-LENCY!?

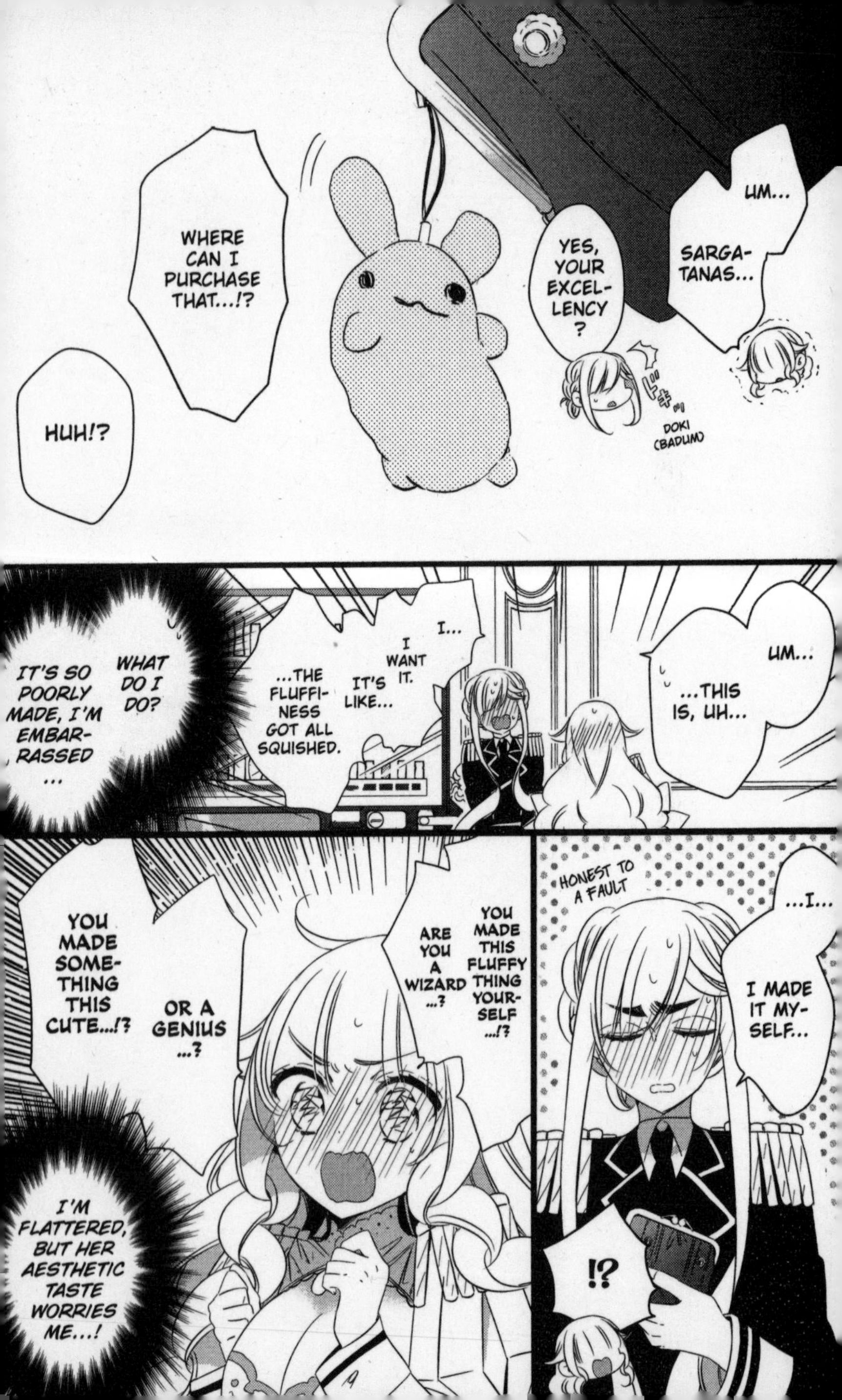
UM... SARGATANAS...
YES, YOUR EXCELLENCY?
DOKI (BADUM)
WHERE CAN I PURCHASE THAT...!?
HUH!?
UM... ...THIS IS, UH...
I... I WANT IT. IT'S LIKE... ...THE FLUFFINESS GOT ALL SQUISHED.
WHAT DO I DO?
IT'S SO POORLY MADE, I'M EMBARRASSED...
HONEST TO A FAULT
...I... I MADE IT MYSELF...
!?
YOU MADE THIS FLUFFY THING YOURSELF...!?
ARE YOU A WIZARD...?
OR A GENIUS...?
YOU MADE SOMETHING THIS CUTE...!?
I'M FLATTERED, BUT HER AESTHETIC TASTE WORRIES ME...!

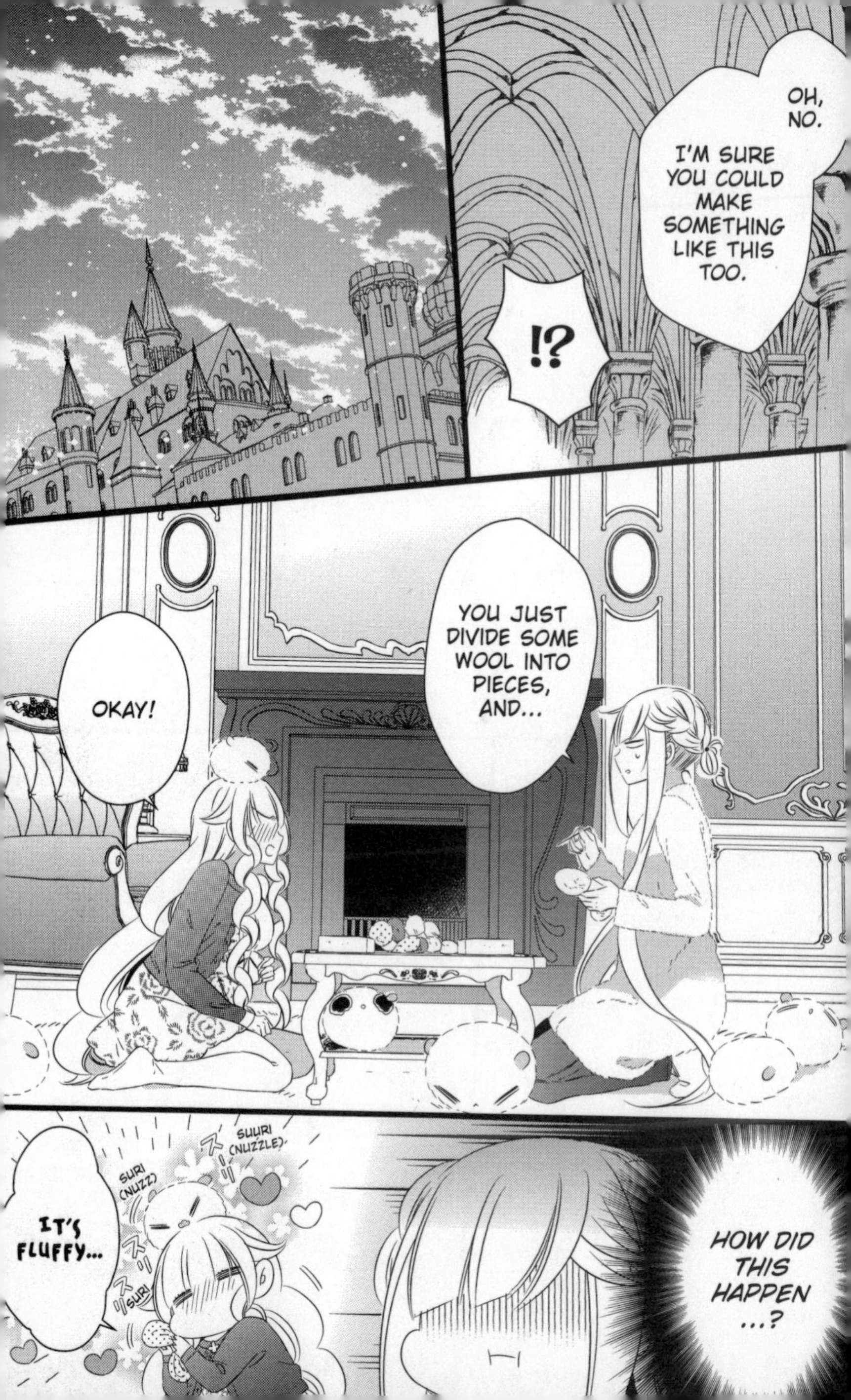
OH, NO.
I'M SURE YOU COULD MAKE SOMETHING LIKE THIS TOO.
!?
YOU JUST DIVIDE SOME WOOL INTO PIECES, AND...
OKAY!
HOW DID THIS HAPPEN ...?
SUURI (NUZZLE)
SURI (NUZZ)
IT'S FLUFFY...
SURI

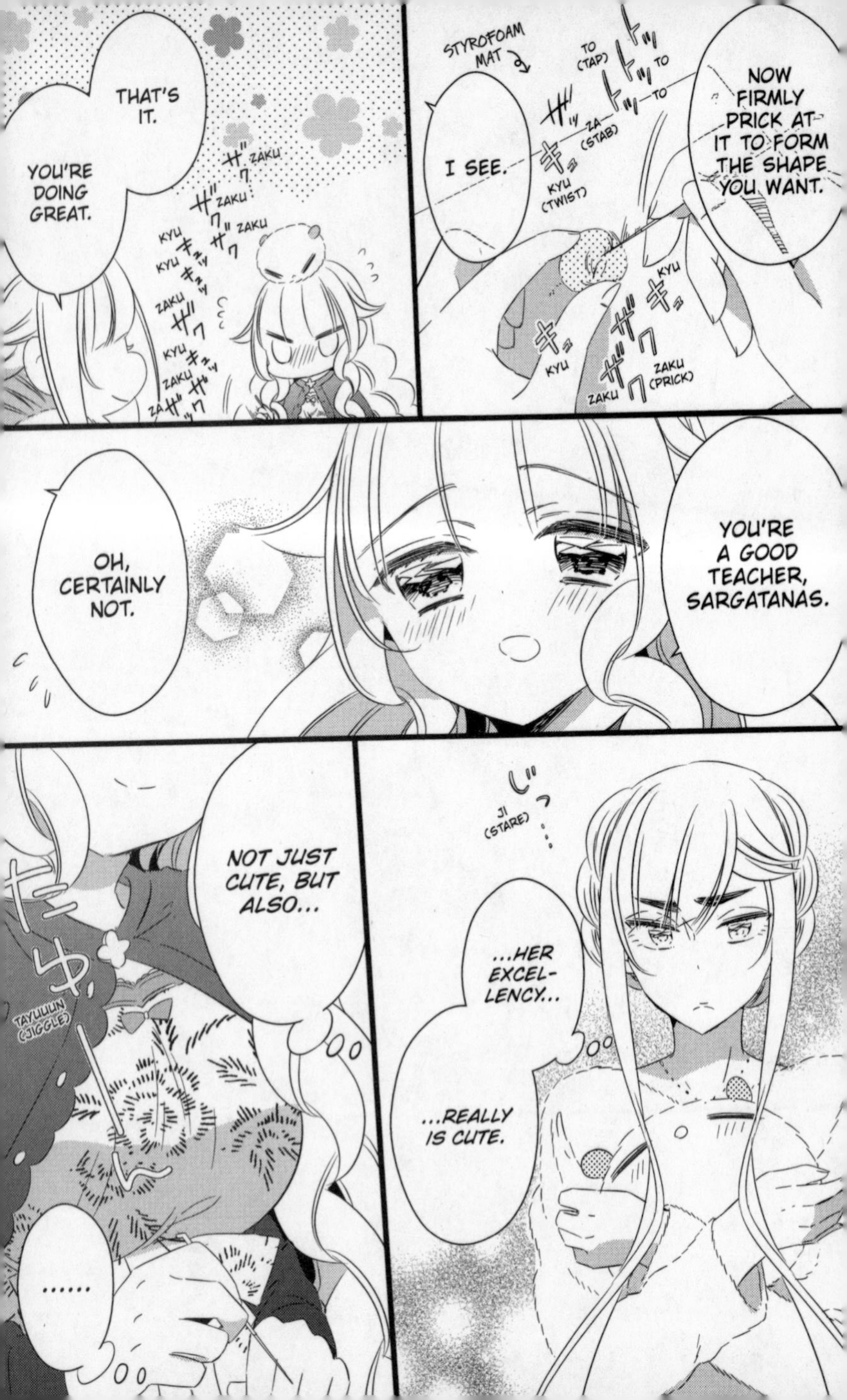

NOW FIRMLY PRICK AT IT TO FORM THE SHAPE YOU WANT.
TO (TAP) TO TO
ZA (STAB)
KYU (TWIST)
STYROFOAM MAT
I SEE.
KYU
KYU
ZAKU (PRICK)
ZAKU
THAT'S IT.
YOU'RE DOING GREAT.
ZAKU
ZAKU
ZAKU
KYU
KYU
ZAKU
KYU
ZAKU
ZA
YOU'RE A GOOD TEACHER, SARGATANAS.
OH, CERTAINLY NOT.
JI (STARE)
...HER EXCEL-LENCY...
...REALLY IS CUTE.
NOT JUST CUTE, BUT ALSO...
TAYUUUN (JIGGLE)
......

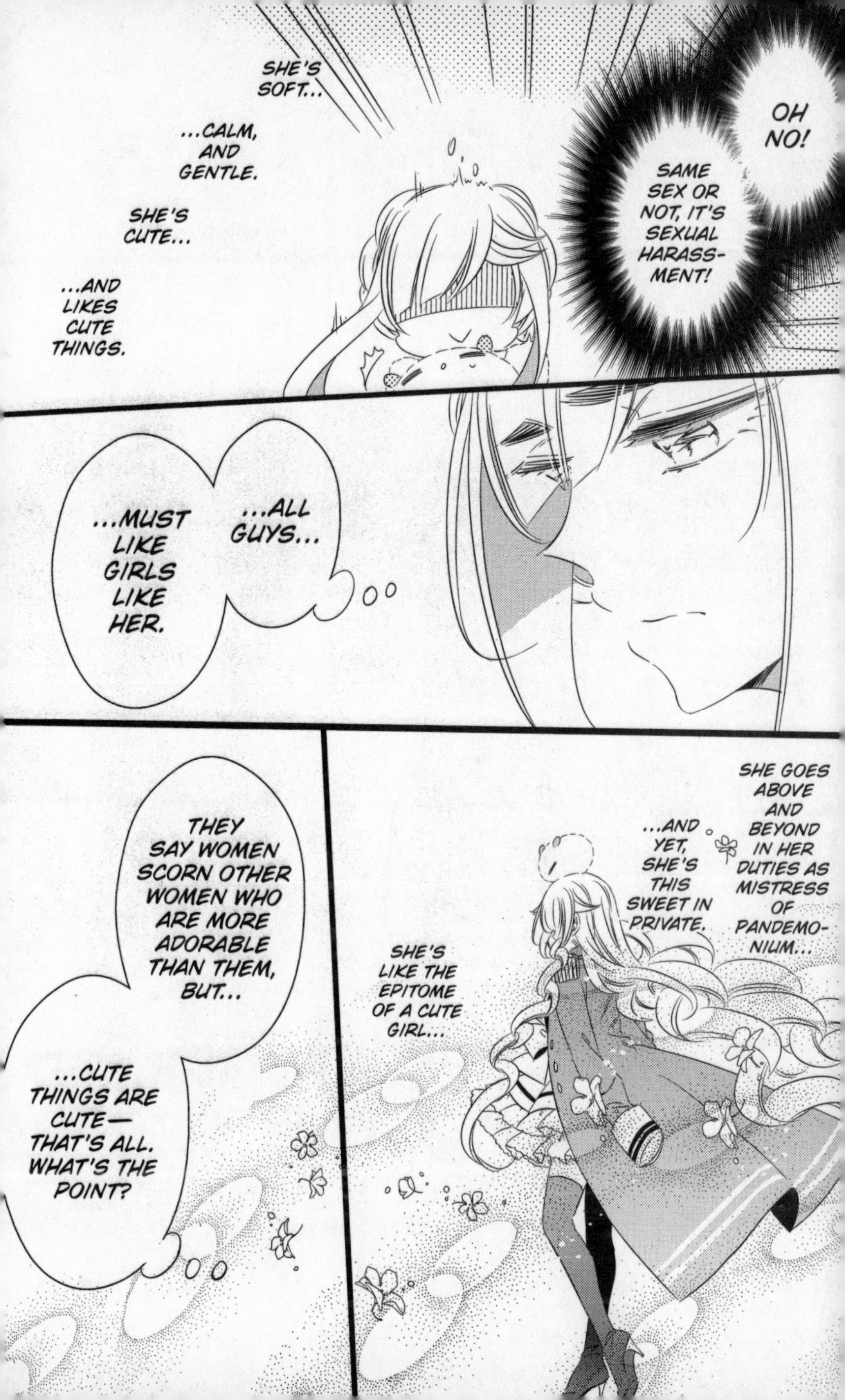
SHE'S SOFT...
...CALM, AND GENTLE.
SHE'S CUTE...
...AND LIKES CUTE THINGS.
OH NO!
SAME SEX OR NOT, IT'S SEXUAL HARASS-MENT!
...ALL GUYS...
...MUST LIKE GIRLS LIKE HER.
SHE GOES ABOVE AND BEYOND IN HER DUTIES AS MISTRESS OF PANDEMO-NIUM...
...AND YET, SHE'S THIS SWEET IN PRIVATE.
SHE'S LIKE THE EPITOME OF A CUTE GIRL...
THEY SAY WOMEN SCORN OTHER WOMEN WHO ARE MORE ADORABLE THAN THEM, BUT...
...CUTE THINGS ARE CUTE— THAT'S ALL. WHAT'S THE POINT?

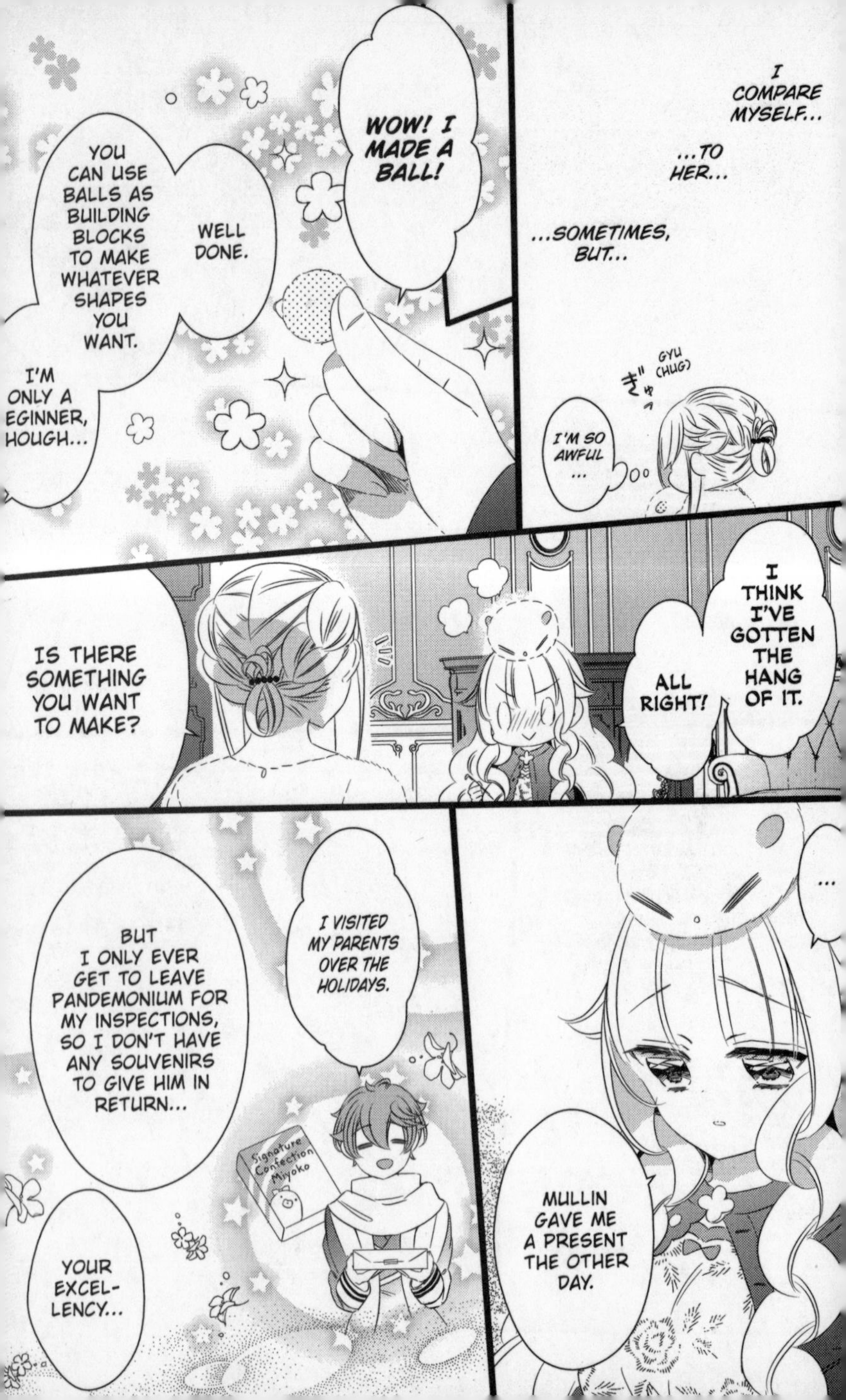
I COMPARE MYSELF...
...TO HER...
...SOMETIMES, BUT...
ぎゅ
GYU (HUG)
I'M SO AWFUL...
WOW! I MADE A BALL!
WELL DONE.
YOU CAN USE BALLS AS BUILDING BLOCKS TO MAKE WHATEVER SHAPES YOU WANT.
I'M ONLY A EGINNER, HOUGH...
I THINK I'VE GOTTEN THE HANG OF IT.
ALL RIGHT!
IS THERE SOMETHING YOU WANT TO MAKE?
...
MULLIN GAVE ME A PRESENT THE OTHER DAY.
I VISITED MY PARENTS OVER THE HOLIDAYS.
BUT I ONLY EVER GET TO LEAVE PANDEMONIUM FOR MY INSPECTIONS, SO I DON'T HAVE ANY SOUVENIRS TO GIVE HIM IN RETURN...
Signature Confection Miyoko
YOUR EXCEL-LENCY...

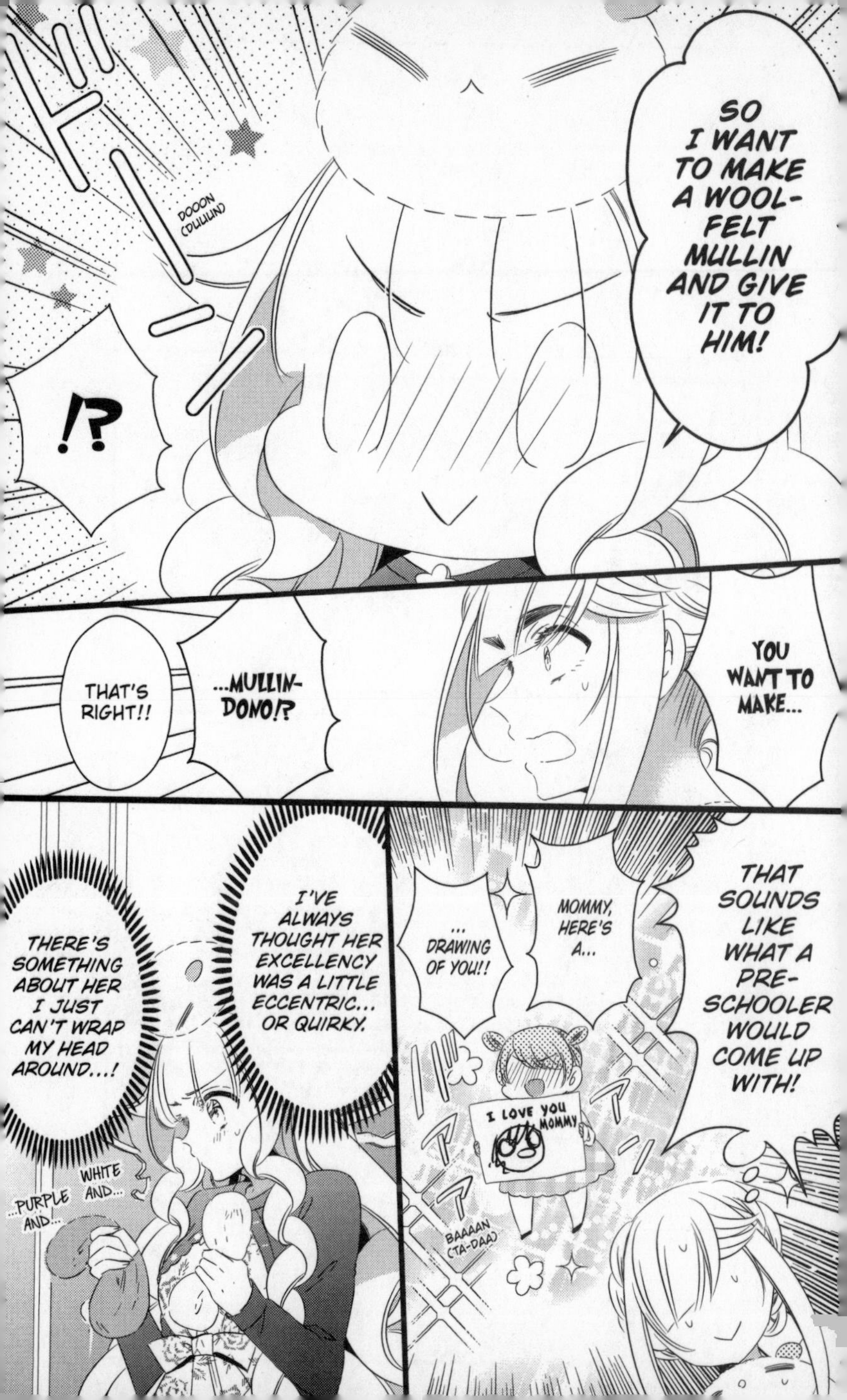
SO I WANT TO MAKE A WOOL-FELT MULLIN AND GIVE IT TO HIM!
DOOON (DUUUN)
!?
YOU WANT TO MAKE...
...MULLIN-DONO!?
THAT'S RIGHT!!
THAT SOUNDS LIKE WHAT A PRE-SCHOOLER WOULD COME UP WITH!
MOMMY, HERE'S A...
...DRAWING OF YOU!!
I LOVE YOU MOMMY
BAAAAN (TA-DAA)
I'VE ALWAYS THOUGHT HER EXCELLENCY WAS A LITTLE ECCENTRIC... OR QUIRKY.
THERE'S SOMETHING ABOUT HER I JUST CAN'T WRAP MY HEAD AROUND...!
WHITE AND...
...PURPLE AND...

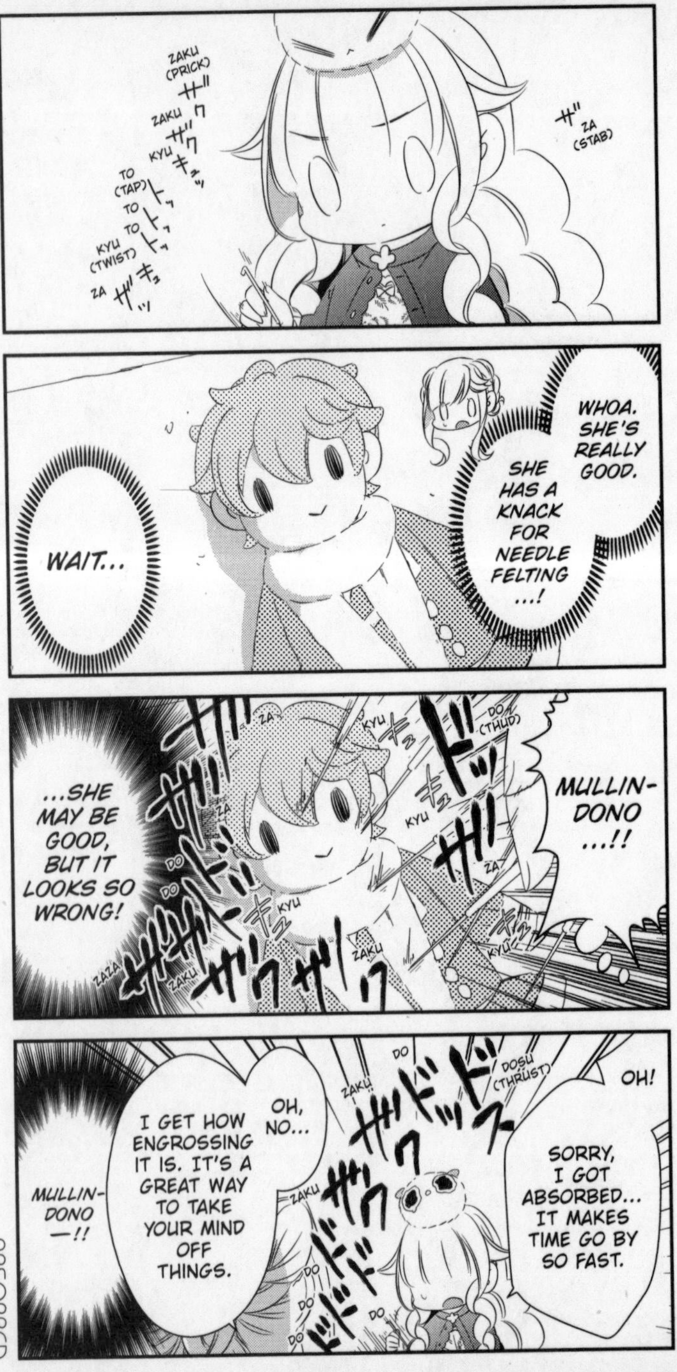
ZA (STAB)
ZAKU (PRICK)
ZAKU
KYU
TO (TAP)
TO
TO
KYU (TWIST)
ZA
WHOA. SHE'S REALLY GOOD.
SHE HAS A KNACK FOR NEEDLE FELTING ...!
WAIT...
MULLIN-DONO ...!!
DO (THUD)
KYU
ZA
KYU
ZA
KYU
KYU
ZAKU
ZA
DO
DO
ZAKU
ZAZA
...SHE MAY BE GOOD, BUT IT LOOKS SO WRONG!
OH!
SORRY, I GOT ABSORBED... IT MAKES TIME GO BY SO FAST.
DOSU (THRUST)
DO
ZAKU
OH, NO...
I GET HOW ENGROSSING IT IS. IT'S A GREAT WAY TO TAKE YOUR MIND OFF THINGS.
ZAKU
DO
DO
DO
DO
MULLIN-DONO—!!

ABSORBED

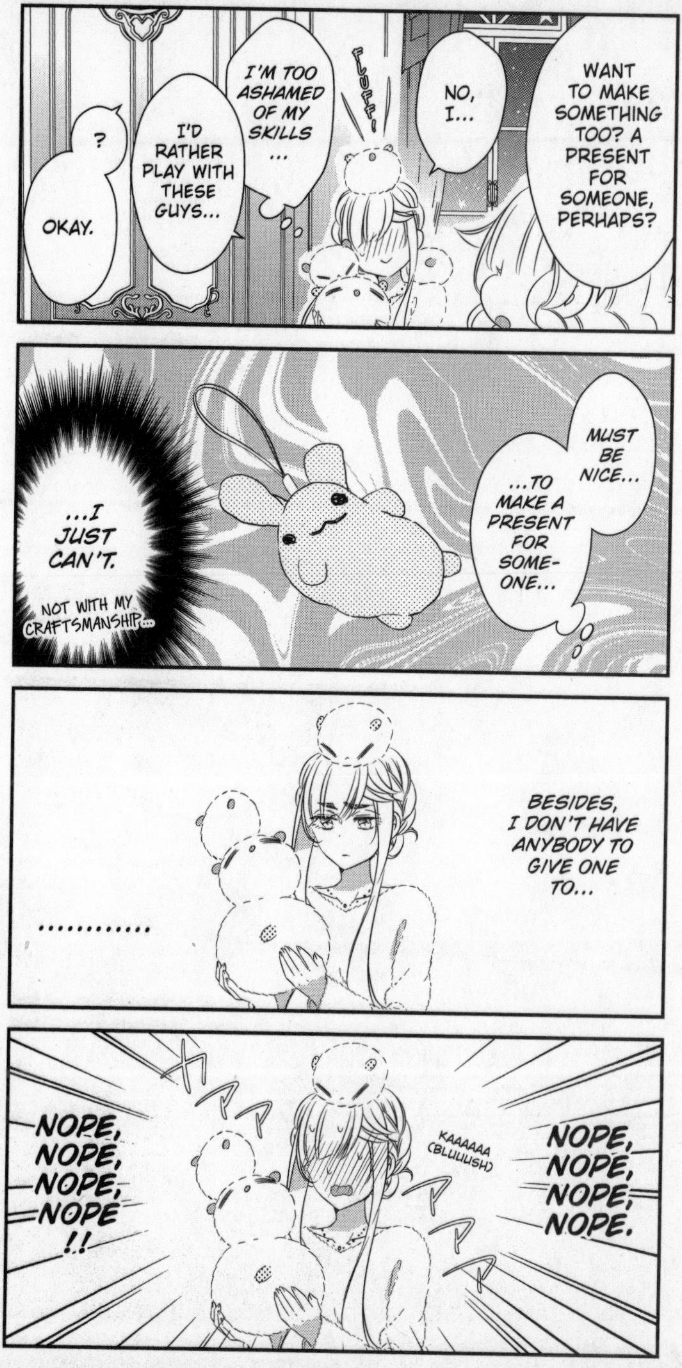
WANT TO MAKE SOMETHING TOO? A PRESENT FOR SOMEONE, PERHAPS?
NO, I...
FLUFF!
I'M TOO ASHAMED OF MY SKILLS ...
I'D RATHER PLAY WITH THESE GUYS...
?
OKAY.
MUST BE NICE...
...TO MAKE A PRESENT FOR SOME-ONE...
...I JUST CAN'T.
NOT WITH MY CRAFTSMANSHIP...
BESIDES, I DON'T HAVE ANYBODY TO GIVE ONE TO...
....
NOPE, NOPE, NOPE, NOPE.
KAAAAAA (BLUUUSH)
NOPE, NOPE, NOPE, NOPE!!

QUIZ: WHO DID SARGATANAS THINK OF?

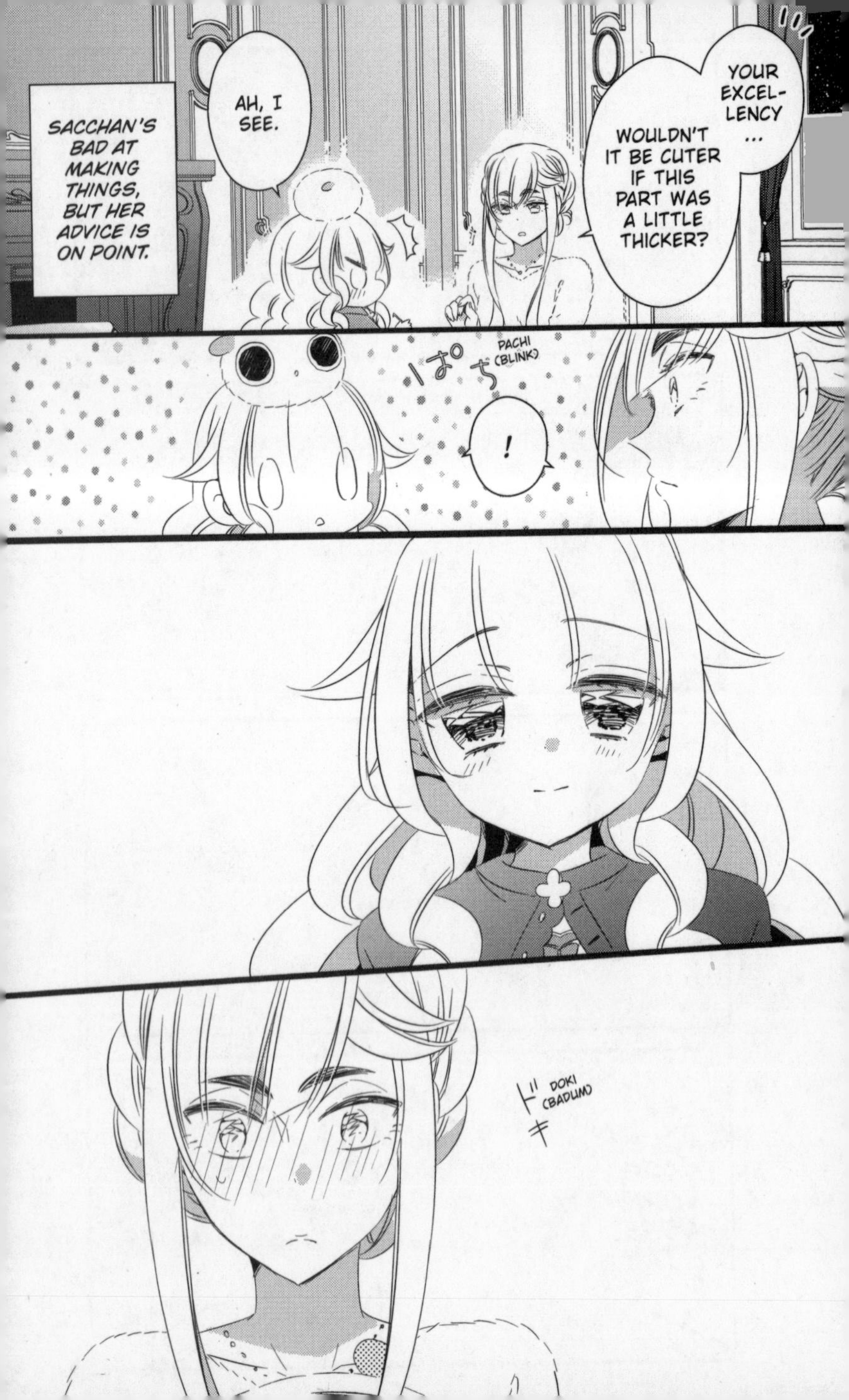
YOUR EXCELLENCY ...
WOULDN'T IT BE CUTER IF THIS PART WAS A LITTLE THICKER?
AH, I SEE.
SACCHAN'S BAD AT MAKING THINGS, BUT HER ADVICE IS ON POINT.
ぱち PACHI (BLINK)
!
ドキ DOKI (BADUM)

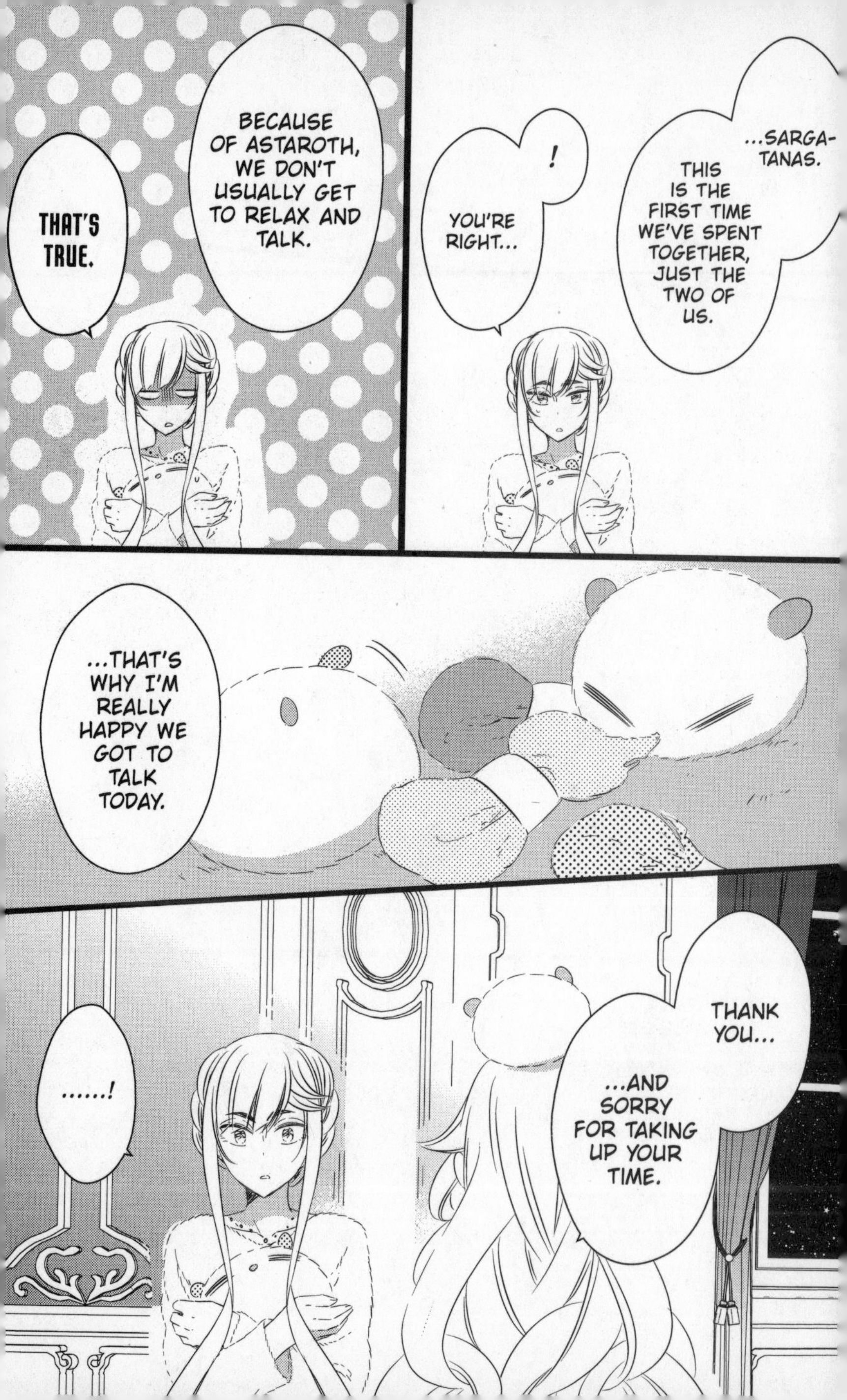
...SARGA-TANAS.
THIS IS THE FIRST TIME WE'VE SPENT TOGETHER, JUST THE TWO OF US.
!
YOU'RE RIGHT...
BECAUSE OF ASTAROTH, WE DON'T USUALLY GET TO RELAX AND TALK.
THAT'S TRUE.
...THAT'S WHY I'M REALLY HAPPY WE GOT TO TALK TODAY.
THANK YOU...
...AND SORRY FOR TAKING UP YOUR TIME.
......!

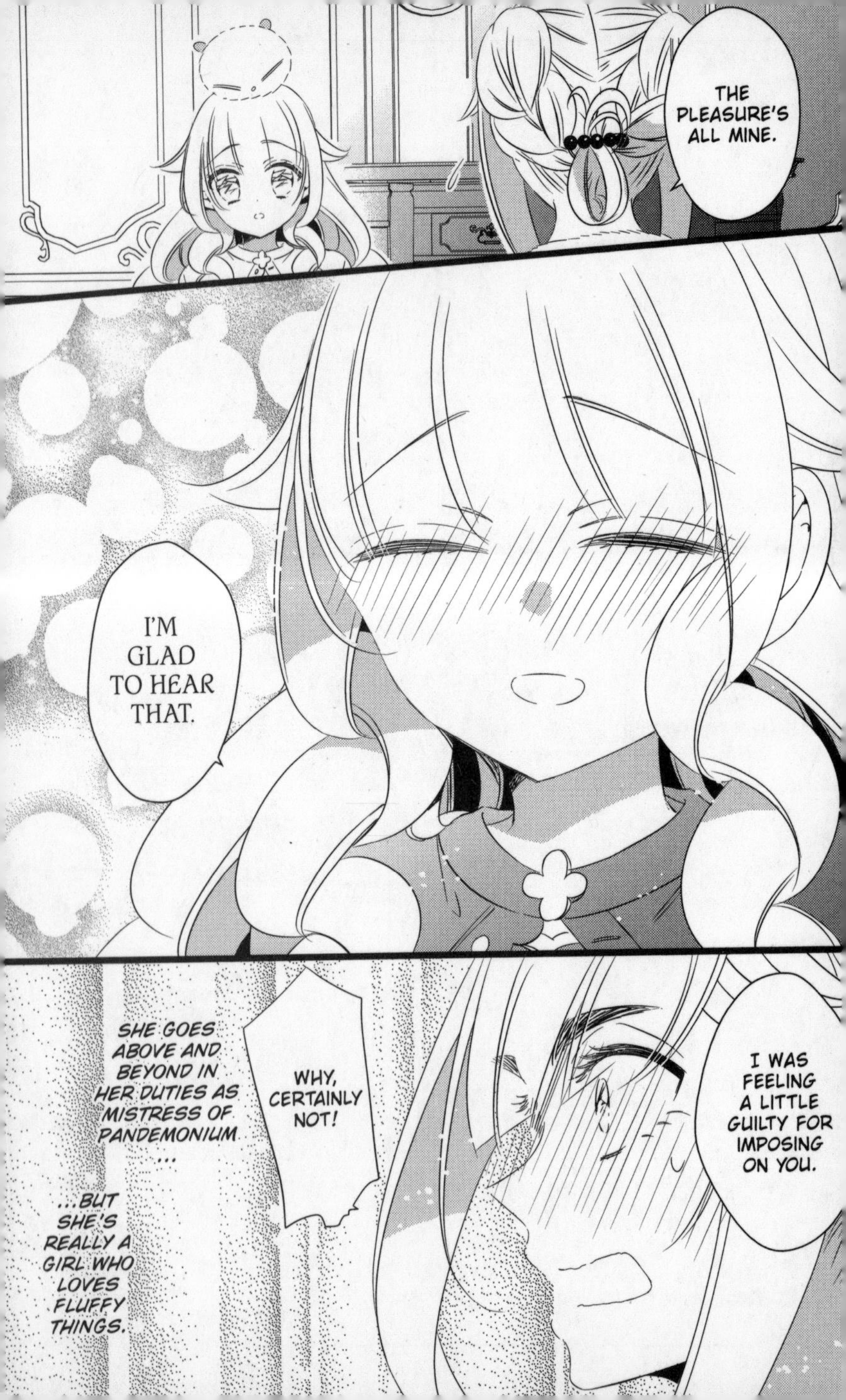
THE PLEASURE'S ALL MINE.
I'M GLAD TO HEAR THAT.
I WAS FEELING A LITTLE GUILTY FOR IMPOSING ON YOU.
WHY, CERTAINLY NOT!
SHE GOES ABOVE AND BEYOND IN HER DUTIES AS MISTRESS OF PANDEMONIUM...
...BUT SHE'S REALLY A GIRL WHO LOVES FLUFFY THINGS.

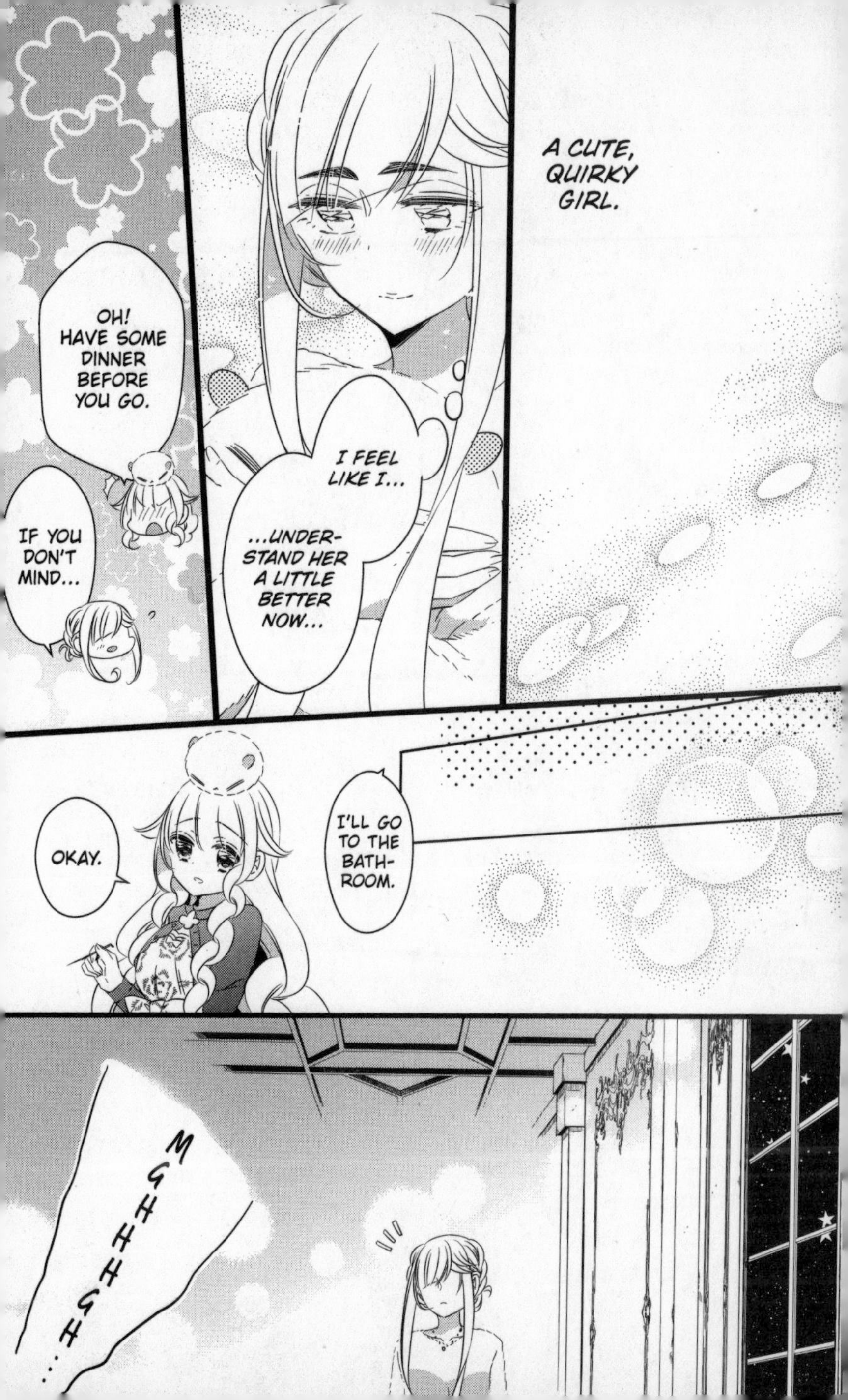
A CUTE, QUIRKY GIRL.
I FEEL LIKE I...
...UNDER-STAND HER A LITTLE BETTER NOW...
OH! HAVE SOME DINNER BEFORE YOU GO.
IF YOU DON'T MIND...
I'LL GO TO THE BATH-ROOM.
OKAY.
MGHHHGH...

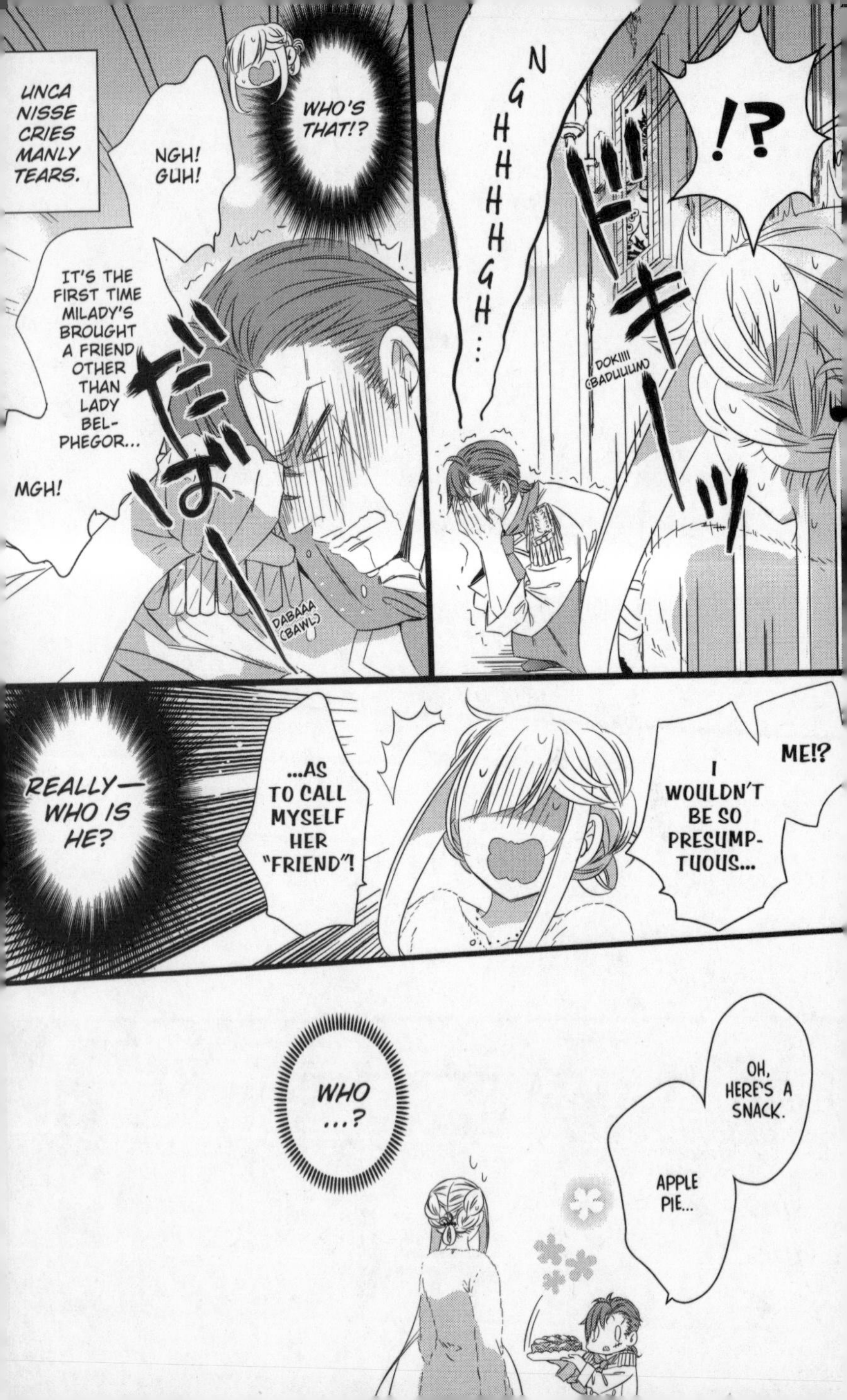
!?
NGHHHHHGH...
DOKIIII (BADUUUM)
WHO'S THAT!?
NGH! GUH!
UNCA NISSE CRIES MANLY TEARS.
IT'S THE FIRST TIME MILADY'S BROUGHT A FRIEND OTHER THAN LADY BEL-PHEGOR...
MGH!
DABAAA (BAWL)
ME!?
I WOULDN'T BE SO PRESUMP-TUOUS...
...AS TO CALL MYSELF HER "FRIEND"!
REALLY— WHO IS HE?
OH, HERE'S A SNACK.
APPLE PIE...
WHO ...?

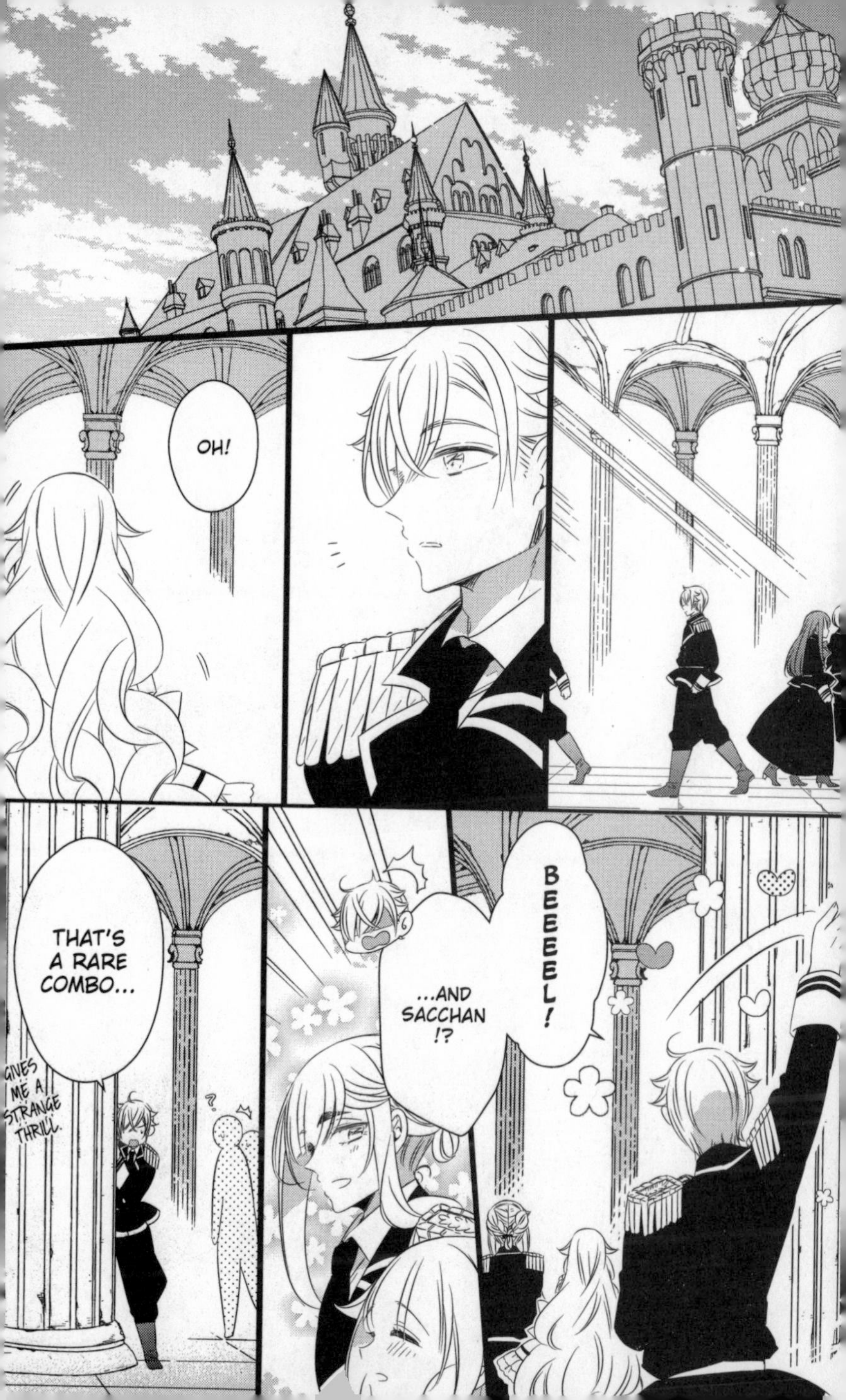
OH!
BEEEEEL!
...AND SACCHAN!?
THAT'S A RARE COMBO...
GIVES ME A STRANGE THRILL.

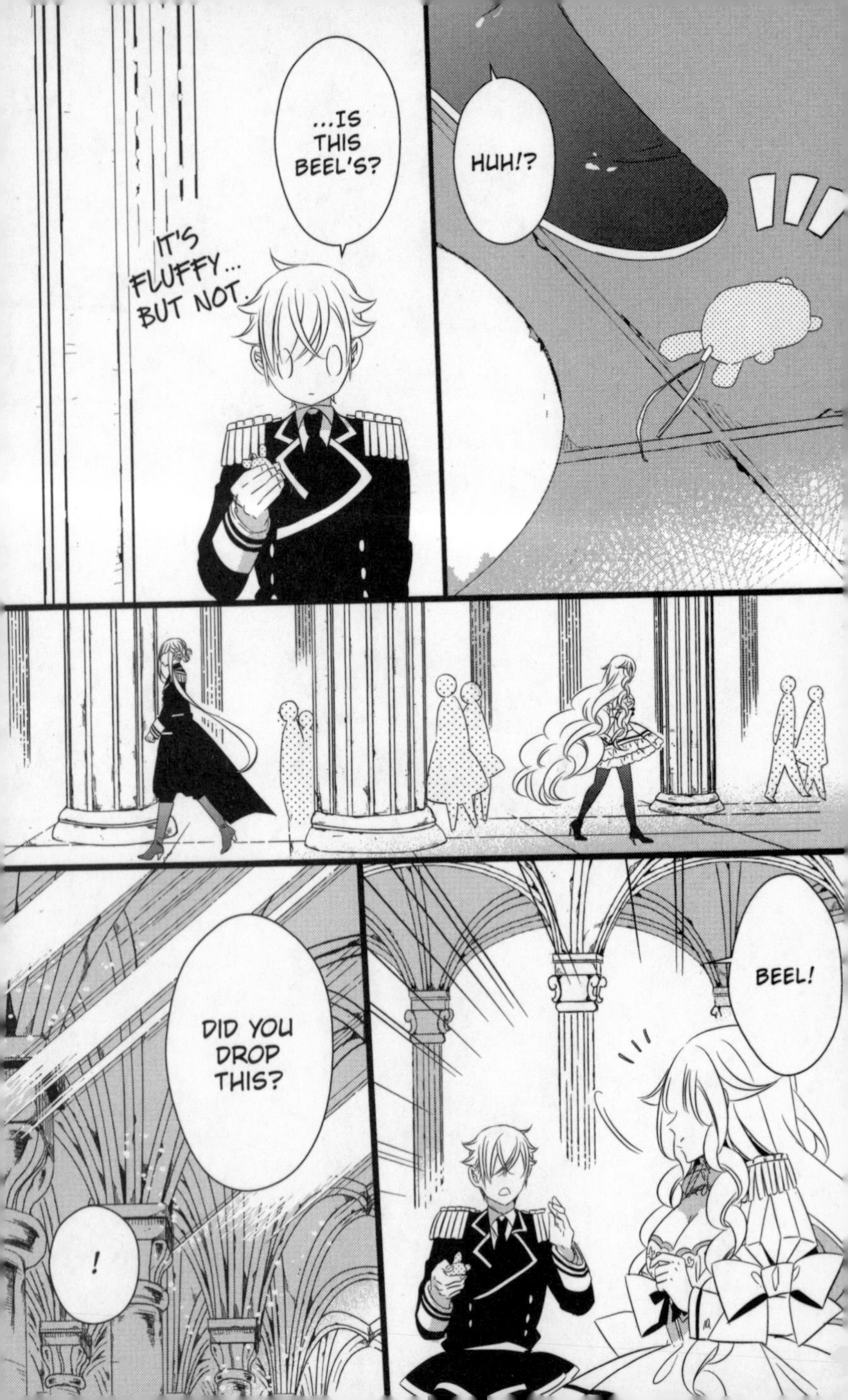
HUH!?
...IS THIS BEEL'S?
IT'S FLUFFY... BUT NOT.
BEEL!
DID YOU DROP THIS?
!

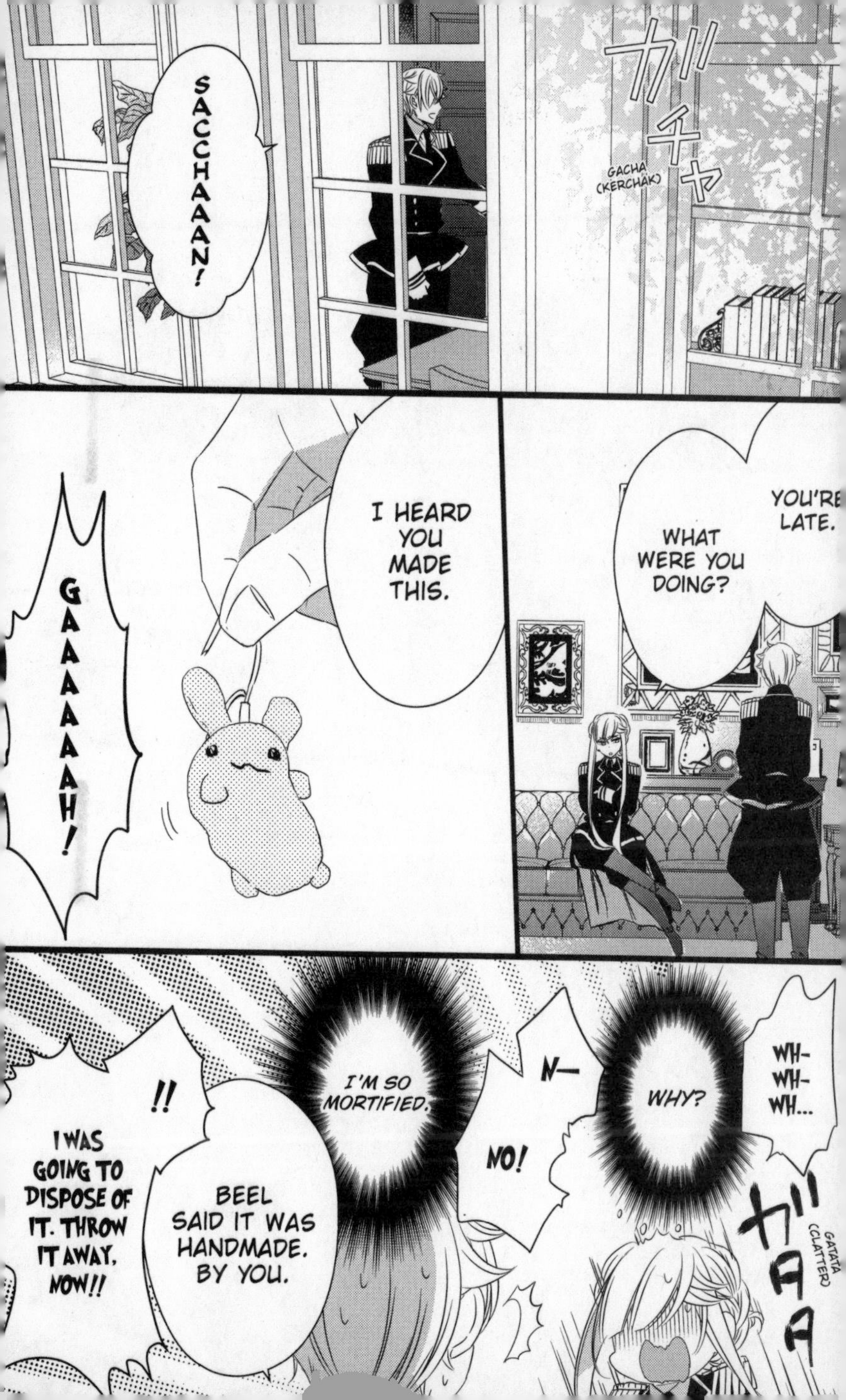
GACHA (KERCHAK)
SACCHAAAN!
YOU'RE LATE.
WHAT WERE YOU DOING?
I HEARD YOU MADE THIS.
GAAAAAAAH!
WH-WH-WH...
GATATA (CLATTER)
WHY?
N—
NO!
I'M SO MORTIFIED.
!!
BEEL SAID IT WAS HANDMADE. BY YOU.
I WAS GOING TO DISPOSE OF IT. THROW IT AWAY, NOW!!

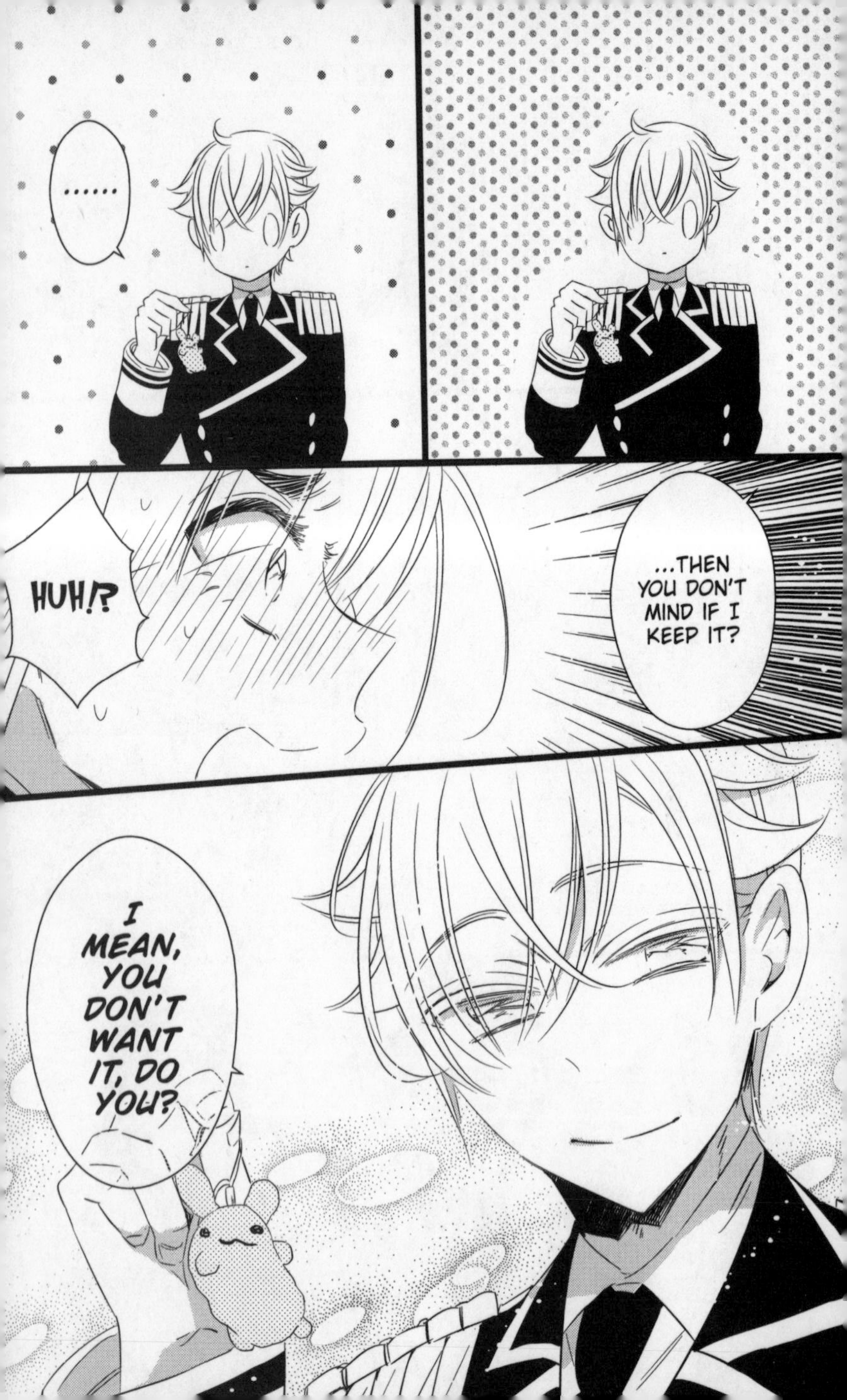
......
...THEN YOU DON'T MIND IF I KEEP IT?
HUH!?
I MEAN, YOU DON'T WANT IT, DO YOU?

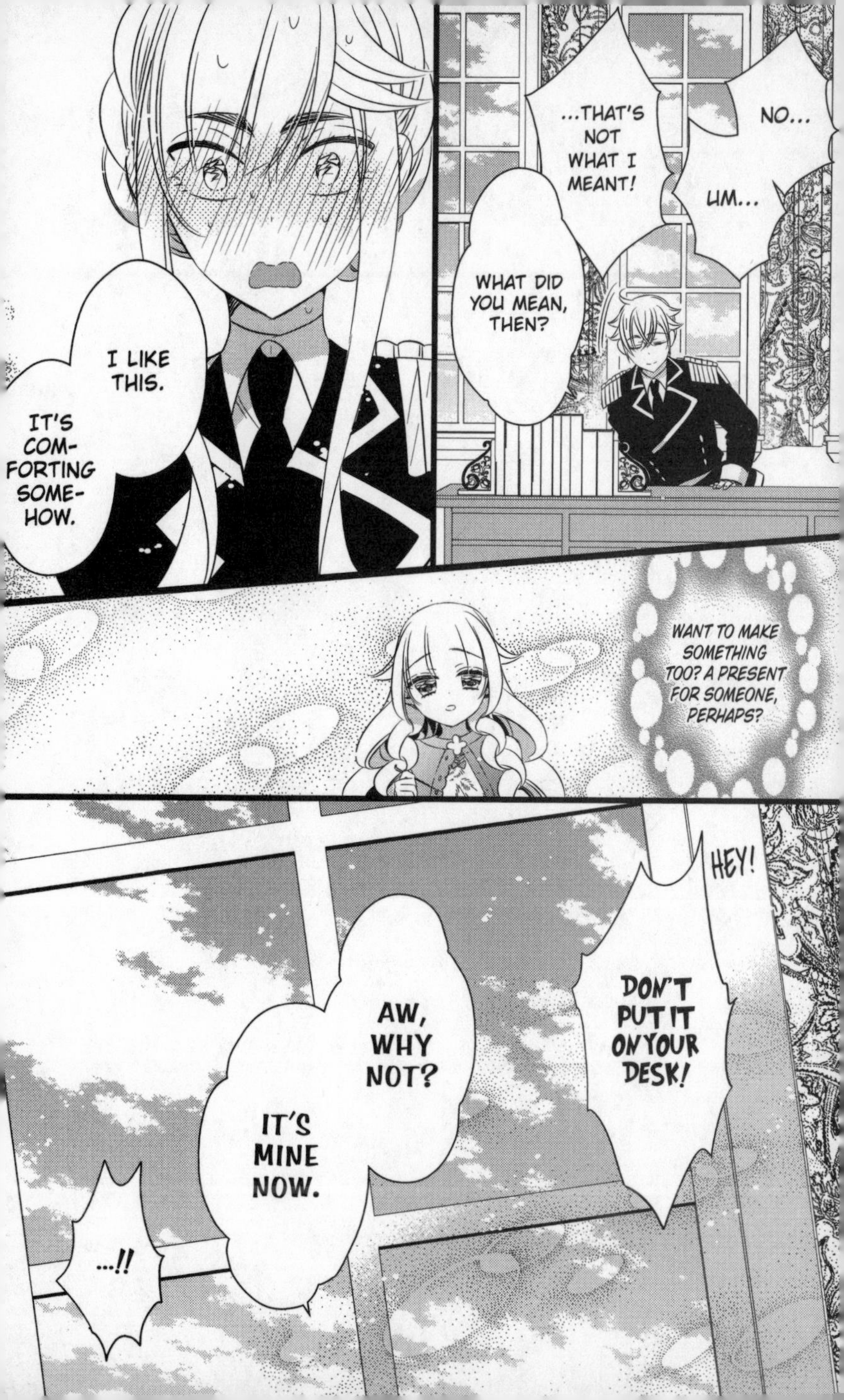

NO...
UM...
...THAT'S NOT WHAT I MEANT!
WHAT DID YOU MEAN, THEN?
I LIKE THIS.
IT'S COMFORTING SOMEHOW.
WANT TO MAKE SOMETHING TOO? A PRESENT FOR SOMEONE, PERHAPS?
HEY!
DON'T PUT IT ON YOUR DESK!
AW, WHY NOT?
IT'S MINE NOW.
...!!

As Miss Beelzebub Likes

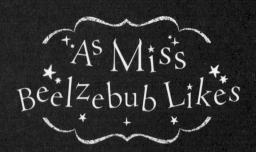

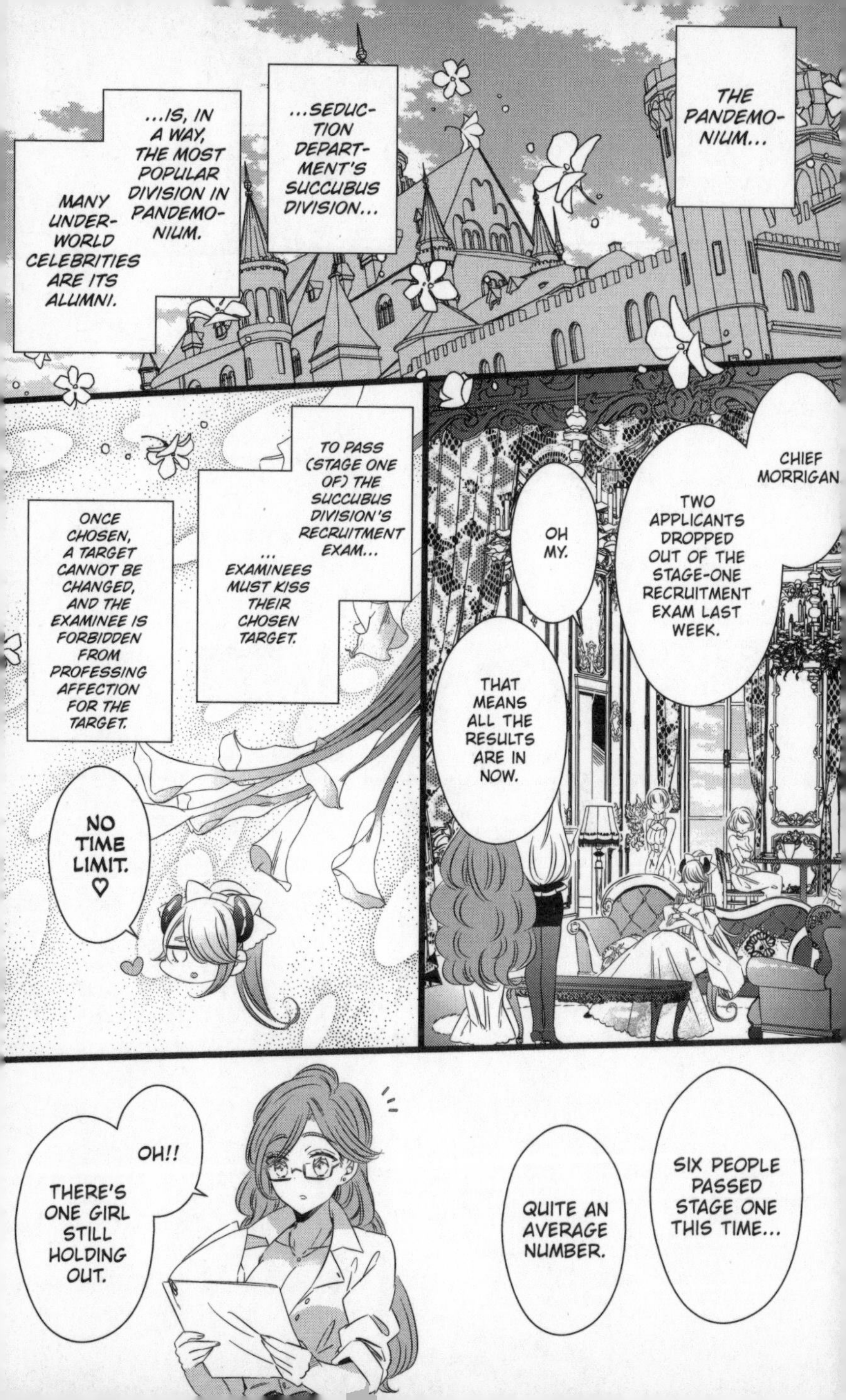
THE PANDEMONIUM...
...SEDUCTION DEPARTMENT'S SUCCUBUS DIVISION...
...IS, IN A WAY, THE MOST POPULAR DIVISION IN PANDEMONIUM.
MANY UNDERWORLD CELEBRITIES ARE ITS ALUMNI.
CHIEF MORRIGAN
TWO APPLICANTS DROPPED OUT OF THE STAGE-ONE RECRUITMENT EXAM LAST WEEK.
OH MY.
THAT MEANS ALL THE RESULTS ARE IN NOW.
TO PASS (STAGE ONE OF) THE SUCCUBUS DIVISION'S RECRUITMENT EXAM...
...EXAMINEES MUST KISS THEIR CHOSEN TARGET.
ONCE CHOSEN, A TARGET CANNOT BE CHANGED, AND THE EXAMINEE IS FORBIDDEN FROM PROFESSING AFFECTION FOR THE TARGET.
NO TIME LIMIT. ♡
SIX PEOPLE PASSED STAGE ONE THIS TIME...
QUITE AN AVERAGE NUMBER.
OH!!
THERE'S ONE GIRL STILL HOLDING OUT.

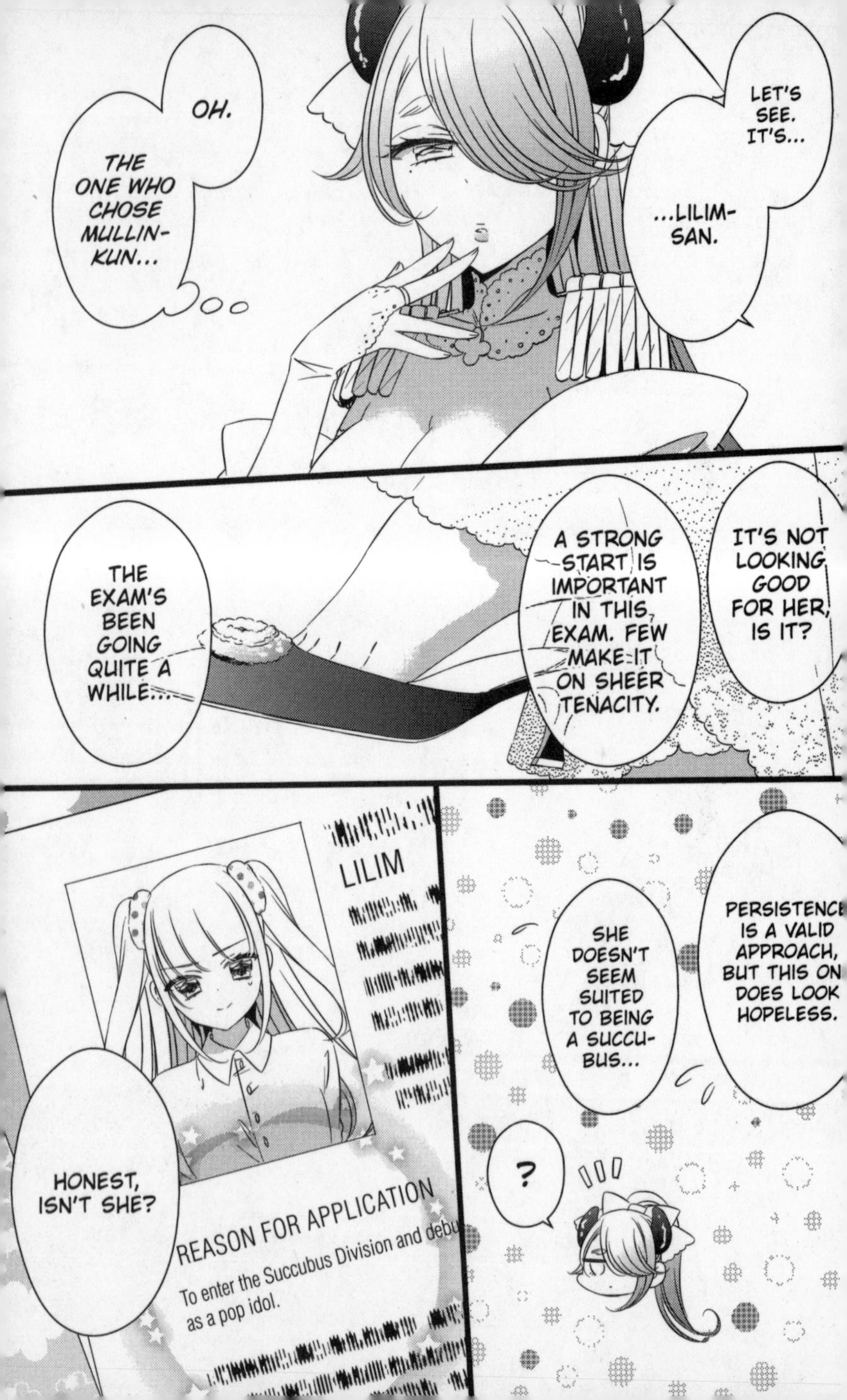
LET'S SEE. IT'S...
...LILIM-SAN.
OH.
THE ONE WHO CHOSE MULLIN-KUN...
IT'S NOT LOOKING GOOD FOR HER, IS IT?
A STRONG START IS IMPORTANT IN THIS EXAM. FEW MAKE IT ON SHEER TENACITY.
THE EXAM'S BEEN GOING QUITE A WHILE...
PERSISTENCE IS A VALID APPROACH, BUT THIS ON DOES LOOK HOPELESS.
SHE DOESN'T SEEM SUITED TO BEING A SUCCUBUS...
?
LILIM
REASON FOR APPLICATION
To enter the Succubus Division and debu as a pop idol.
HONEST, ISN'T SHE?

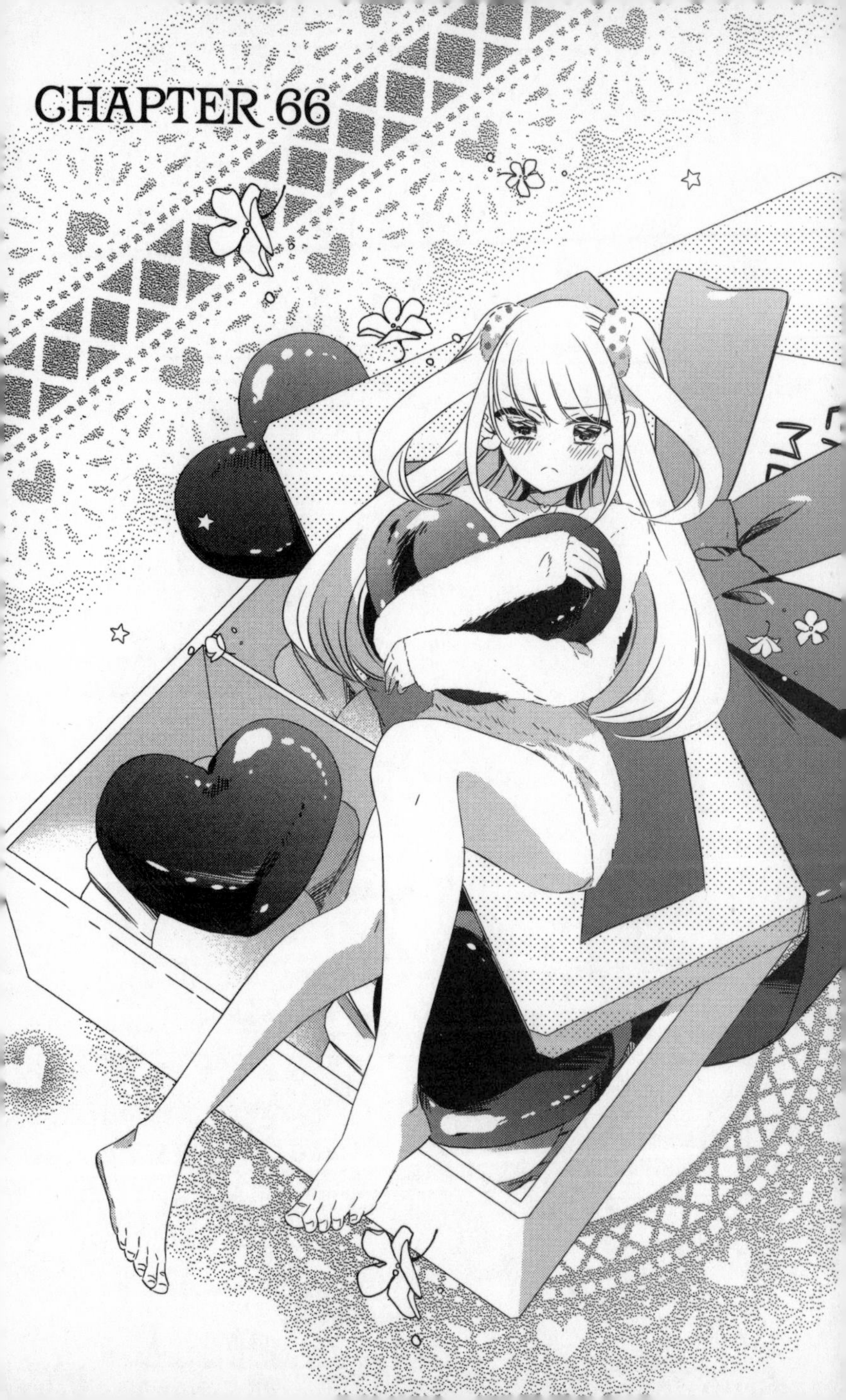
CHAPTER 66

NOT UP ALREADY

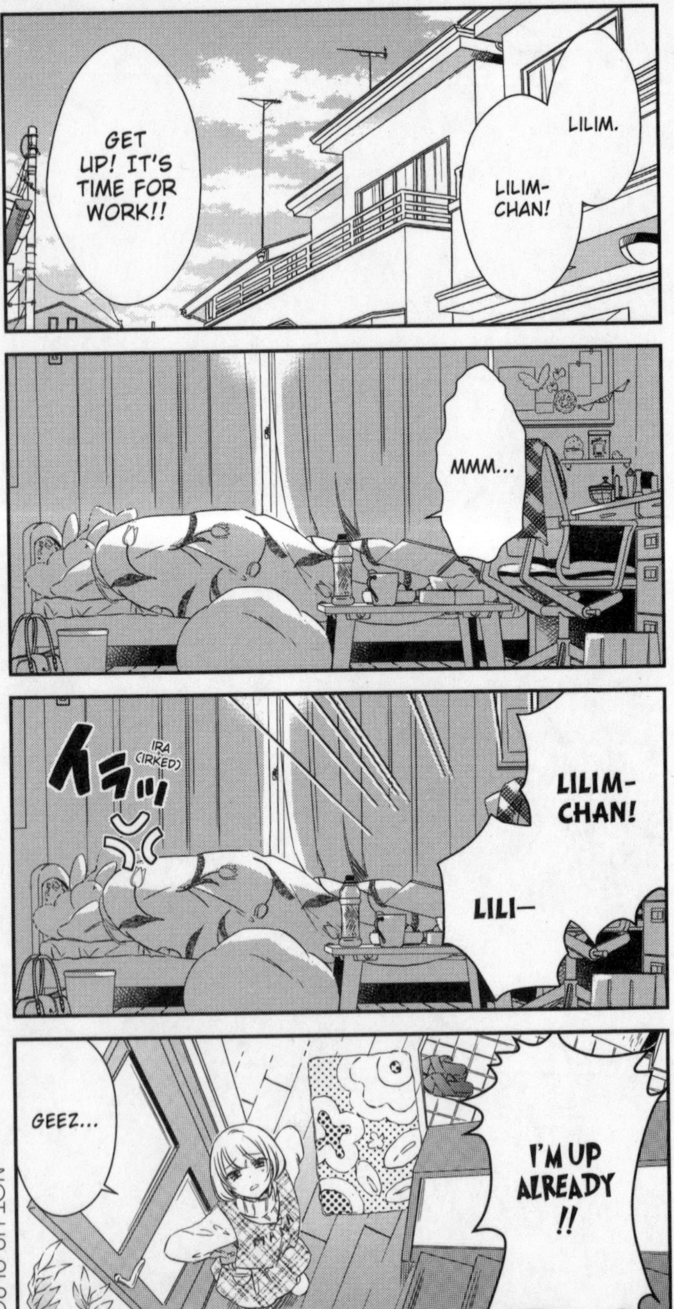
LILIM.
LILIM-CHAN!
GET UP! IT'S TIME FOR WORK!!
MMM...
LILIM-CHAN!
LILI—
IRA (IRKED)
I'M UP ALREADY!!
GEEZ...

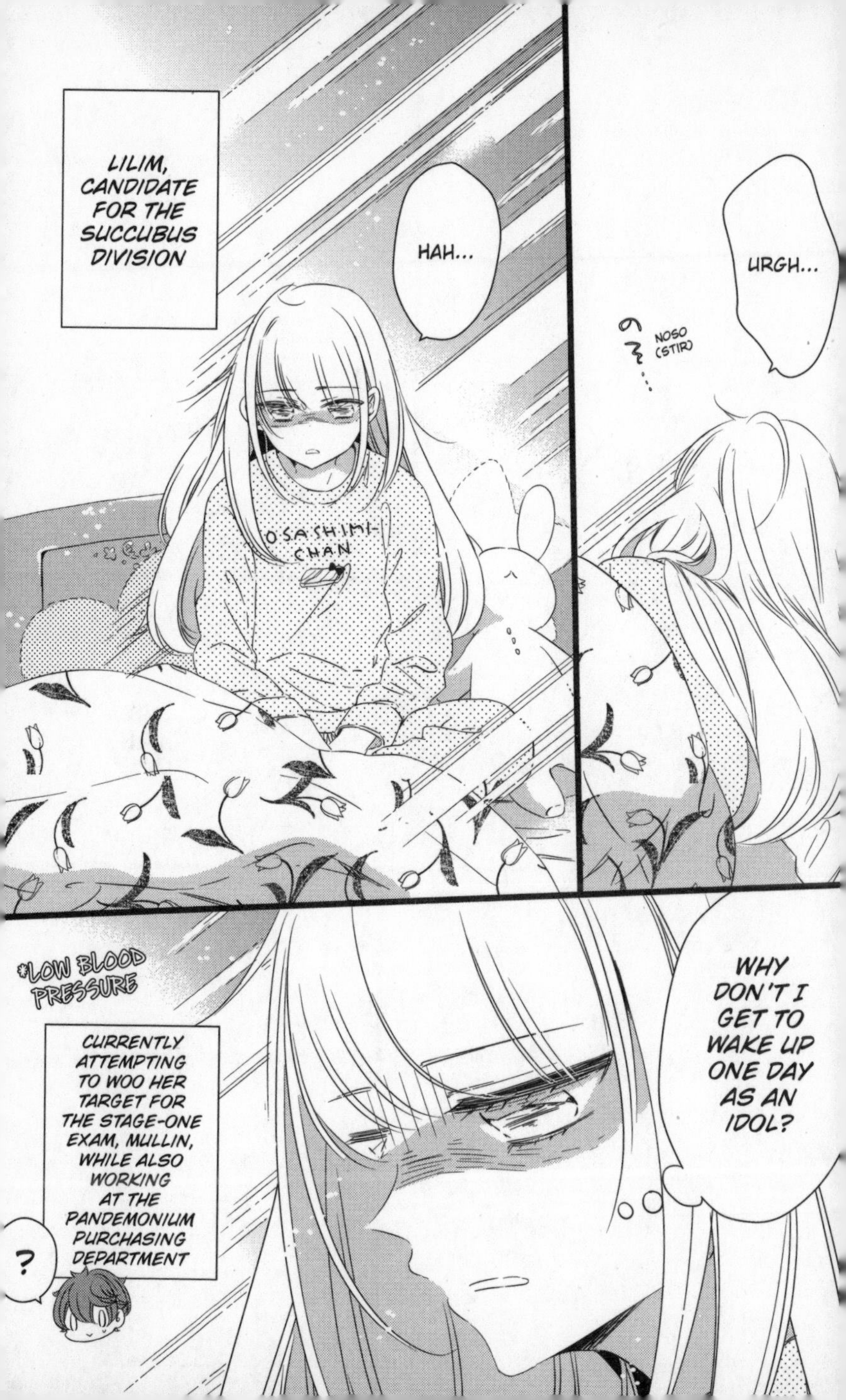
URGH...
NOSO (STIR)
HAH...
LILIM, CANDIDATE FOR THE SUCCUBUS DIVISION
WHY DON'T I GET TO WAKE UP ONE DAY AS AN IDOL?
*LOW BLOOD PRESSURE
CURRENTLY ATTEMPTING TO WOO HER TARGET FOR THE STAGE-ONE EXAM, MULLIN, WHILE ALSO WORKING AT THE PANDEMONIUM PURCHASING DEPARTMENT
?

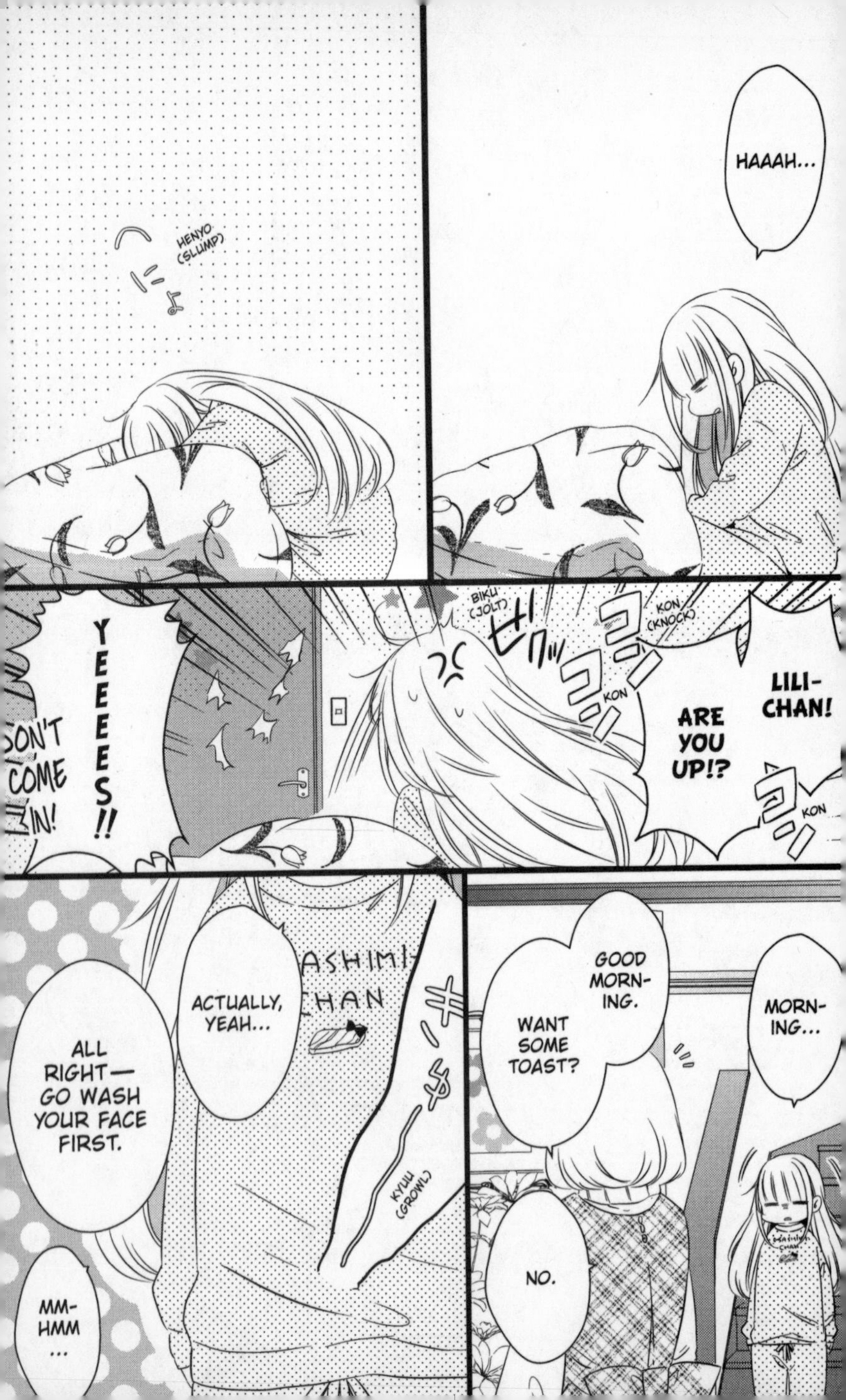
HAAAH...
HENYO (SLUMP)
LILI-CHAN!
KON (KNOCK)
BIKU (JOLT)
ARE YOU UP!?
KON
KON
YEEEEES!!
DON'T COME IN!
MORN-ING...
GOOD MORN-ING.
WANT SOME TOAST?
NO.
ACTUALLY, YEAH...
KYUU (GROWL)
ALL RIGHT— GO WASH YOUR FACE FIRST.
MM-HMM...

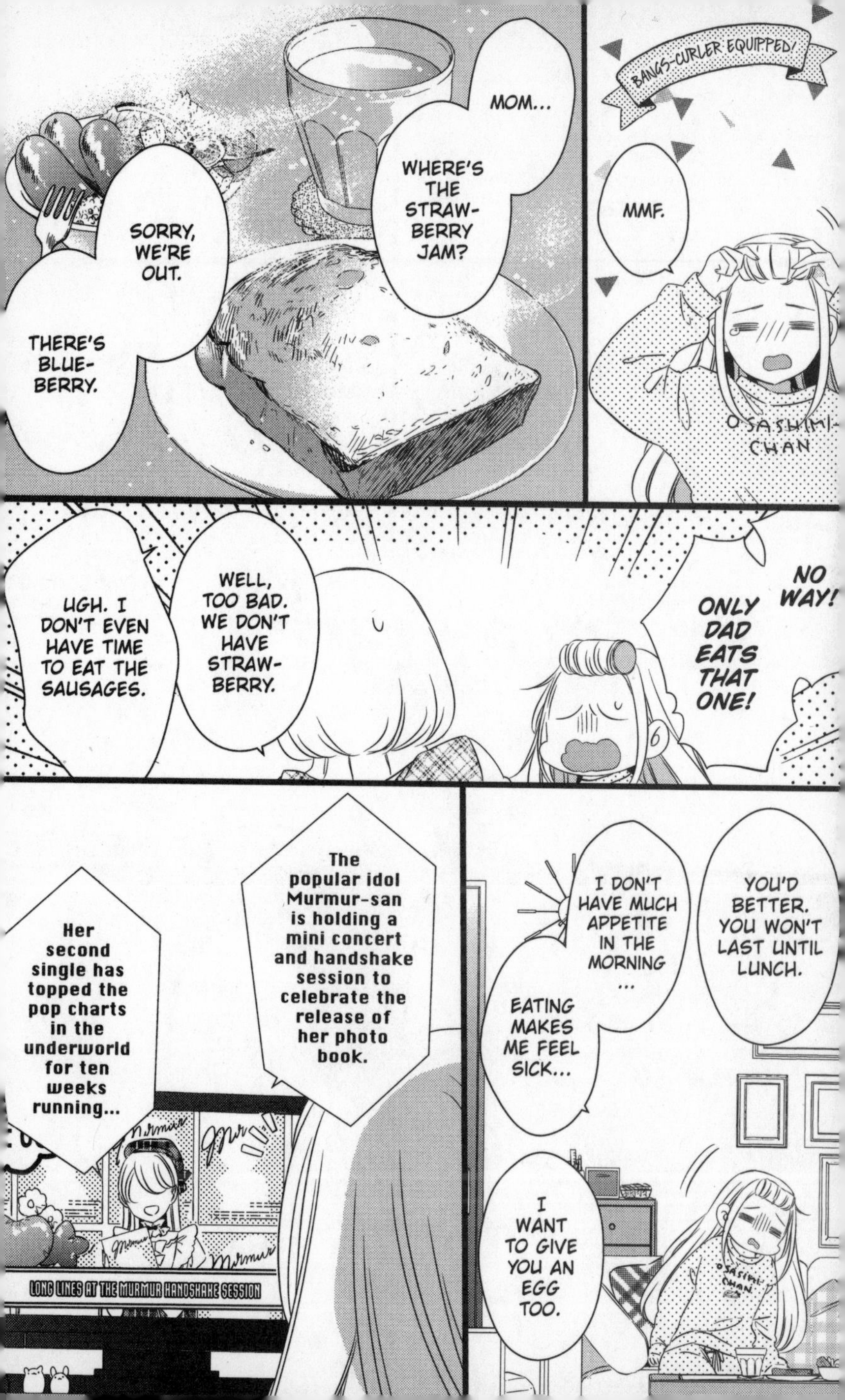
BANGS-CURLER EQUIPPED!
MMF.
O SASHIMI-CHAN
MOM...
WHERE'S THE STRAWBERRY JAM?
SORRY, WE'RE OUT.
THERE'S BLUEBERRY.
NO WAY!
ONLY DAD EATS THAT ONE!
WELL, TOO BAD. WE DON'T HAVE STRAWBERRY.
UGH. I DON'T EVEN HAVE TIME TO EAT THE SAUSAGES.
YOU'D BETTER. YOU WON'T LAST UNTIL LUNCH.
I DON'T HAVE MUCH APPETITE IN THE MORNING...
EATING MAKES ME FEEL SICK...
I WANT TO GIVE YOU AN EGG TOO.
O SASHIMI-CHAN
The popular idol Murmur-san is holding a mini concert and handshake session to celebrate the release of her photo book.
Her second single has topped the pop charts in the underworld for ten weeks running...
LONG LINES AT THE MURMUR HANDSHAKE SESSION

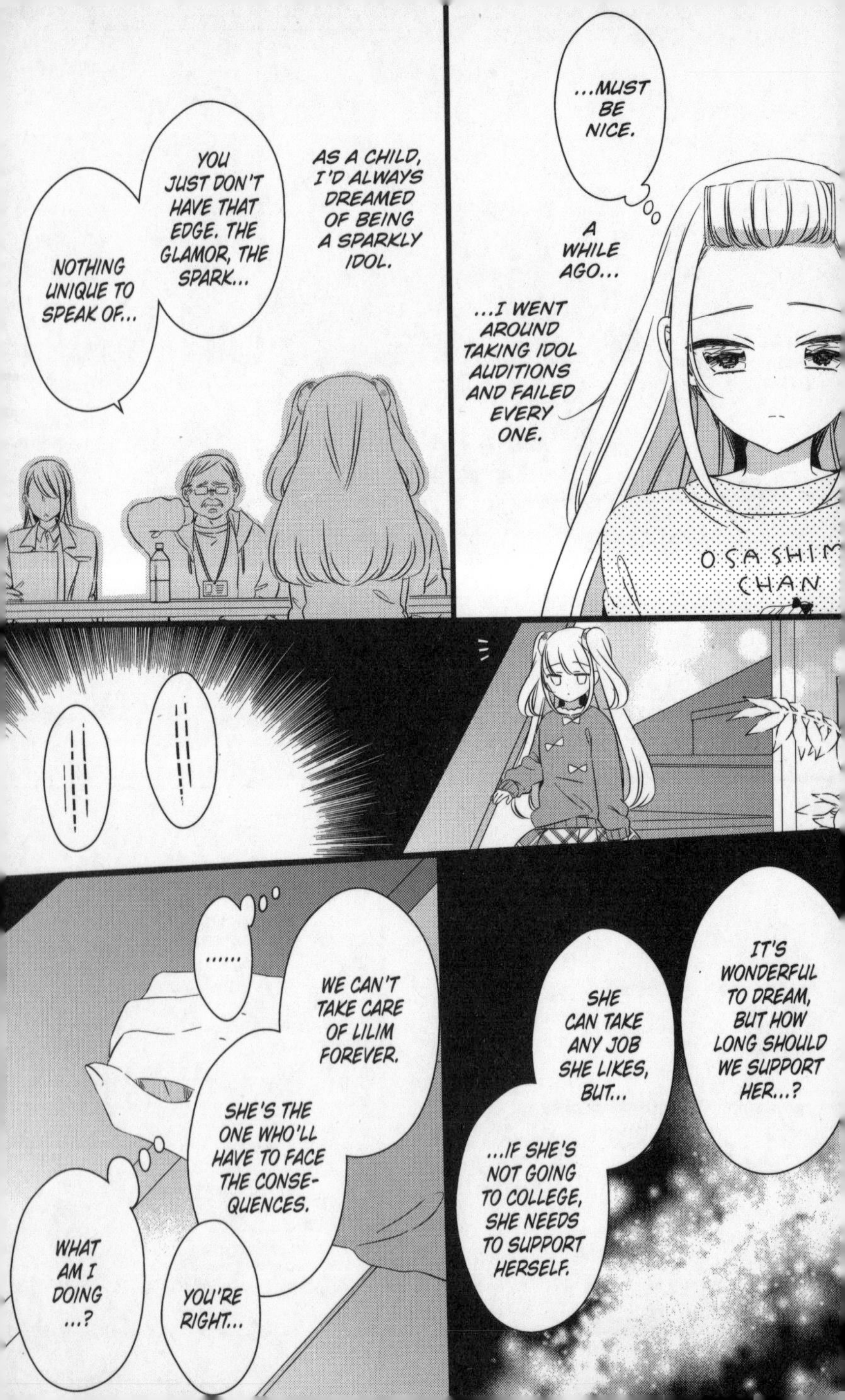
...MUST BE NICE.
A WHILE AGO...
...I WENT AROUND TAKING IDOL AUDITIONS AND FAILED EVERY ONE.
OSASHIM CHAN
AS A CHILD, I'D ALWAYS DREAMED OF BEING A SPARKLY IDOL.
YOU JUST DON'T HAVE THAT EDGE. THE GLAMOR, THE SPARK...
NOTHING UNIQUE TO SPEAK OF...
IT'S WONDERFUL TO DREAM, BUT HOW LONG SHOULD WE SUPPORT HER...?
SHE CAN TAKE ANY JOB SHE LIKES, BUT...
...IF SHE'S NOT GOING TO COLLEGE, SHE NEEDS TO SUPPORT HERSELF.
......
WE CAN'T TAKE CARE OF LILIM FOREVER.
SHE'S THE ONE WHO'LL HAVE TO FACE THE CONSEQUENCES.
YOU'RE RIGHT...
WHAT AM I DOING ...?

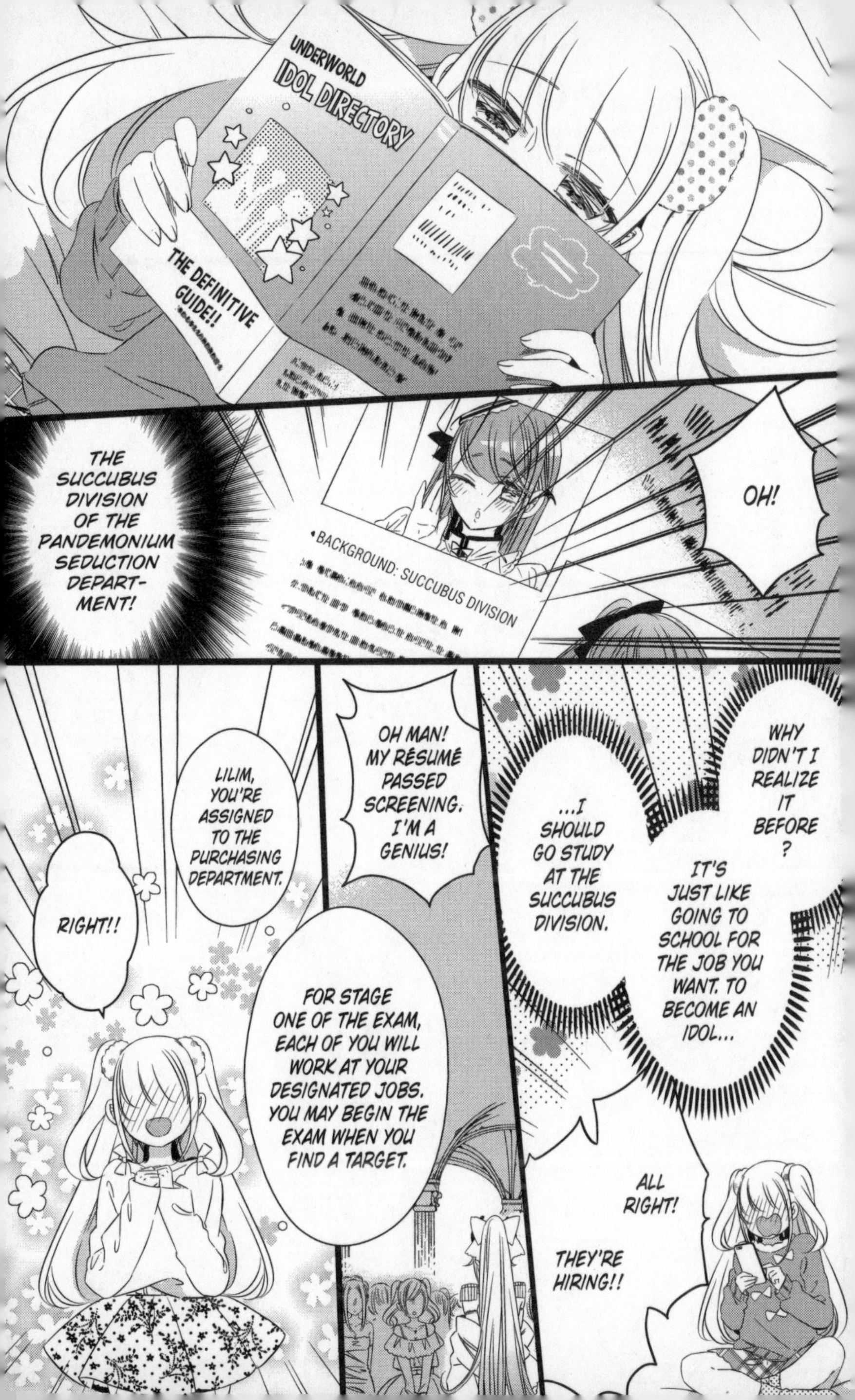

UNDERWORLD IDOL DIRECTORY
THE DEFINITIVE GUIDE!!
OH!
BACKGROUND: SUCCUBUS DIVISION
THE SUCCUBUS DIVISION OF THE PANDEMONIUM SEDUCTION DEPART-MENT!
WHY DIDN'T I REALIZE IT BEFORE?
IT'S JUST LIKE GOING TO SCHOOL FOR THE JOB YOU WANT. TO BECOME AN IDOL...
...I SHOULD GO STUDY AT THE SUCCUBUS DIVISION.
ALL RIGHT!
THEY'RE HIRING!!
OH MAN! MY RÉSUMÉ PASSED SCREENING. I'M A GENIUS!
FOR STAGE ONE OF THE EXAM, EACH OF YOU WILL WORK AT YOUR DESIGNATED JOBS. YOU MAY BEGIN THE EXAM WHEN YOU FIND A TARGET.
LILIM, YOU'RE ASSIGNED TO THE PURCHASING DEPARTMENT.
RIGHT!!

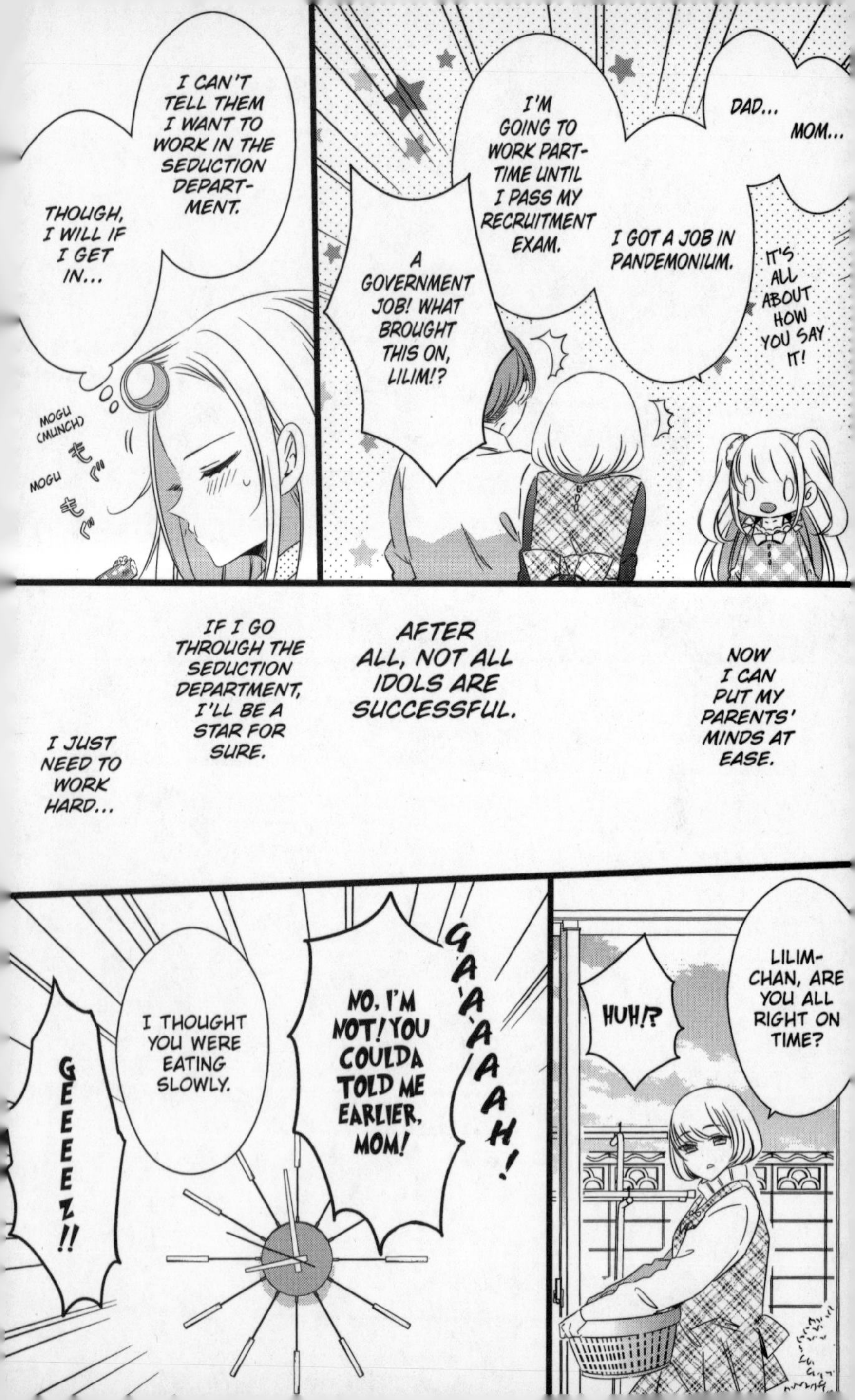
DAD...
MOM...
I'M GOING TO WORK PART-TIME UNTIL I PASS MY RECRUITMENT EXAM.
I GOT A JOB IN PANDEMONIUM.
IT'S ALL ABOUT HOW YOU SAY IT!
A GOVERNMENT JOB! WHAT BROUGHT THIS ON, LILIM!?
I CAN'T TELL THEM I WANT TO WORK IN THE SEDUCTION DEPARTMENT.
THOUGH, I WILL IF I GET IN...
MOGU (MUNCH)
もぐ
MOGU
もぐ
NOW I CAN PUT MY PARENTS' MINDS AT EASE.
AFTER ALL, NOT ALL IDOLS ARE SUCCESSFUL.
IF I GO THROUGH THE SEDUCTION DEPARTMENT, I'LL BE A STAR FOR SURE.
I JUST NEED TO WORK HARD...
LILIM-CHAN, ARE YOU ALL RIGHT ON TIME?
HUH!?
GAAAAAAH!
NO, I'M NOT! YOU COULDA TOLD ME EARLIER, MOM!
I THOUGHT YOU WERE EATING SLOWLY.
GEEEEEZ!!

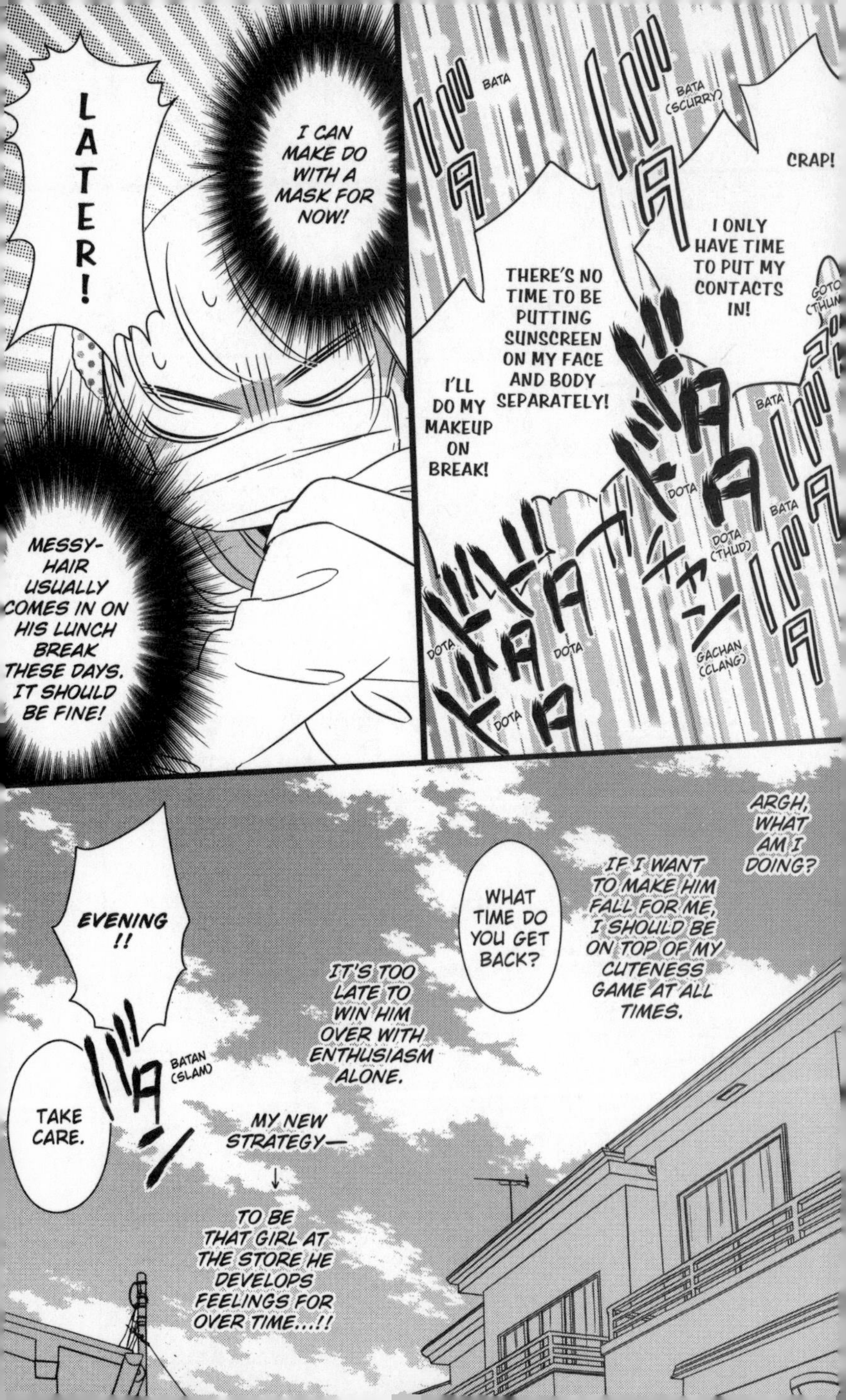
CRAP!
BATA (SCURRY)
I ONLY HAVE TIME TO PUT MY CONTACTS IN!
BATA
THERE'S NO TIME TO BE PUTTING SUNSCREEN ON MY FACE AND BODY SEPARATELY!
I'LL DO MY MAKEUP ON BREAK!
BATA
BATA
DOTA
DOTA (THUD)
GACHAN (CLANG)
DOTA
DOTA
DOTA
LATER!
I CAN MAKE DO WITH A MASK FOR NOW!
MESSY-HAIR USUALLY COMES IN ON HIS LUNCH BREAK THESE DAYS. IT SHOULD BE FINE!
ARGH, WHAT AM I DOING?
IF I WANT TO MAKE HIM FALL FOR ME, I SHOULD BE ON TOP OF MY CUTENESS GAME AT ALL TIMES.
WHAT TIME DO YOU GET BACK?
IT'S TOO LATE TO WIN HIM OVER WITH ENTHUSIASM ALONE.
EVENING!!
BATAN (SLAM)
TAKE CARE.
MY NEW STRATEGY—
↓
TO BE THAT GIRL AT THE STORE HE DEVELOPS FEELINGS FOR OVER TIME...!!

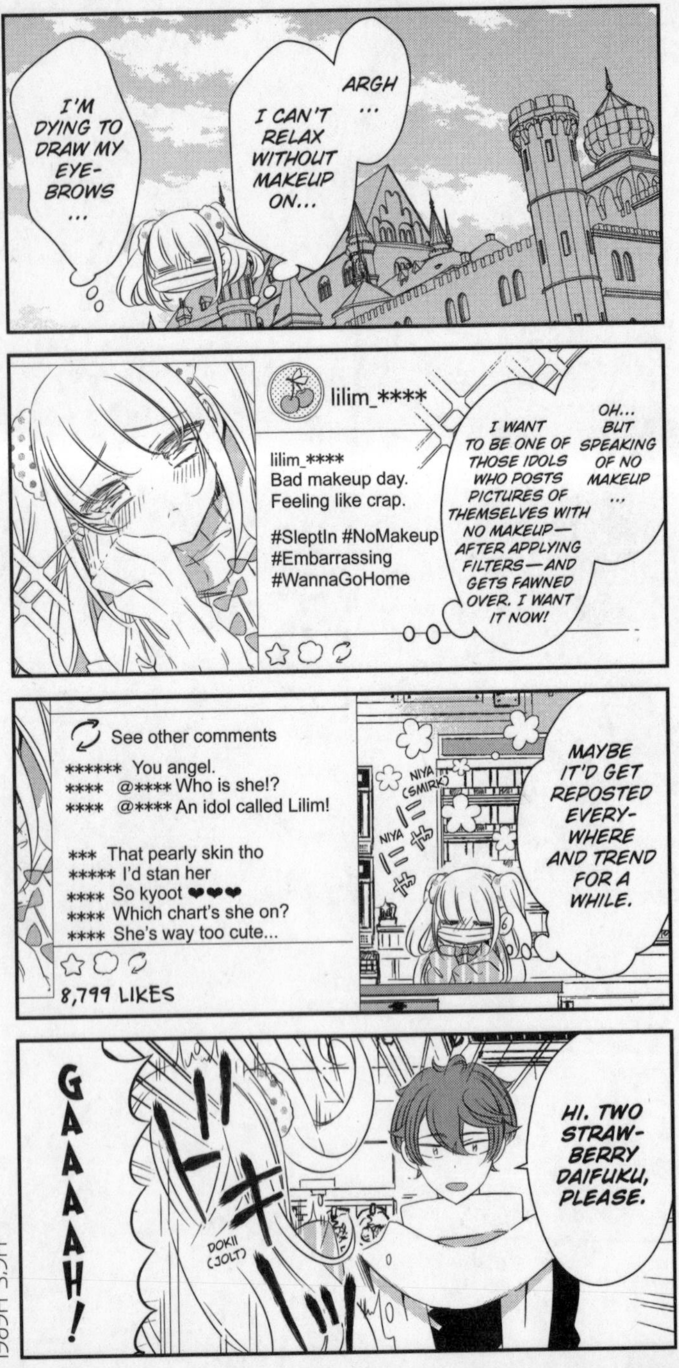
ARGH… I CAN'T RELAX WITHOUT MAKEUP ON…
I'M DYING TO DRAW MY EYE-BROWS…
OH… BUT SPEAKING OF NO MAKEUP…
I WANT TO BE ONE OF THOSE IDOLS WHO POSTS PICTURES OF THEMSELVES WITH NO MAKEUP—AFTER APPLYING FILTERS—AND GETS FAWNED OVER. I WANT IT NOW!
lilim_****
lilim_****
Bad makeup day.
Feeling like crap.
#SleptIn #NoMakeup
#Embarrassing
#WannaGoHome
MAYBE IT'D GET REPOSTED EVERY-WHERE AND TREND FOR A WHILE.
NIYA (SMIRK)
NIYA
See other comments
****** You angel.
**** @**** Who is she!?
**** @**** An idol called Lilim!
*** That pearly skin tho
***** I'd stan her
**** So kyoot ❤❤❤
**** Which chart's she on?
**** She's way too cute...
8,799 LIKES
HI. TWO STRAW-BERRY DAIFUKU, PLEASE.
DOKII (JOLT)
GAAAAAH!

HE'S HERE!

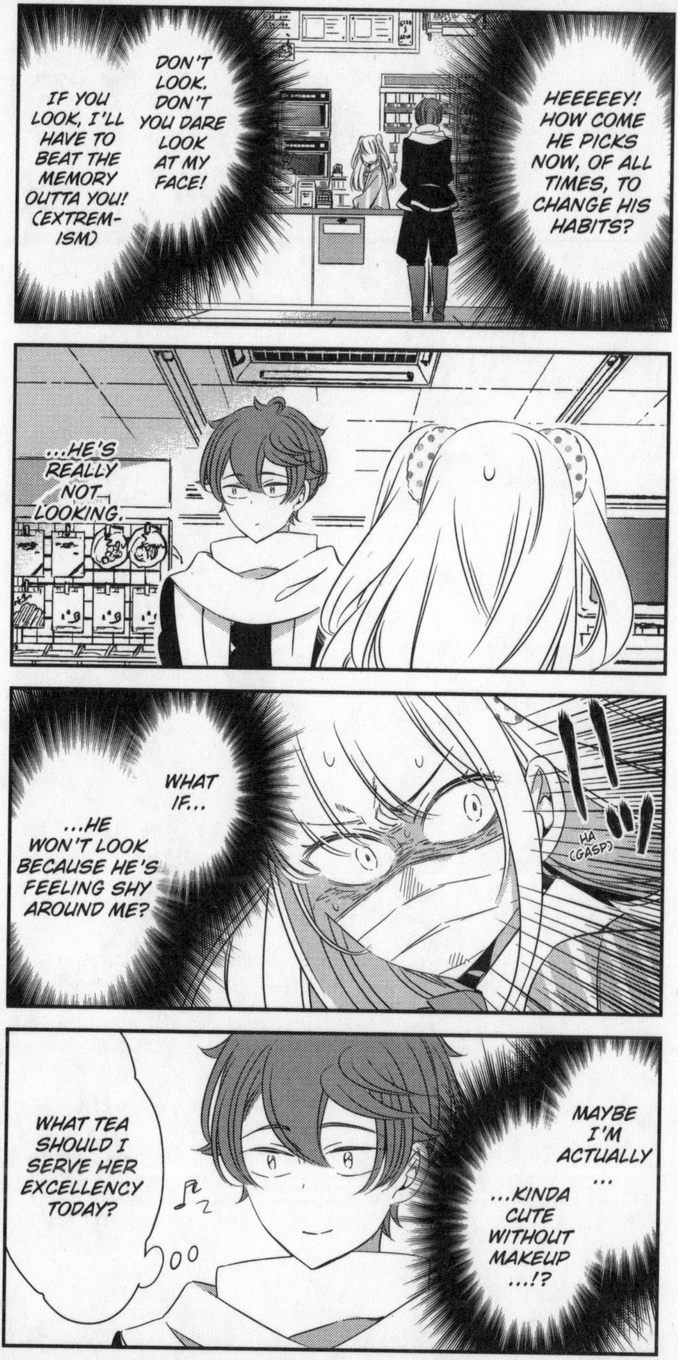
HEEEEEY! HOW COME HE PICKS NOW, OF ALL TIMES, TO CHANGE HIS HABITS?
DON'T LOOK. DON'T YOU DARE LOOK AT MY FACE!
IF YOU LOOK, I'LL HAVE TO BEAT THE MEMORY OUTTA YOU! (EXTREMISM)
...HE'S REALLY NOT LOOKING.
HA (GASP)
WHAT IF...
...HE WON'T LOOK BECAUSE HE'S FEELING SHY AROUND ME?
MAYBE I'M ACTUALLY ...
...KINDA CUTE WITHOUT MAKEUP ...!?
WHAT TEA SHOULD I SERVE HER EXCELLENCY TODAY?

STRANGELY POSITIVE THINKING

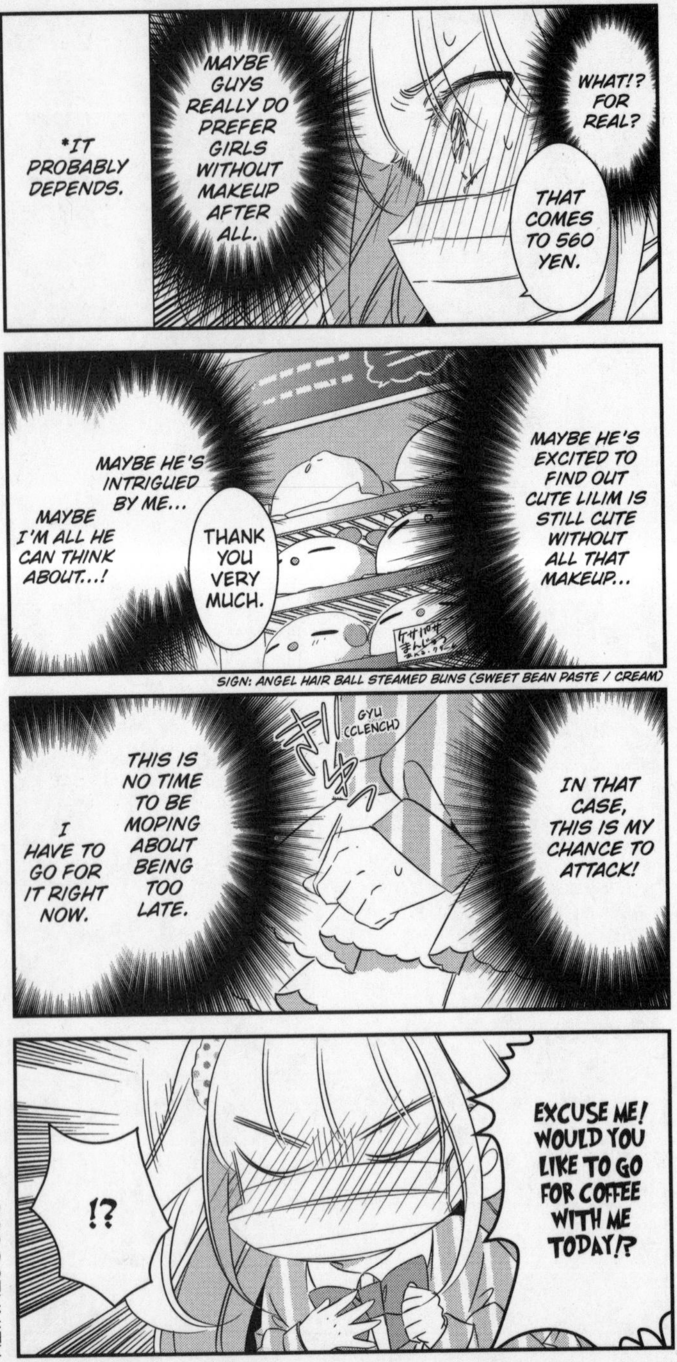
WHAT!? FOR REAL?
THAT COMES TO 560 YEN.
MAYBE GUYS REALLY DO PREFER GIRLS WITHOUT MAKEUP AFTER ALL.
*IT PROBABLY DEPENDS.
MAYBE HE'S EXCITED TO FIND OUT CUTE LILIM IS STILL CUTE WITHOUT ALL THAT MAKEUP...
THANK YOU VERY MUCH.
MAYBE HE'S INTRIGUED BY ME...
MAYBE I'M ALL HE CAN THINK ABOUT...!
SIGN: ANGEL HAIR BALL STEAMED BUNS (SWEET BEAN PASTE / CREAM)
GYU (CLENCH)
IN THAT CASE, THIS IS MY CHANCE TO ATTACK!
THIS IS NO TIME TO BE MOPING ABOUT BEING TOO LATE.
I HAVE TO GO FOR IT RIGHT NOW.
EXCUSE ME! WOULD YOU LIKE TO GO FOR COFFEE WITH ME TODAY!?
!?

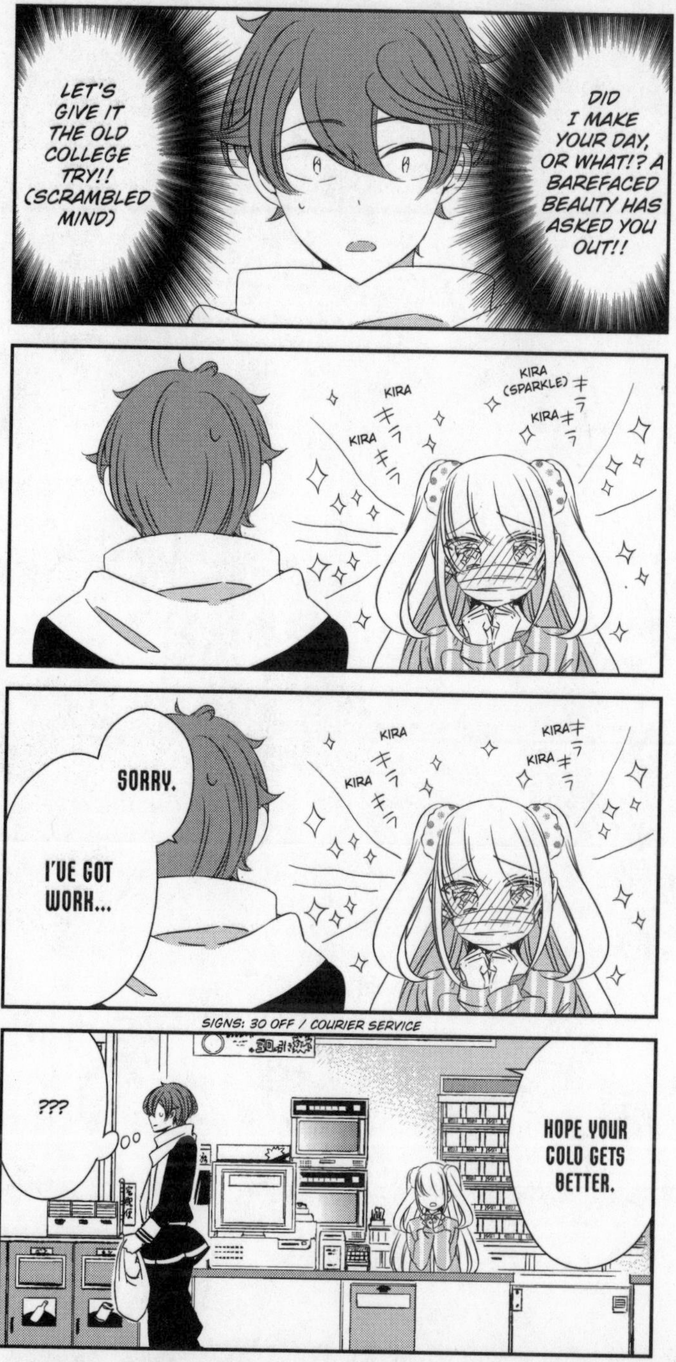
DID I MAKE YOUR DAY, OR WHAT!? A BAREFACED BEAUTY HAS ASKED YOU OUT!!
LET'S GIVE IT THE OLD COLLEGE TRY!! (SCRAMBLED MIND)
KIRA (SPARKLE) キラ
KIRA キラ
KIRA キラ
KIRA キラ
KIRA キラ
KIRA キラ
KIRA キラ
KIRA キラ
SORRY.
I'VE GOT WORK...
SIGNS: 30 OFF / COURIER SERVICE
HOPE YOUR COLD GETS BETTER.
???

THE THOUGHT "MAYBE ANOTHER DAY" DOESN'T OCCUR TO MULLIN

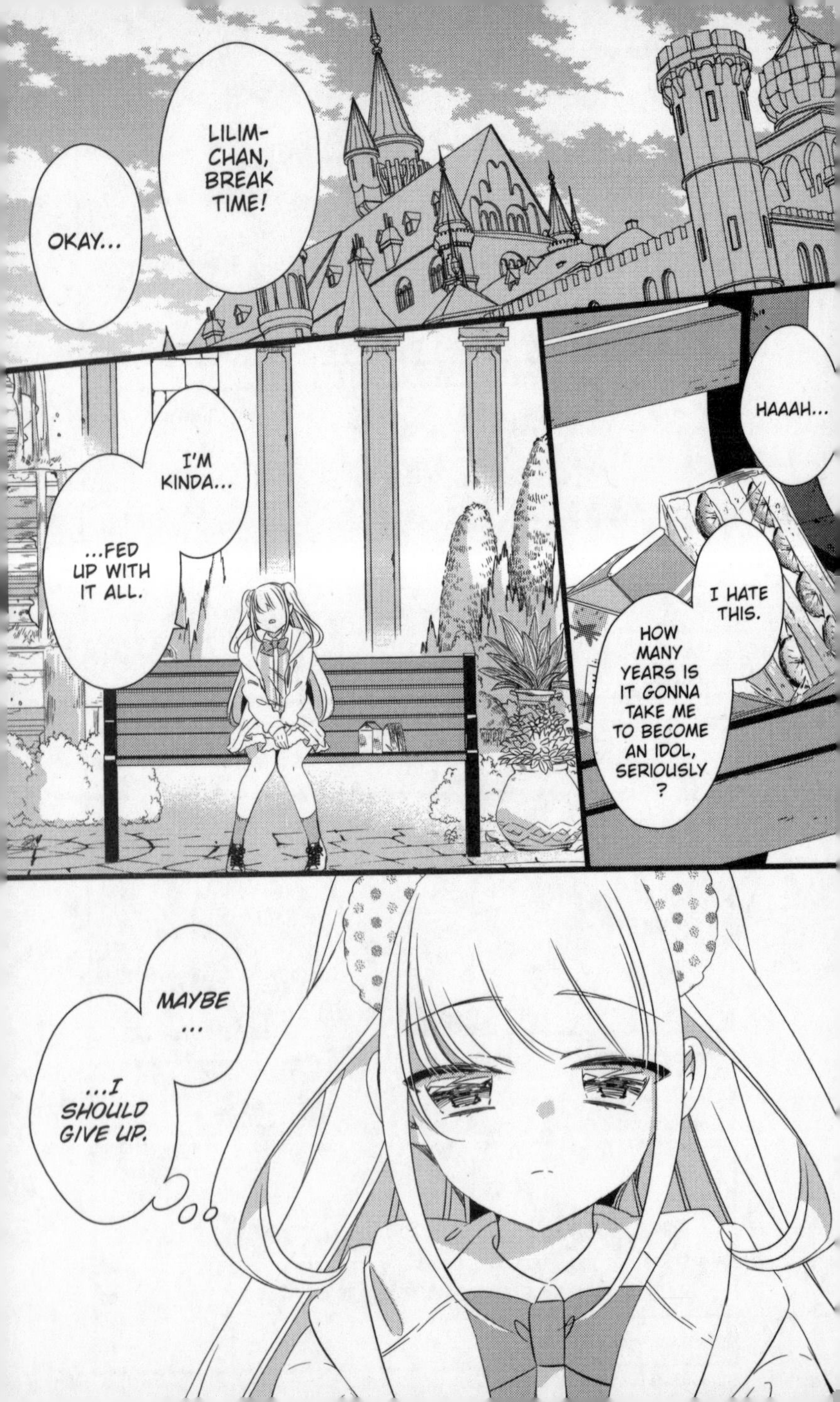
LILIM-CHAN, BREAK TIME!
OKAY...
HAAAH...
I HATE THIS.
HOW MANY YEARS IS IT GONNA TAKE ME TO BECOME AN IDOL, SERIOUSLY?
I'M KINDA...
...FED UP WITH IT ALL.
MAYBE ...
...I SHOULD GIVE UP.

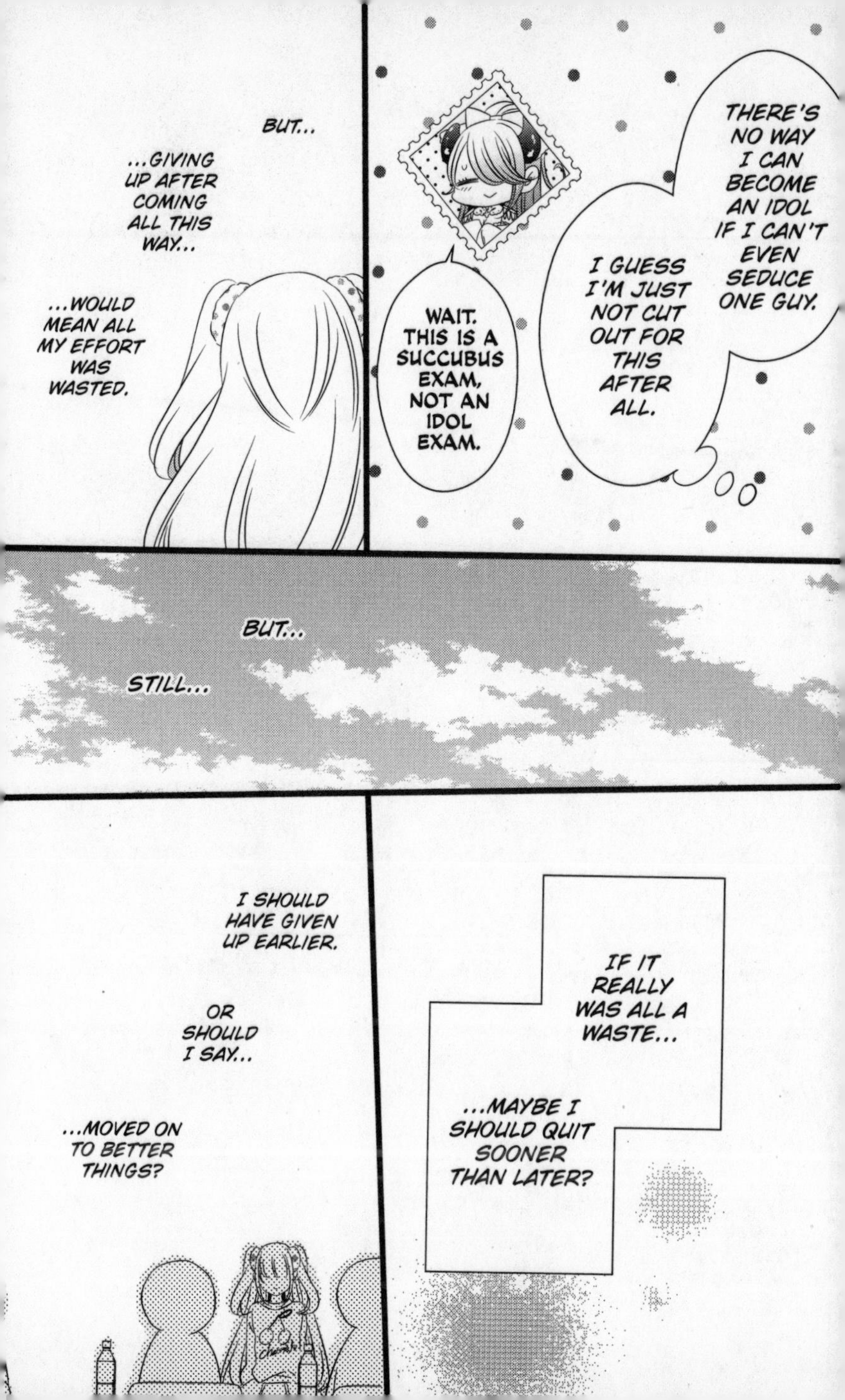
THERE'S NO WAY I CAN BECOME AN IDOL IF I CAN'T EVEN SEDUCE ONE GUY.
I GUESS I'M JUST NOT CUT OUT FOR THIS AFTER ALL.
WAIT. THIS IS A SUCCUBUS EXAM, NOT AN IDOL EXAM.
BUT...
...GIVING UP AFTER COMING ALL THIS WAY...
...WOULD MEAN ALL MY EFFORT WAS WASTED.
BUT...
STILL...
IF IT REALLY WAS ALL A WASTE...
...MAYBE I SHOULD QUIT SOONER THAN LATER?
I SHOULD HAVE GIVEN UP EARLIER.
OR SHOULD I SAY...
...MOVED ON TO BETTER THINGS?

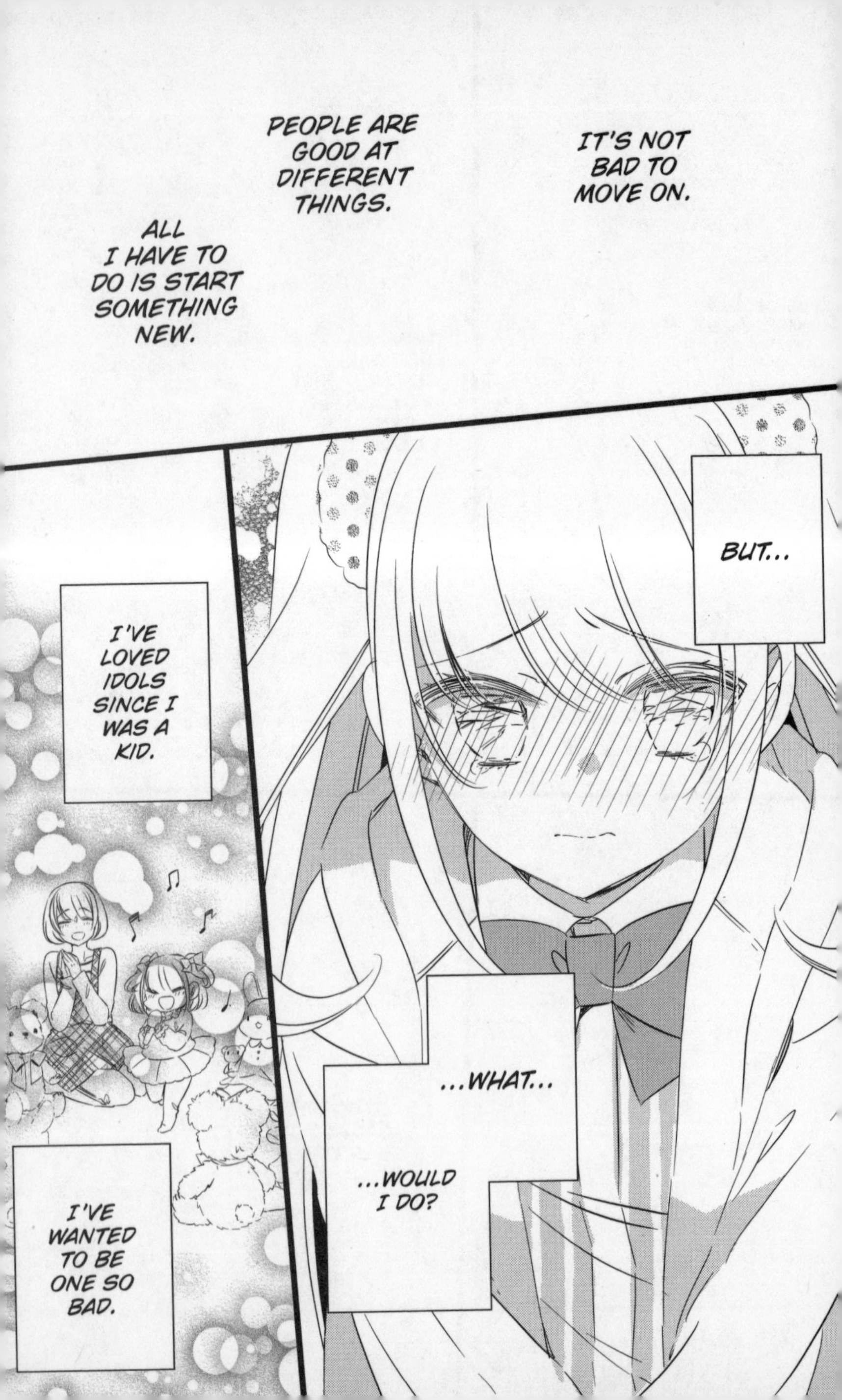
IT'S NOT BAD TO MOVE ON.
PEOPLE ARE GOOD AT DIFFERENT THINGS.
ALL I HAVE TO DO IS START SOMETHING NEW.
BUT...
...WHAT...
...WOULD I DO?
I'VE LOVED IDOLS SINCE I WAS A KID.
I'VE WANTED TO BE ONE SO BAD.

GETTING ANGRIER AND ANGRIER

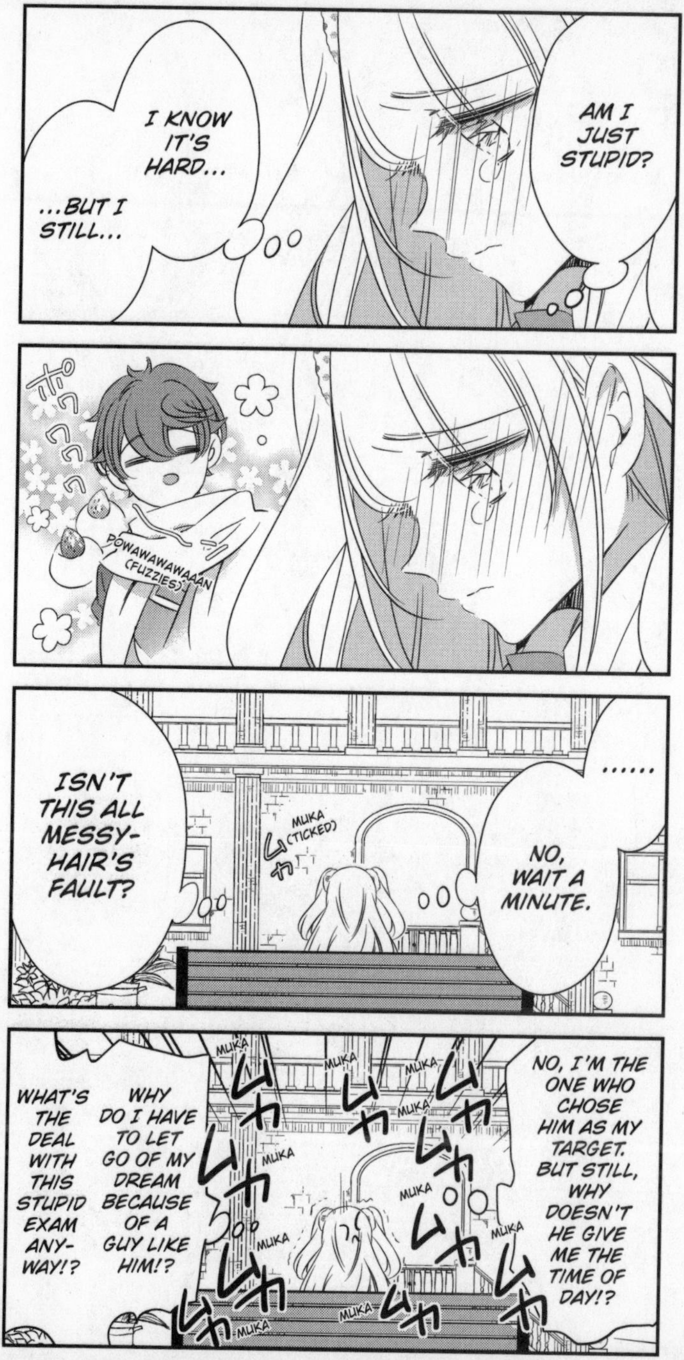
AM I JUST STUPID?
I KNOW IT'S HARD...
...BUT I STILL...
POWAWAWAWAAAN (FUZZIES)
......
NO, WAIT A MINUTE.
MUKA (TICKED)
ISN'T THIS ALL MESSY-HAIR'S FAULT?
NO, I'M THE ONE WHO CHOSE HIM AS MY TARGET. BUT STILL, WHY DOESN'T HE GIVE ME THE TIME OF DAY!?
MUKA MUKA MUKA MUKA MUKA MUKA MUKA MUKA MUKA MUKA
WHY DO I HAVE TO LET GO OF MY DREAM BECAUSE OF A GUY LIKE HIM!?
WHAT'S THE DEAL WITH THIS STUPID EXAM ANYWAY!?

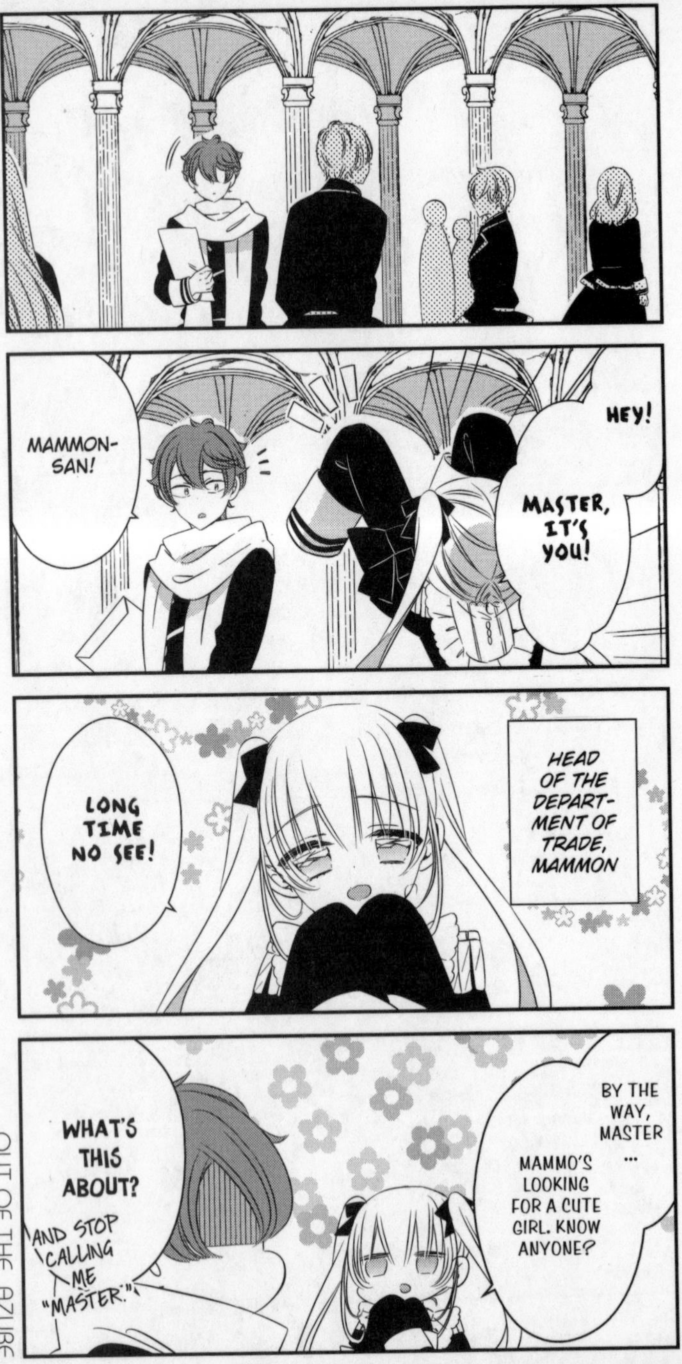
HEY!
MASTER, IT'S YOU!
MAMMON-SAN!
HEAD OF THE DEPARTMENT OF TRADE, MAMMON
LONG TIME NO SEE!
BY THE WAY, MASTER ...
MAMMO'S LOOKING FOR A CUTE GIRL. KNOW ANYONE?
WHAT'S THIS ABOUT?
AND STOP CALLING ME "MASTER."

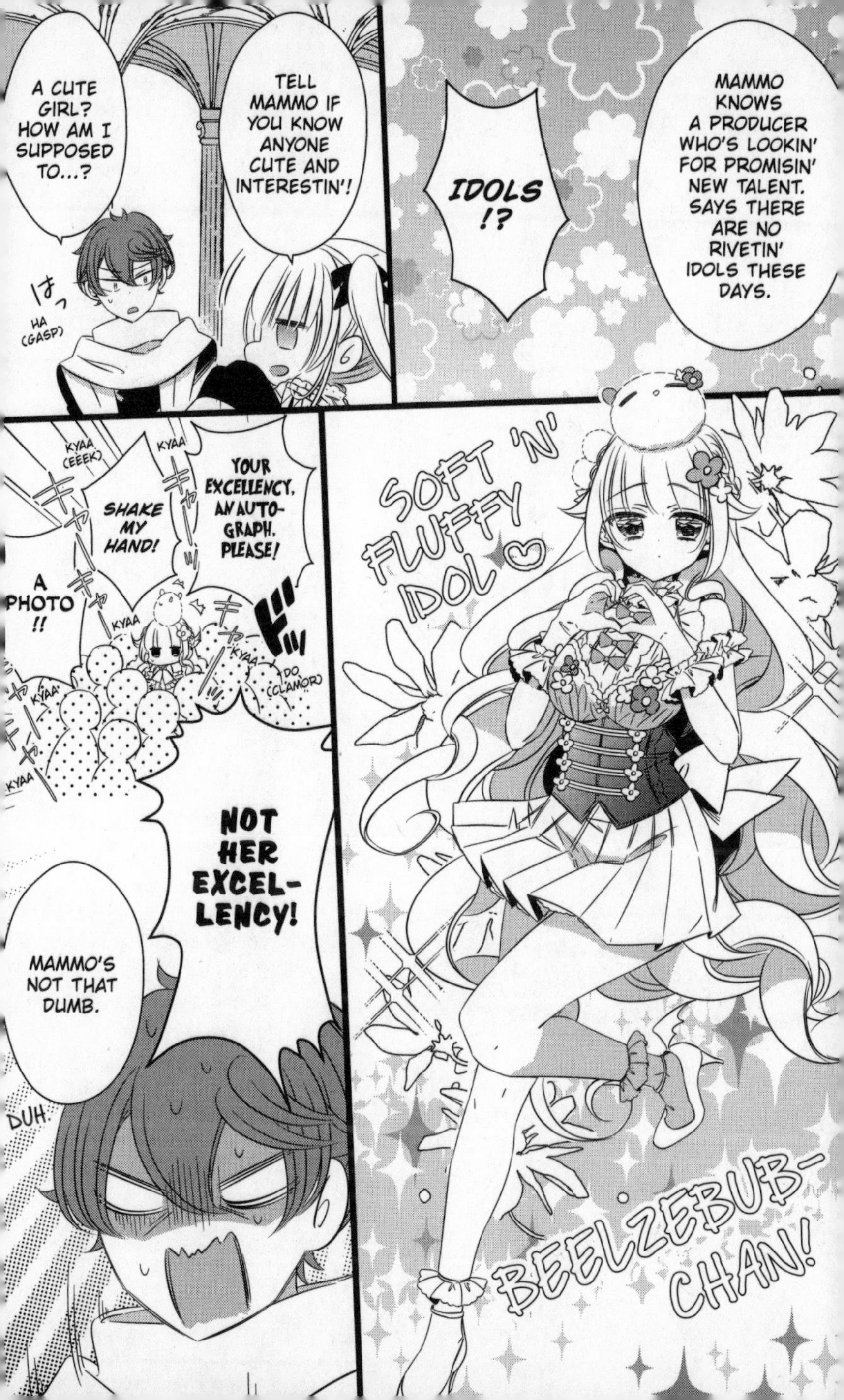

MAMMO KNOWS A PRODUCER WHO'S LOOKIN' FOR PROMISIN' NEW TALENT. SAYS THERE ARE NO RIVETIN' IDOLS THESE DAYS.
IDOLS!?
TELL MAMMO IF YOU KNOW ANYONE CUTE AND INTERESTIN'!
A CUTE GIRL? HOW AM I SUPPOSED TO...?
はっ
HA (GASP)
SOFT 'N' FLUFFY IDOL ♡
BEELZEBUB-CHAN!
YOUR EXCELLENCY, AN AUTO-GRAPH, PLEASE!
KYAA
SHAKE MY HAND!
KYAA (EEEK)
A PHOTO!!
ド
DO (CLAMOR)
KYAA
KYAA
KYAA
KYAA
NOT HER EXCEL-LENCY!
MAMMO'S NOT THAT DUMB.
DUH.

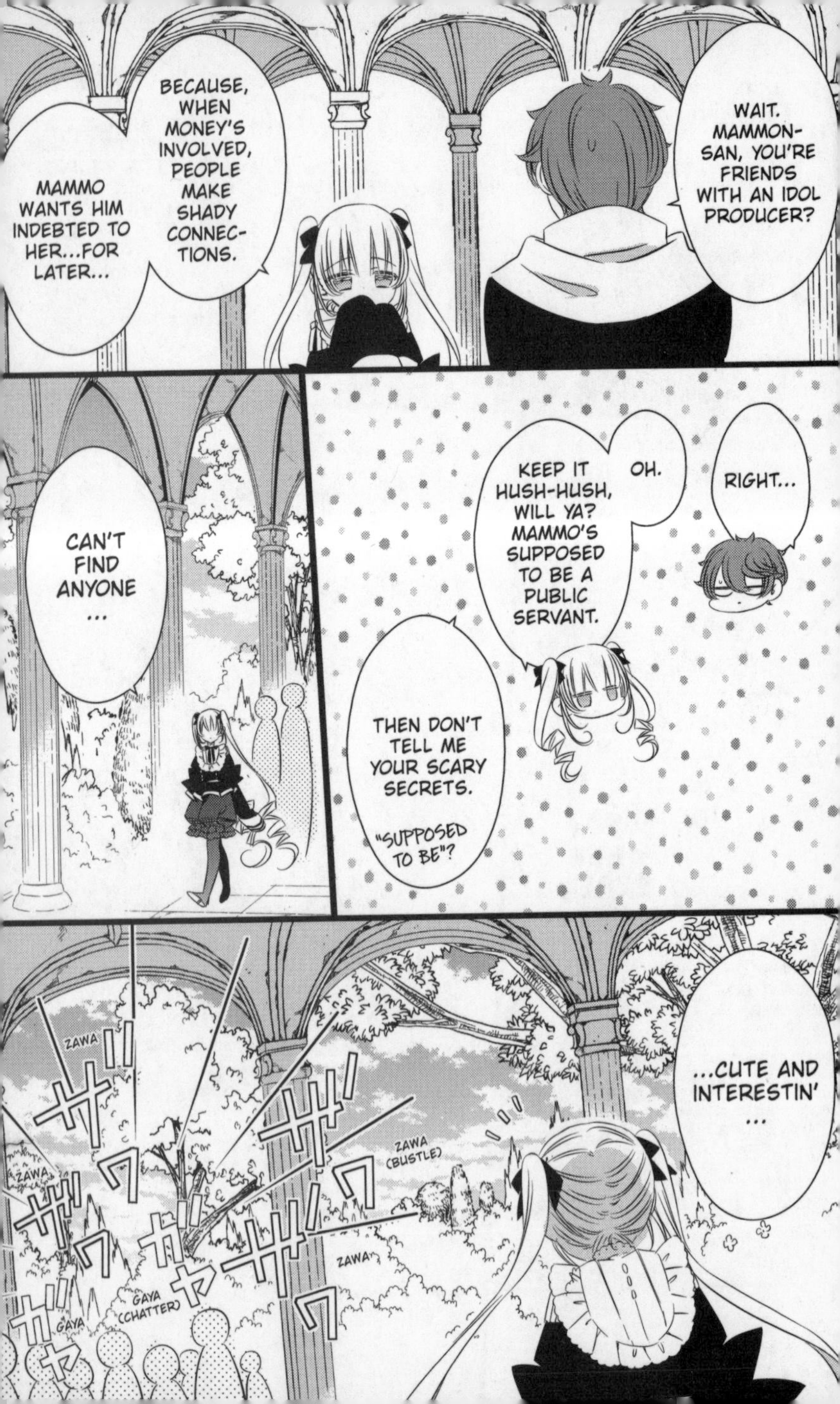
WAIT. MAMMON-SAN, YOU'RE FRIENDS WITH AN IDOL PRODUCER?
BECAUSE, WHEN MONEY'S INVOLVED, PEOPLE MAKE SHADY CONNECTIONS.
MAMMO WANTS HIM INDEBTED TO HER...FOR LATER...
RIGHT...
OH.
KEEP IT HUSH-HUSH, WILL YA? MAMMO'S SUPPOSED TO BE A PUBLIC SERVANT.
THEN DON'T TELL ME YOUR SCARY SECRETS.
"SUPPOSED TO BE"?
CAN'T FIND ANYONE ...
...CUTE AND INTERESTIN' ...
ZAWA (BUSTLE)
ZAWA
ZAWA
ZAWA
GAYA (CHATTER)
GAYA

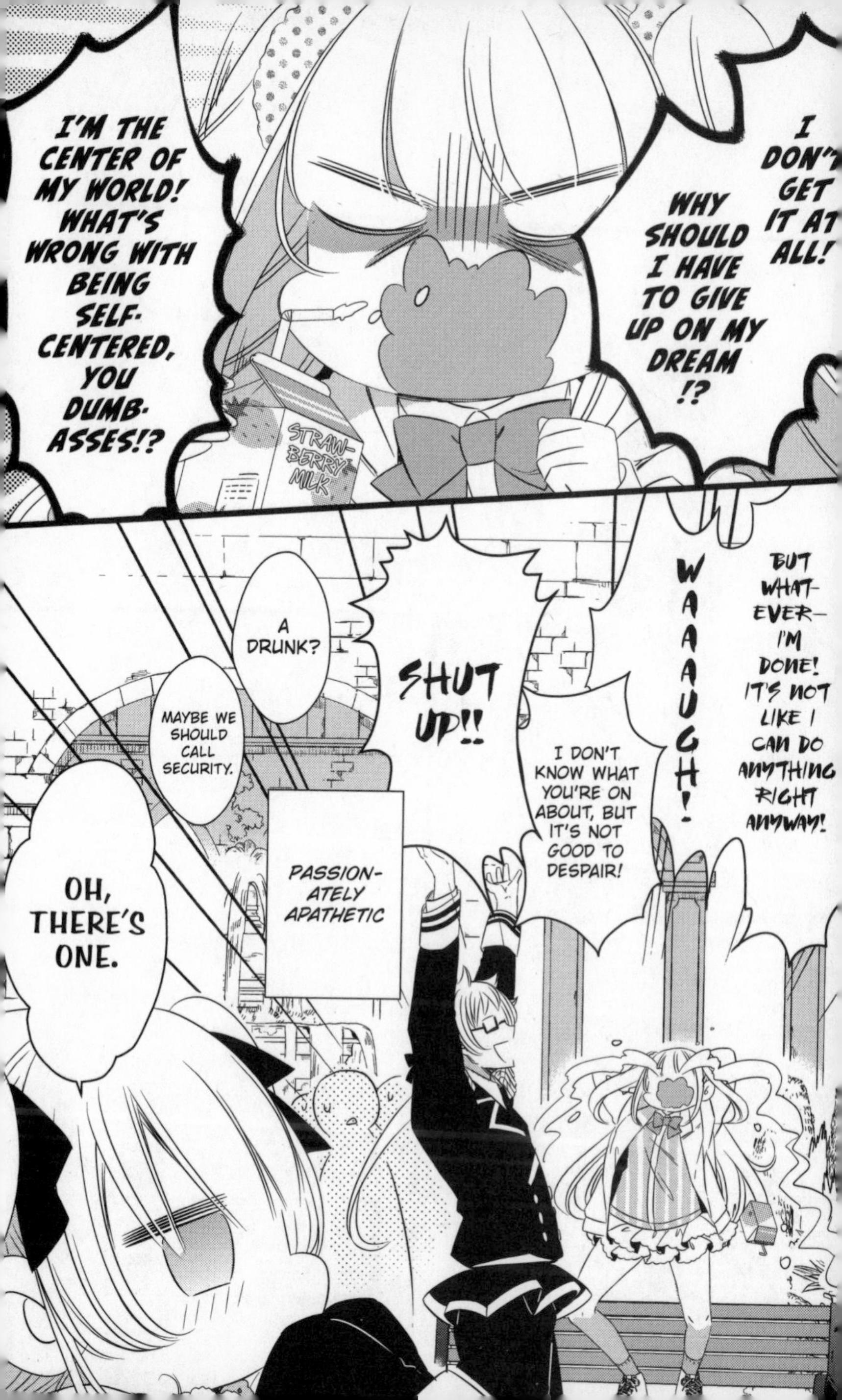
I DON'T GET IT AT ALL!
WHY SHOULD I HAVE TO GIVE UP ON MY DREAM!?
I'M THE CENTER OF MY WORLD! WHAT'S WRONG WITH BEING SELF-CENTERED, YOU DUMBASSES!?
STRAWBERRY MILK
BUT WHATEVER— I'M DONE! IT'S NOT LIKE I CAN DO ANYTHING RIGHT ANYWAY!
WAAAAUGH!
I DON'T KNOW WHAT YOU'RE ON ABOUT, BUT IT'S NOT GOOD TO DESPAIR!
SHUT UP!!
A DRUNK?
MAYBE WE SHOULD CALL SECURITY.
PASSIONATELY APATHETIC
OH, THERE'S ONE.

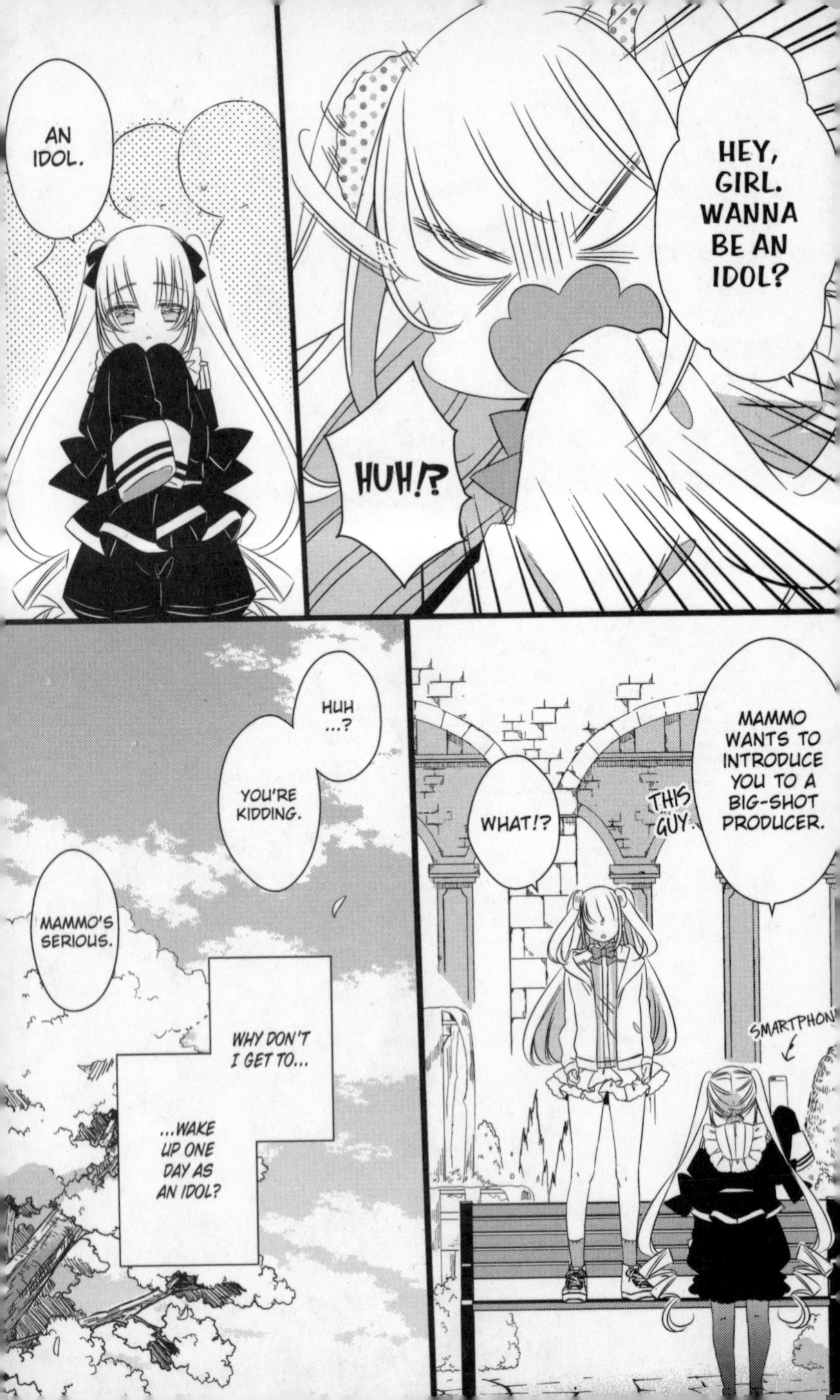
HEY, GIRL. WANNA BE AN IDOL?
HUH!?
AN IDOL.
MAMMO WANTS TO INTRODUCE YOU TO A BIG-SHOT PRODUCER.
THIS GUY.
WHAT!?
SMARTPHON
HUH ...?
YOU'RE KIDDING.
MAMMO'S SERIOUS.
WHY DON'T I GET TO...
...WAKE UP ONE DAY AS AN IDOL?

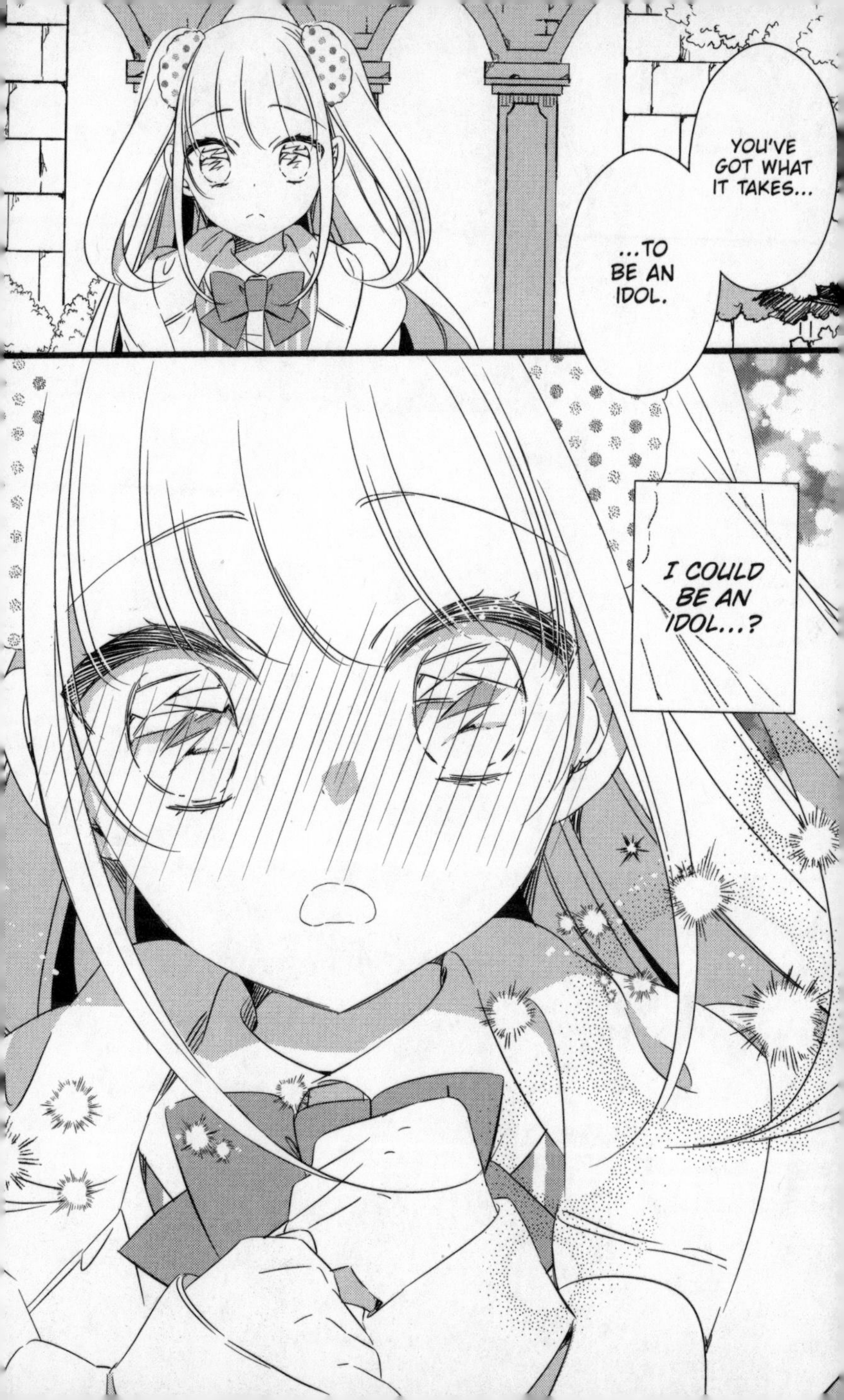
YOU'VE GOT WHAT IT TAKES...
...TO BE AN IDOL.
I COULD BE AN IDOL...?

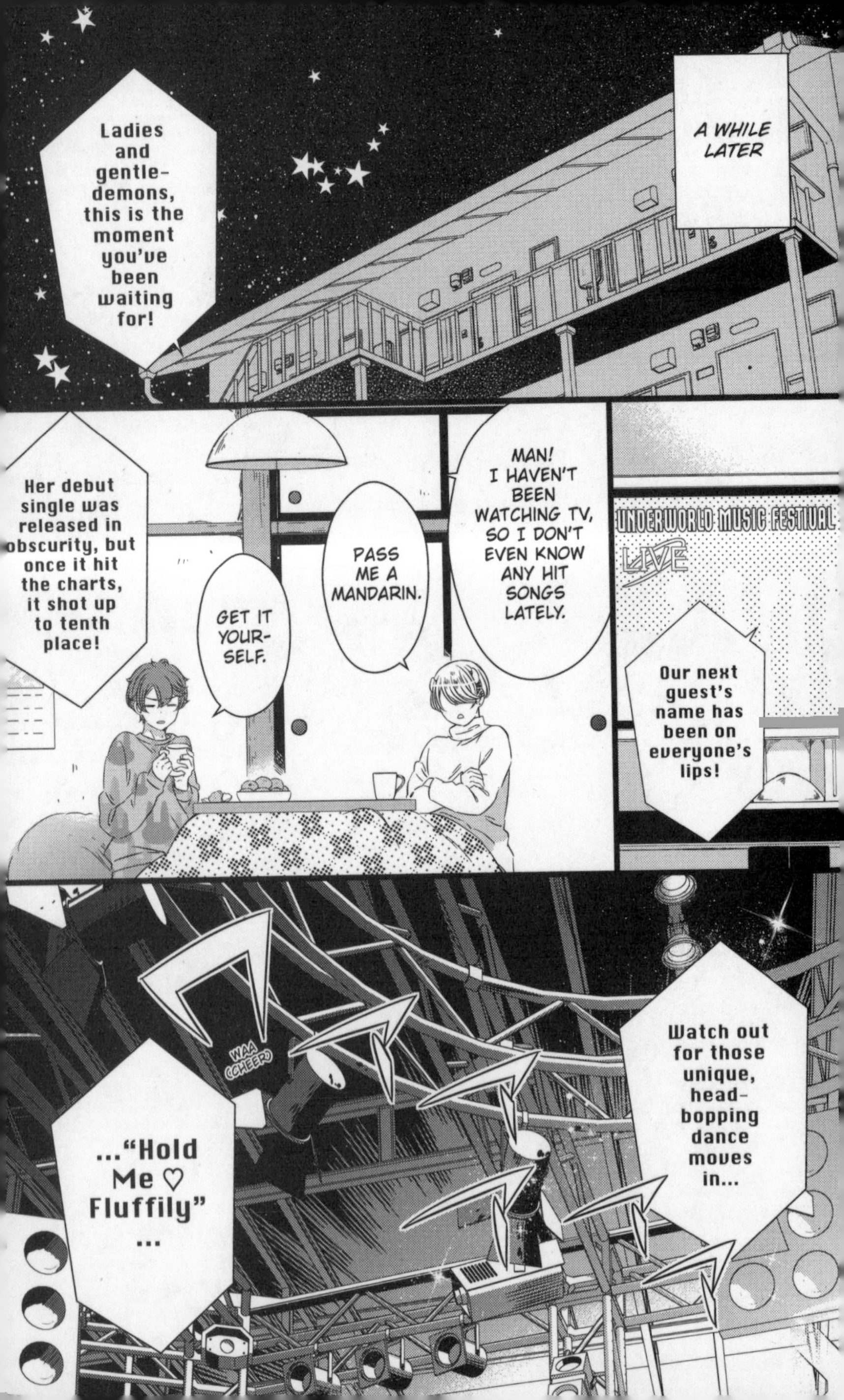
A WHILE LATER
Ladies and gentle-demons, this is the moment you've been waiting for!
UNDERWORLD MUSIC FESTIVAL
LIVE
Our next guest's name has been on everyone's lips!
MAN! I HAVEN'T BEEN WATCHING TV, SO I DON'T EVEN KNOW ANY HIT SONGS LATELY.
PASS ME A MANDARIN.
GET IT YOURSELF.
Her debut single was released in obscurity, but once it hit the charts, it shot up to tenth place!
Watch out for those unique, head-bopping dance moves in...
WAA (CHEER)
..."Hold Me ♡ Fluffily" ...

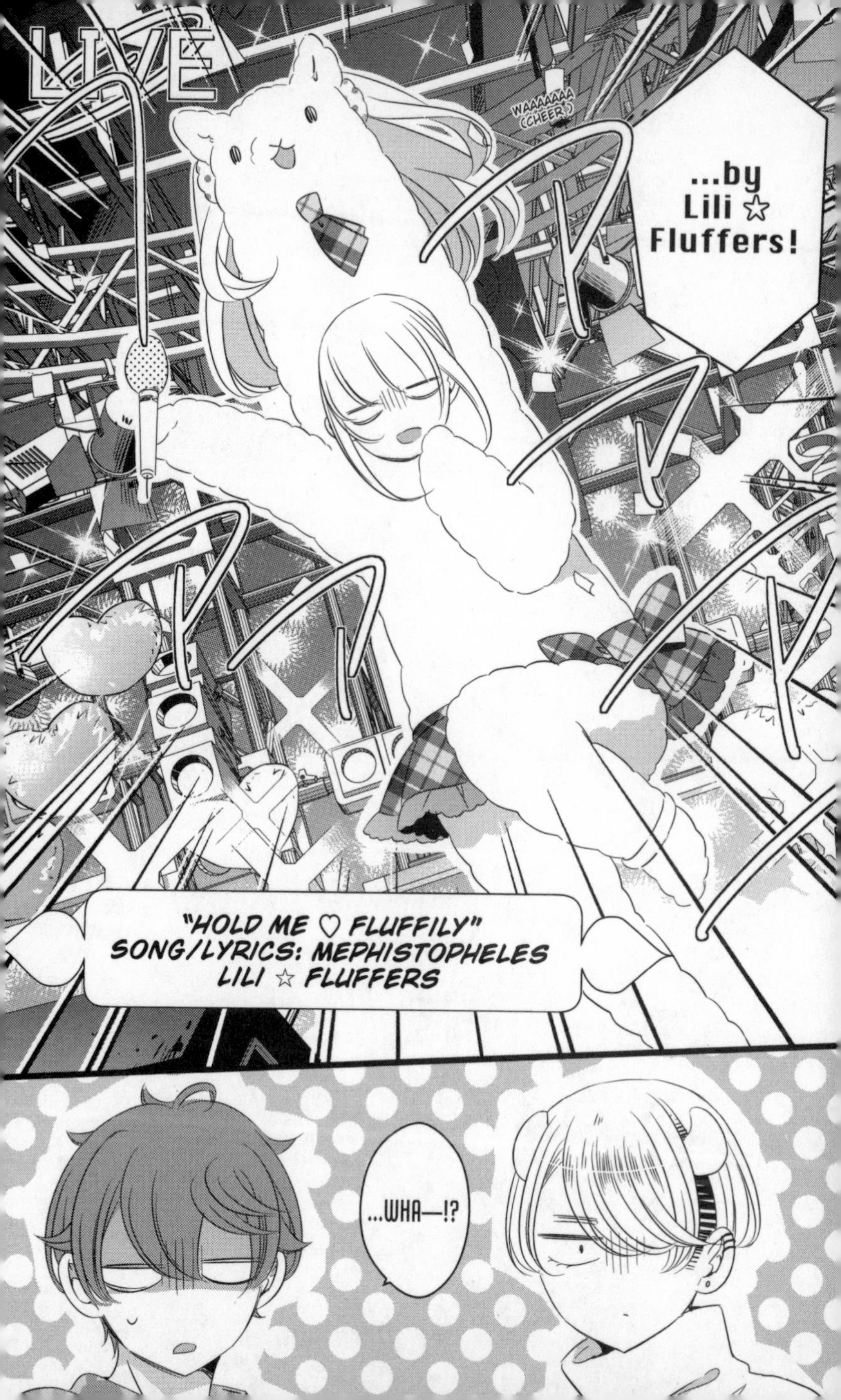
...by Lili ☆ Fluffers!
WAAAAAAA (CHEER)
LIVE
"HOLD ME ♡ FLUFFILY"
SONG/LYRICS: MEPHISTOPHELES
LILI ☆ FLUFFERS
...WHA—!?

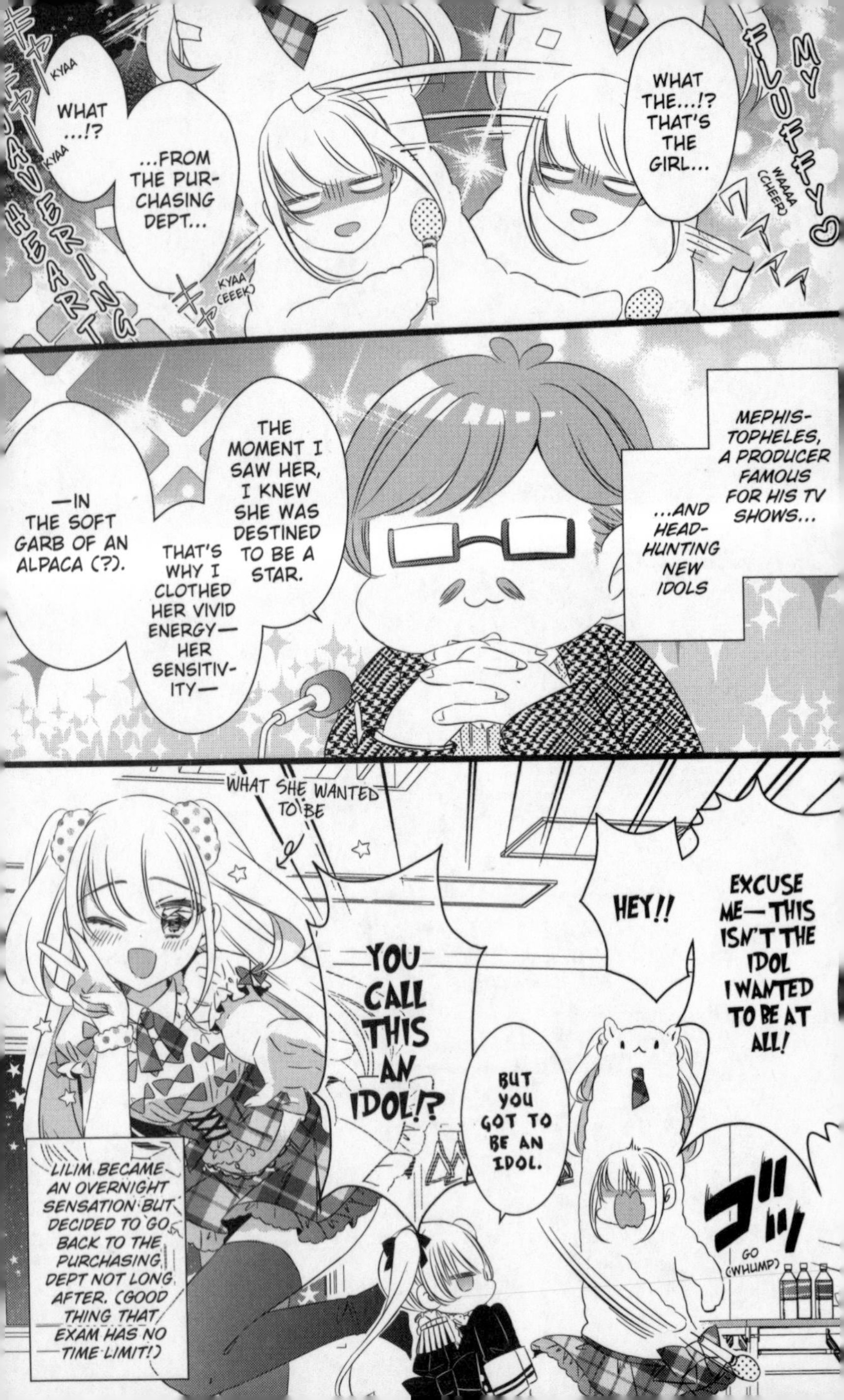
MY FLUFFY♡
WAAAA (CHEER)
WHAT THE...!? THAT'S THE GIRL...
...FROM THE PURCHASING DEPT...
WHAT ...!?
KYAA
KYAA
KYAA (EEEK)
MEPHISTOPHELES, A PRODUCER FAMOUS FOR HIS TV SHOWS...
...AND HEAD-HUNTING NEW IDOLS
THE MOMENT I SAW HER, I KNEW SHE WAS DESTINED TO BE A STAR.
THAT'S WHY I CLOTHED HER VIVID ENERGY—HER SENSITIVITY—
—IN THE SOFT GARB OF AN ALPACA (?).
EXCUSE ME—THIS ISN'T THE IDOL I WANTED TO BE AT ALL!
HEY!!
YOU CALL THIS AN IDOL!?
WHAT SHE WANTED TO BE
GO (WHUMP)
BUT YOU GOT TO BE AN IDOL.
LILIM BECAME AN OVERNIGHT SENSATION BUT DECIDED TO GO BACK TO THE PURCHASING DEPT NOT LONG AFTER. (GOOD THING THAT EXAM HAS NO TIME LIMIT!)

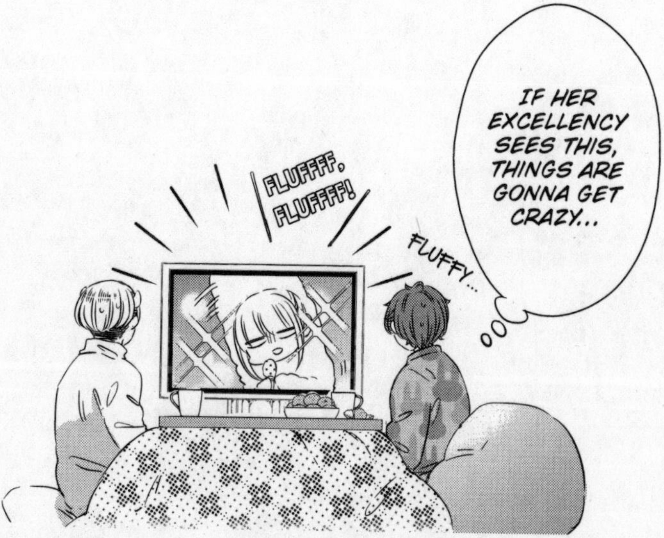
IF HER EXCELLENCY SEES THIS, THINGS ARE GONNA GET CRAZY...
FLUFFY...
FLUFFFF, FLUFFFF!

As Miss Beelzebub Likes

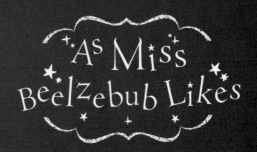

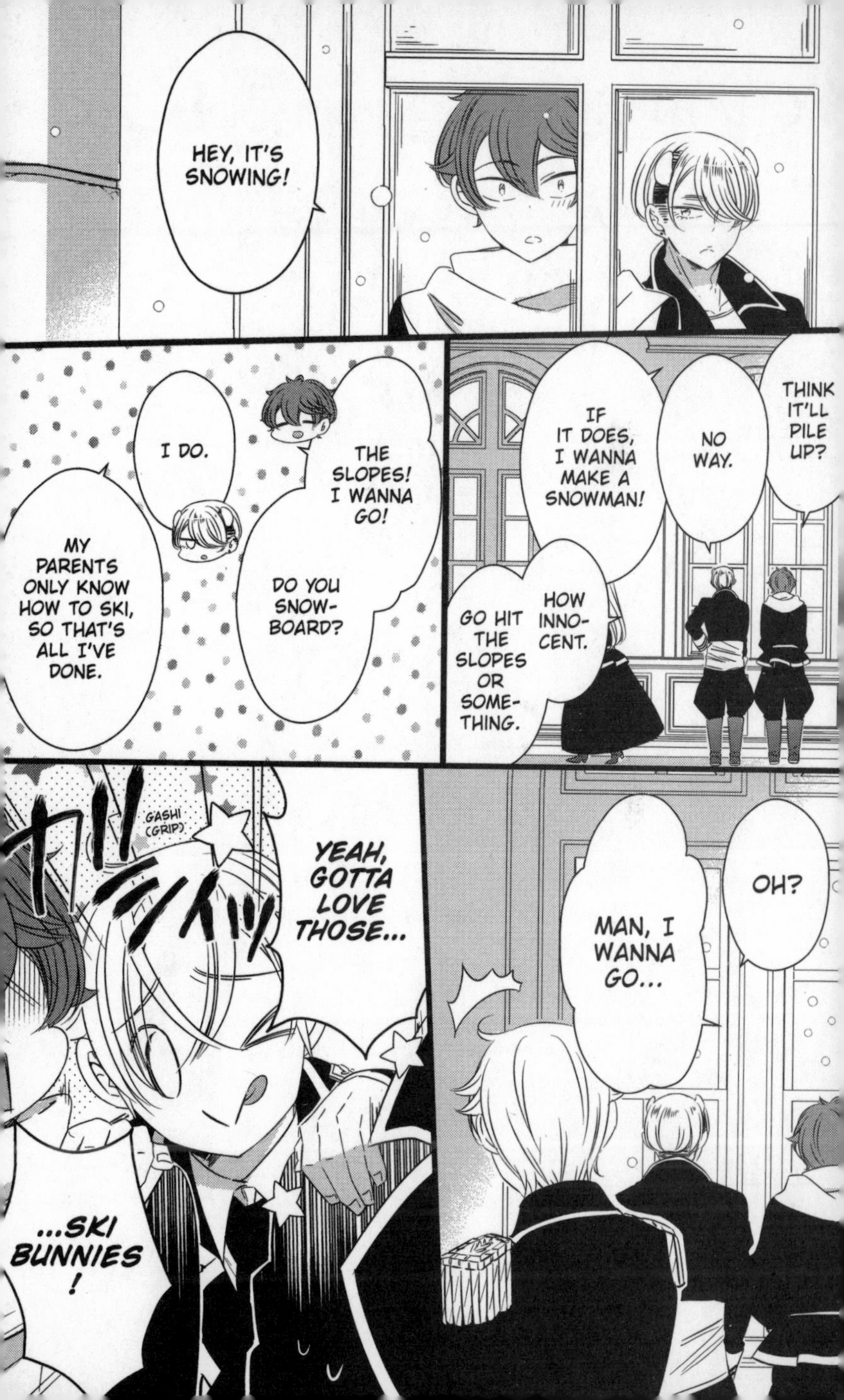
HEY, IT'S SNOWING!
THINK IT'LL PILE UP?
NO WAY.
IF IT DOES, I WANNA MAKE A SNOWMAN!
HOW INNOCENT.
GO HIT THE SLOPES OR SOMETHING.
THE SLOPES! I WANNA GO!
DO YOU SNOWBOARD?
I DO.
MY PARENTS ONLY KNOW HOW TO SKI, SO THAT'S ALL I'VE DONE.
OH?
MAN, I WANNA GO...
GASHI (GRIP)
YEAH, GOTTA LOVE THOSE...
...SKI BUNNIES!

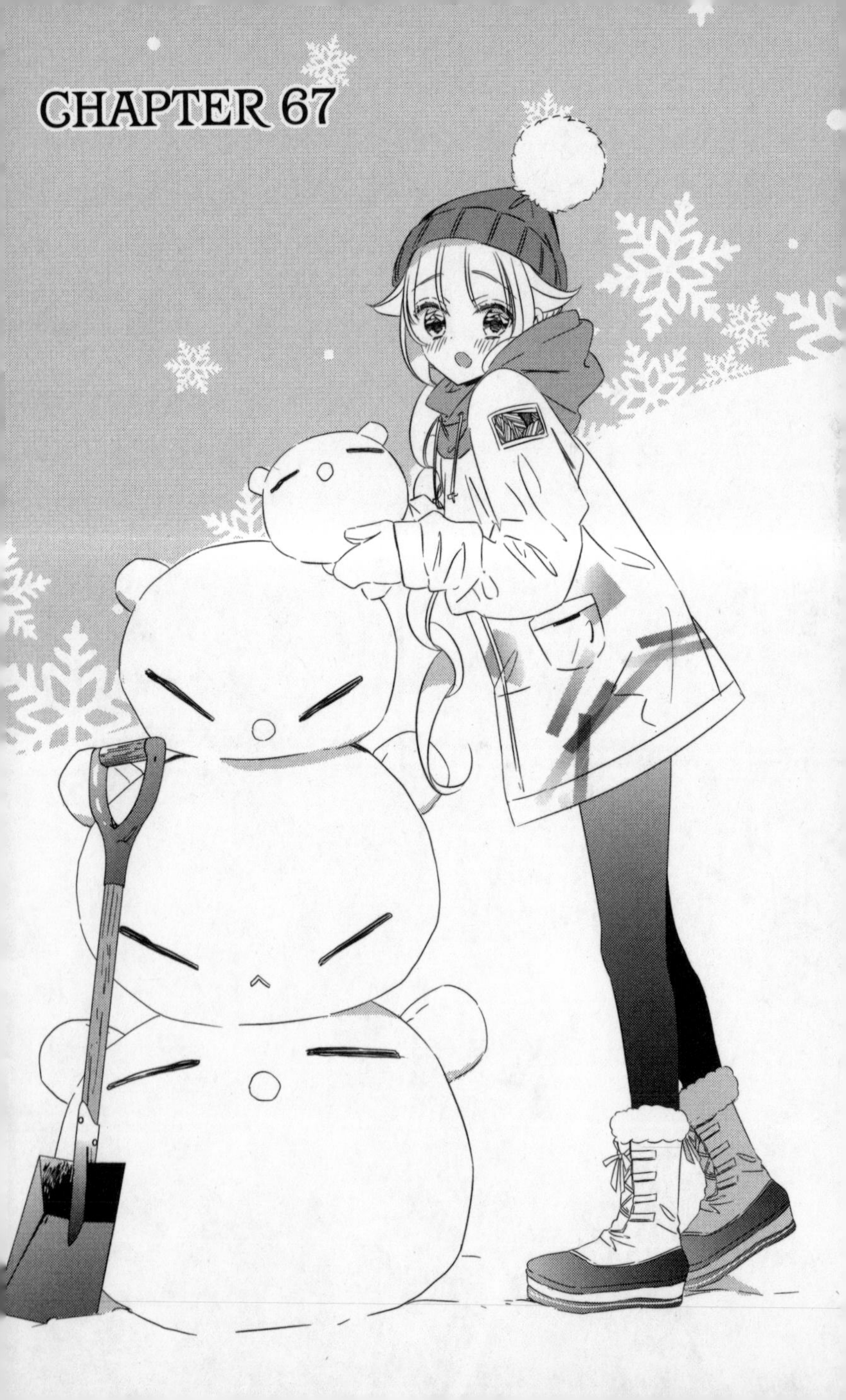
CHAPTER 67

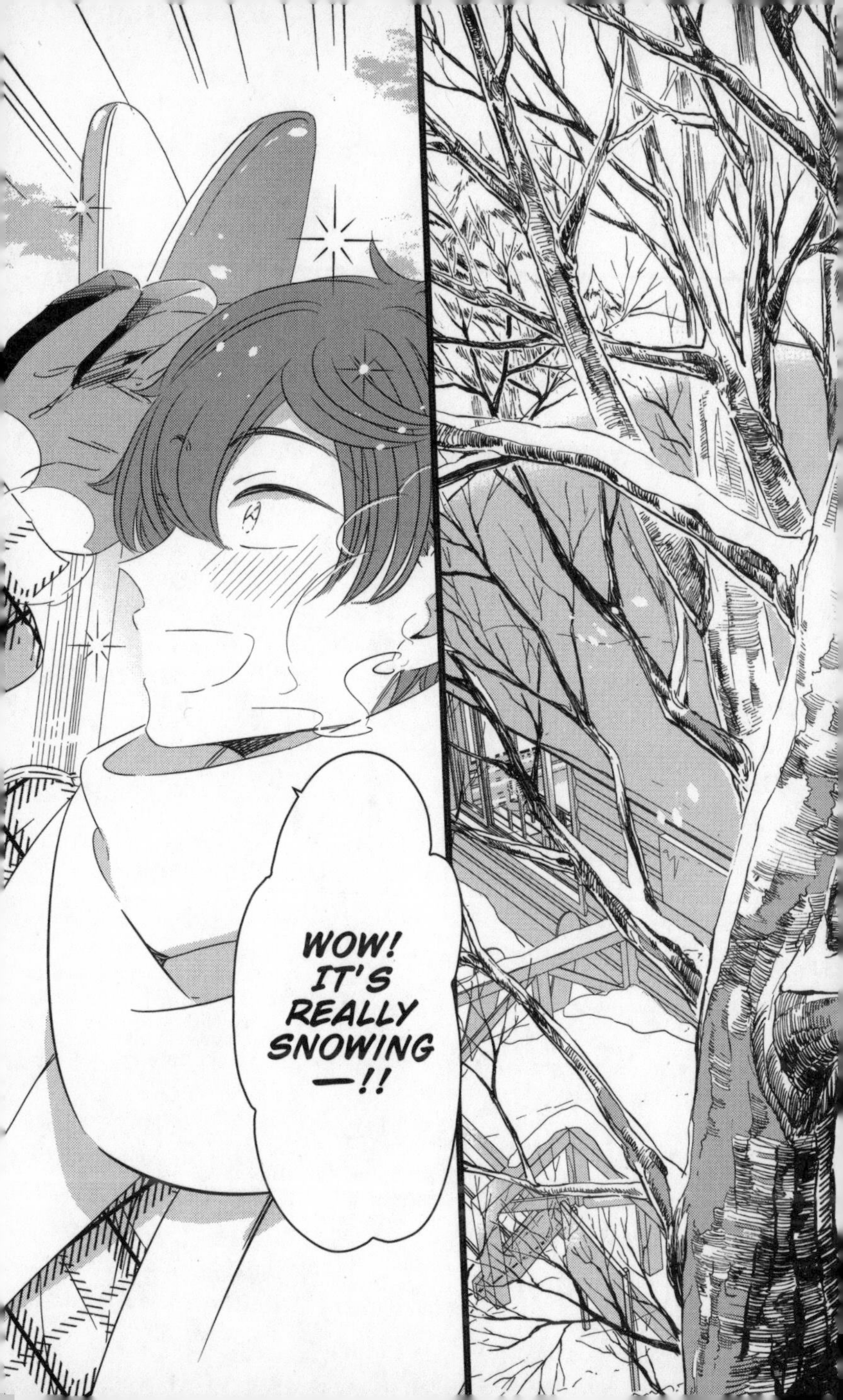
WOW! IT'S REALLY SNOWING—!!

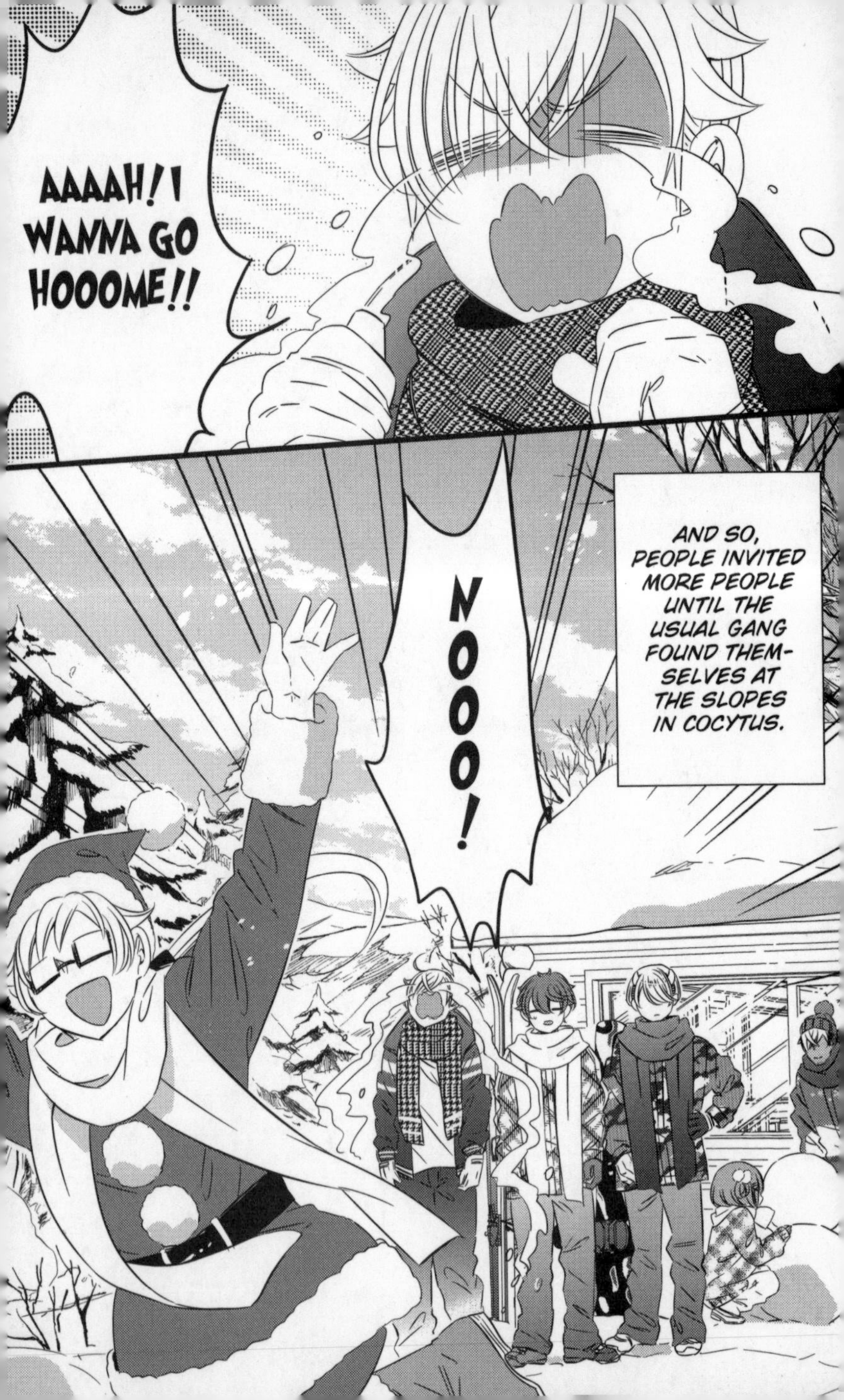
AAAAH! I WANNA GO HOOOME!!
AND SO, PEOPLE INVITED MORE PEOPLE UNTIL THE USUAL GANG FOUND THEM-SELVES AT THE SLOPES IN COCYTUS.
NOOO!

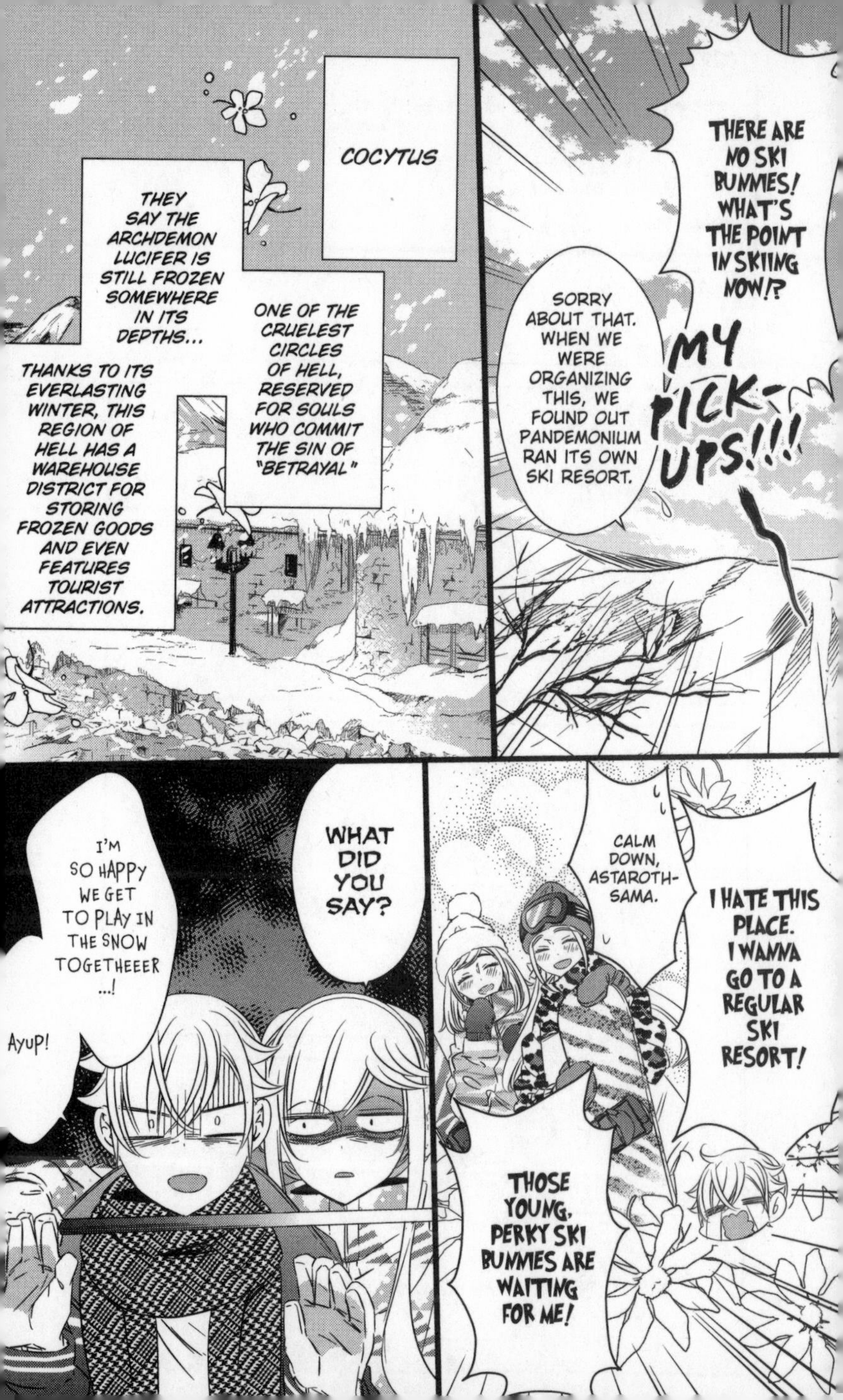
THERE ARE NO SKI BUNNIES! WHAT'S THE POINT IN SKIING NOW!?
MY PICK-UPS!!!
SORRY ABOUT THAT. WHEN WE WERE ORGANIZING THIS, WE FOUND OUT PANDEMONIUM RAN ITS OWN SKI RESORT.
COCYTUS
THEY SAY THE ARCHDEMON LUCIFER IS STILL FROZEN SOMEWHERE IN ITS DEPTHS...
ONE OF THE CRUELEST CIRCLES OF HELL, RESERVED FOR SOULS WHO COMMIT THE SIN OF "BETRAYAL"
THANKS TO ITS EVERLASTING WINTER, THIS REGION OF HELL HAS A WAREHOUSE DISTRICT FOR STORING FROZEN GOODS AND EVEN FEATURES TOURIST ATTRACTIONS.
I HATE THIS PLACE. I WANNA GO TO A REGULAR SKI RESORT!
CALM DOWN, ASTAROTH-SAMA.
THOSE YOUNG, PERKY SKI BUNNIES ARE WAITING FOR ME!
WHAT DID YOU SAY?
I'M SO HAPPY WE GET TO PLAY IN THE SNOW TOGETHEEER...!
AYUP!

GOOD GOING, GOCCHIN

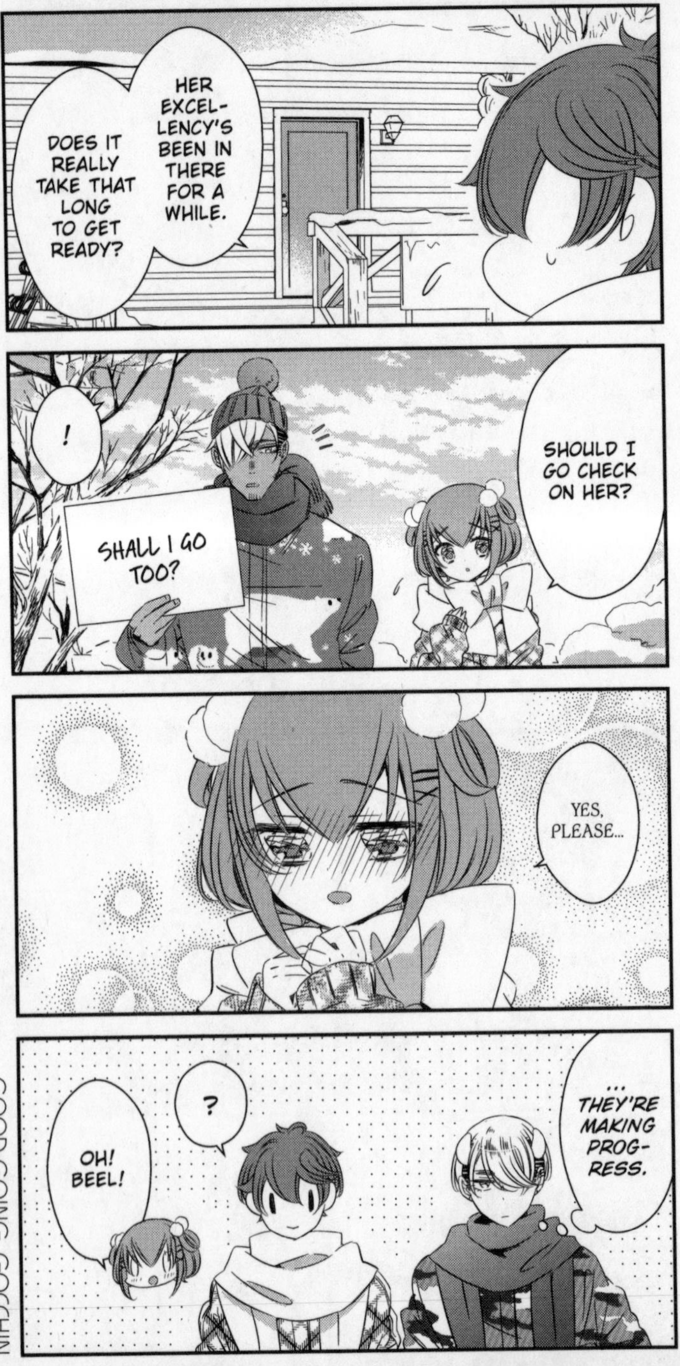
HER EXCEL-LENCY'S BEEN IN THERE FOR A WHILE.
DOES IT REALLY TAKE THAT LONG TO GET READY?
SHOULD I GO CHECK ON HER?
!
SHALL I GO TOO?
YES, PLEASE...
... THEY'RE MAKING PROG-RESS.
?
OH! BEEL!

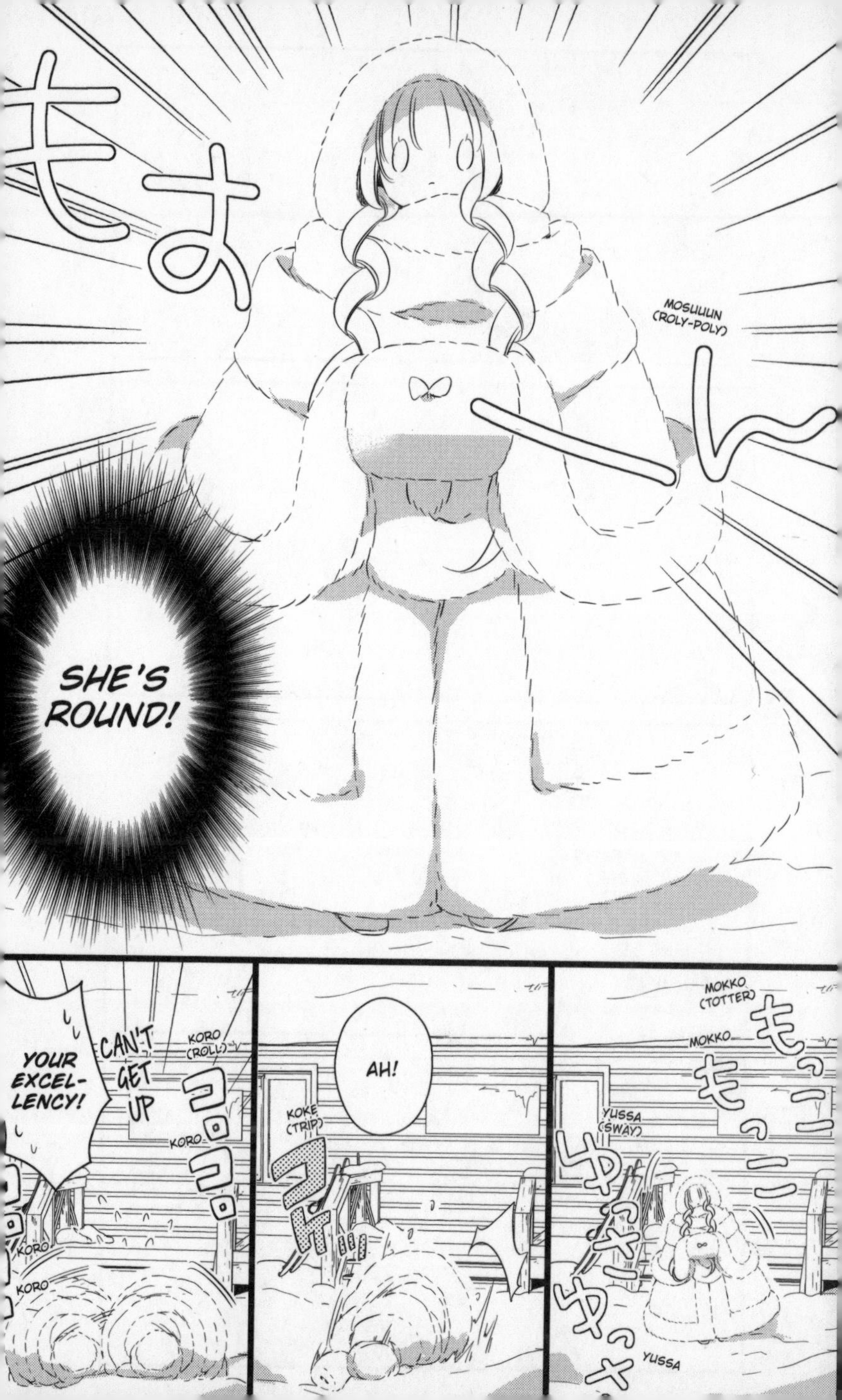

MOSUUUN (ROLY-POLY)
SHE'S ROUND!
MOKKO (TOTTER)
MOKKO
YUSSA (SWAY)
YUSSA
AH!
KOKE (TRIP)
YOUR EXCEL-LENCY!
CAN'T GET UP
KORO (ROLL)
KORO
KORO
KORO

FEELING KINDA BASHFUL

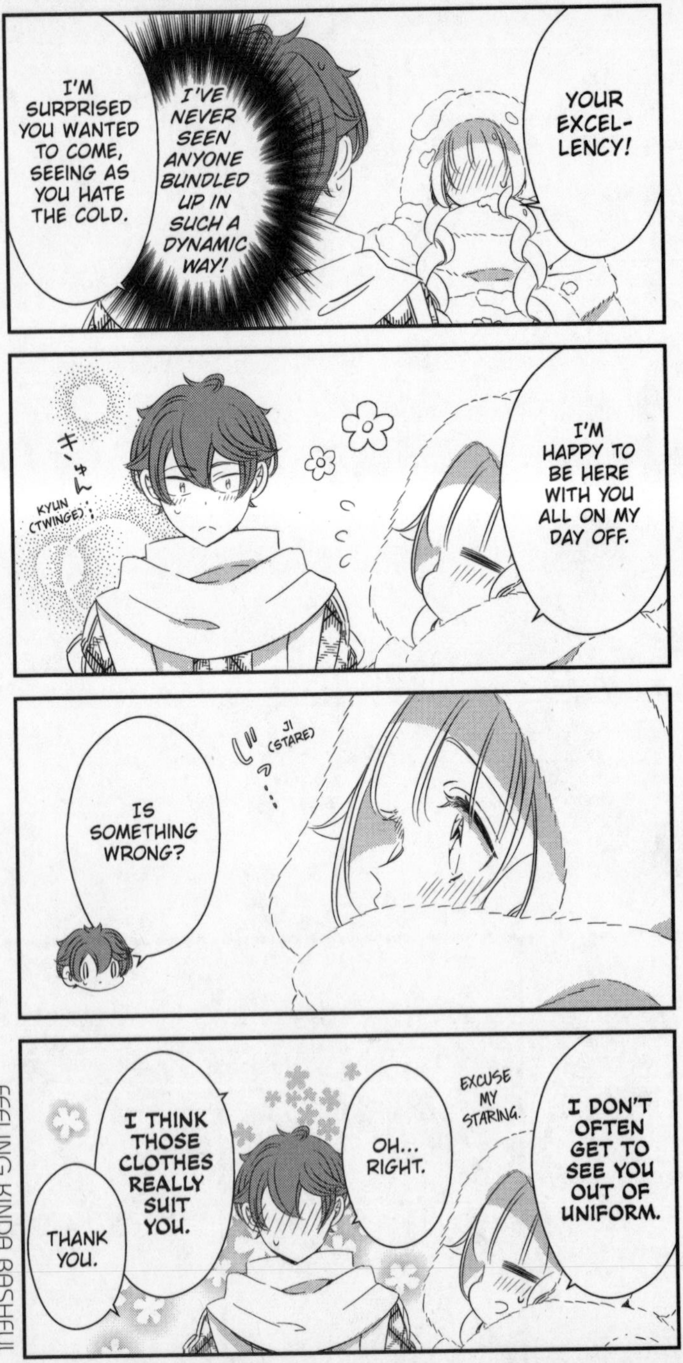
YOUR EXCEL-LENCY!
I'VE NEVER SEEN ANYONE BUNDLED UP IN SUCH A DYNAMIC WAY!
I'M SURPRISED YOU WANTED TO COME, SEEING AS YOU HATE THE COLD.
I'M HAPPY TO BE HERE WITH YOU ALL ON MY DAY OFF.
キュン
KYUN (TWINGE)
じ
JI (STARE)
IS SOMETHING WRONG?
I DON'T OFTEN GET TO SEE YOU OUT OF UNIFORM.
EXCUSE MY STARING.
OH... RIGHT.
I THINK THOSE CLOTHES REALLY SUIT YOU.
THANK YOU.

SUITS YOU, AS IN "YOU'RE LIKE A BABY SEAL"

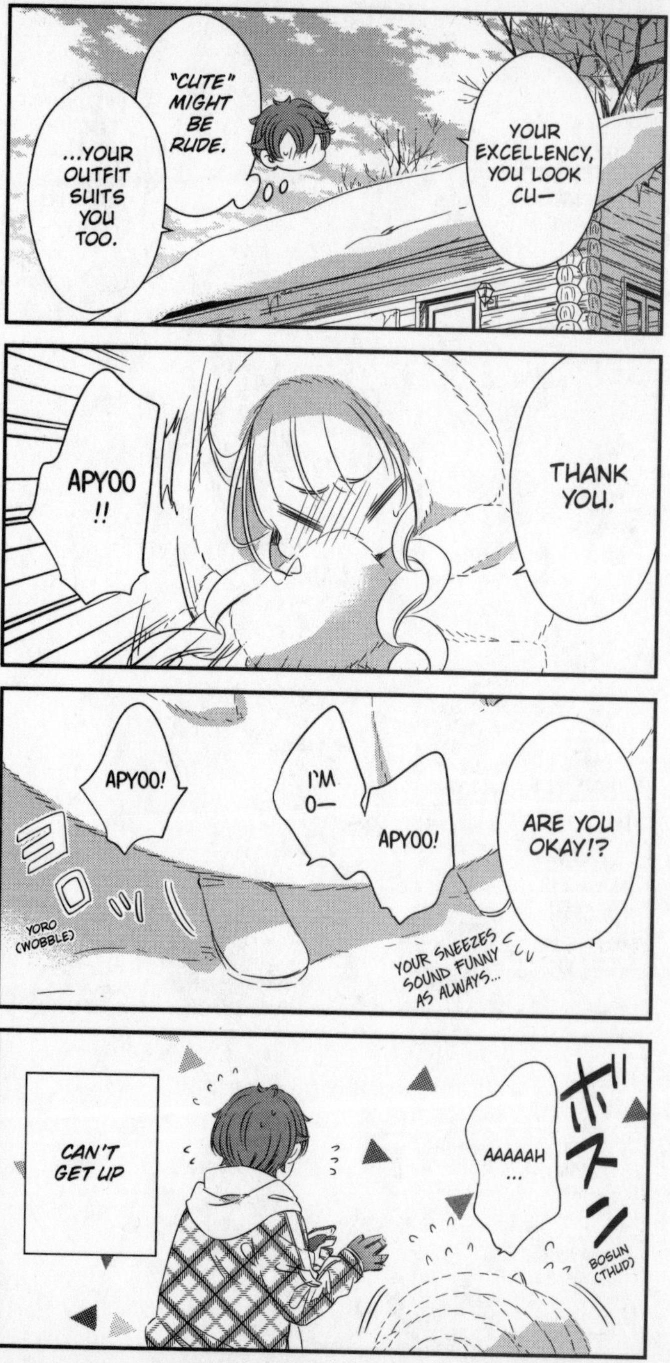
YOUR EXCELLENCY, YOU LOOK CU—
"CUTE" MIGHT BE RUDE.
...YOUR OUTFIT SUITS YOU TOO.
THANK YOU.
APYOO !!
ARE YOU OKAY!?
YOUR SNEEZES SOUND FUNNY AS ALWAYS...
I'M O—
APYOO!
APYOO!
ヨロッ
YORO (WOBBLE)
ボスン
BOSUN (THUD)
AAAAAH ...
CAN'T GET UP

NOTHING NEW HERE

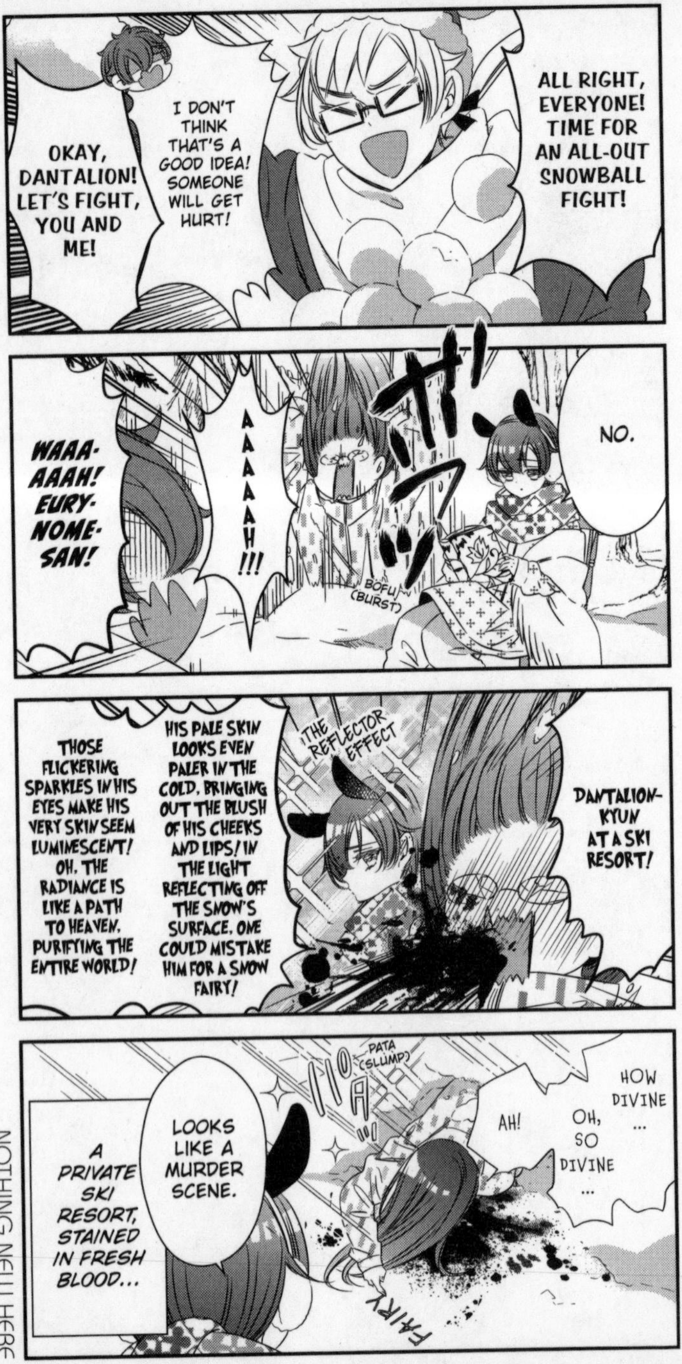
ALL RIGHT, EVERYONE! TIME FOR AN ALL-OUT SNOWBALL FIGHT!
I DON'T THINK THAT'S A GOOD IDEA! SOMEONE WILL GET HURT!
OKAY, DANTALION! LET'S FIGHT, YOU AND ME!
NO.
BOFU! (BURST)
AAAAAAH!!!
WAAA-AAAH! EURY-NOME-SAN!
DANTALION-KYUN AT A SKI RESORT!
THE REFLECTOR EFFECT
HIS PALE SKIN LOOKS EVEN PALER IN THE COLD, BRINGING OUT THE BLUSH OF HIS CHEEKS AND LIPS! IN THE LIGHT REFLECTING OFF THE SNOW'S SURFACE, ONE COULD MISTAKE HIM FOR A SNOW FAIRY!
THOSE FLICKERING SPARKLES IN HIS EYES MAKE HIS VERY SKIN SEEM LUMINESCENT! OH, THE RADIANCE IS LIKE A PATH TO HEAVEN, PURIFYING THE ENTIRE WORLD!
HOW DIVINE ...
OH, SO DIVINE ...
AH!
PATA (SLUMP)
LOOKS LIKE A MURDER SCENE.
A PRIVATE SKI RESORT, STAINED IN FRESH BLOOD...
FAIRY

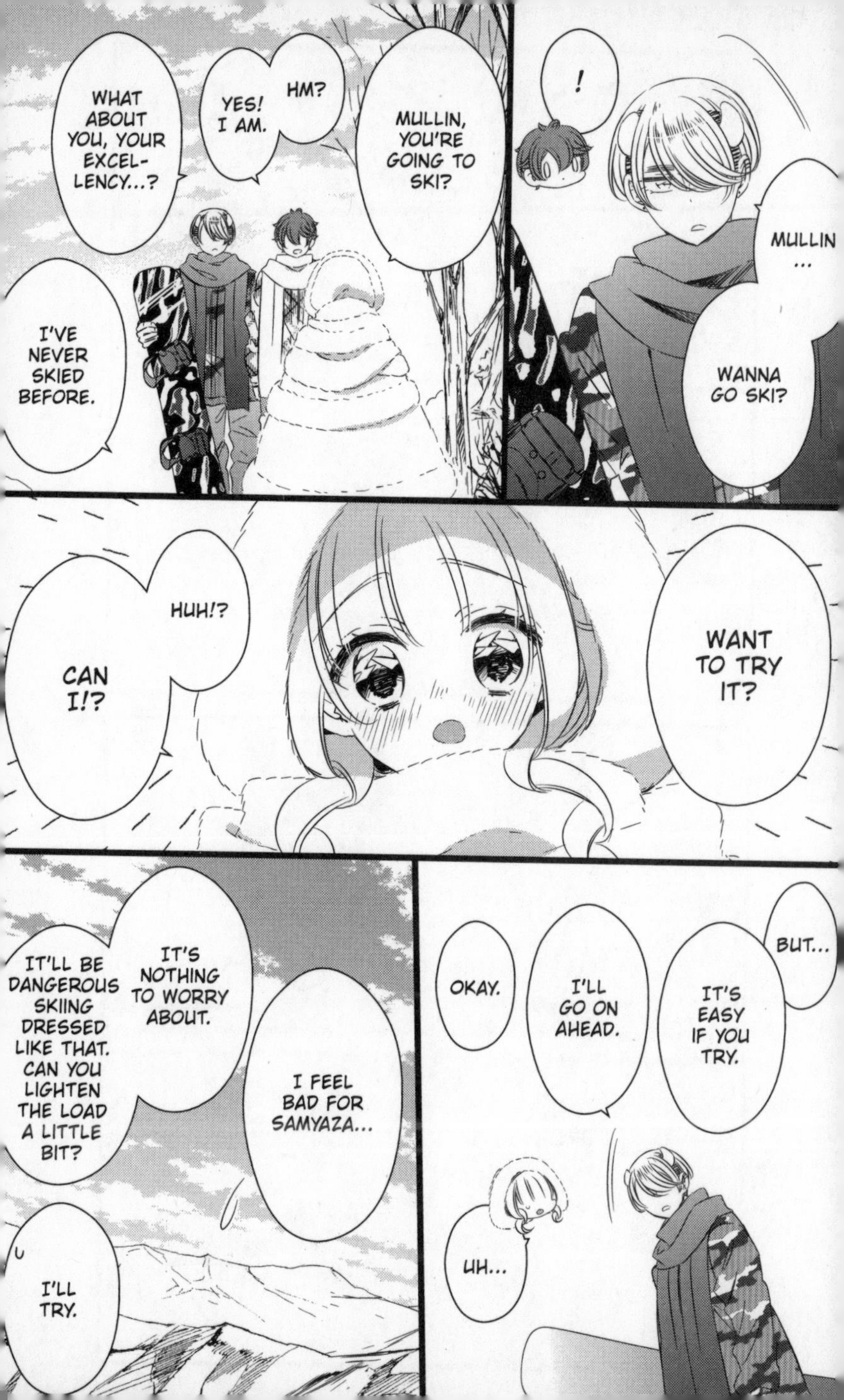
!
MULLIN ...
WANNA GO SKI?
MULLIN, YOU'RE GOING TO SKI?
HM?
YES! I AM.
WHAT ABOUT YOU, YOUR EXCEL-LENCY...?
I'VE NEVER SKIED BEFORE.
WANT TO TRY IT?
HUH!?
CAN I!?
BUT...
IT'S EASY IF YOU TRY.
I'LL GO ON AHEAD.
OKAY.
UH...
IT'S NOTHING TO WORRY ABOUT.
IT'LL BE DANGEROUS SKIING DRESSED LIKE THAT. CAN YOU LIGHTEN THE LOAD A LITTLE BIT?
I FEEL BAD FOR SAMYAZA...
U
I'LL TRY.

POOR SAM

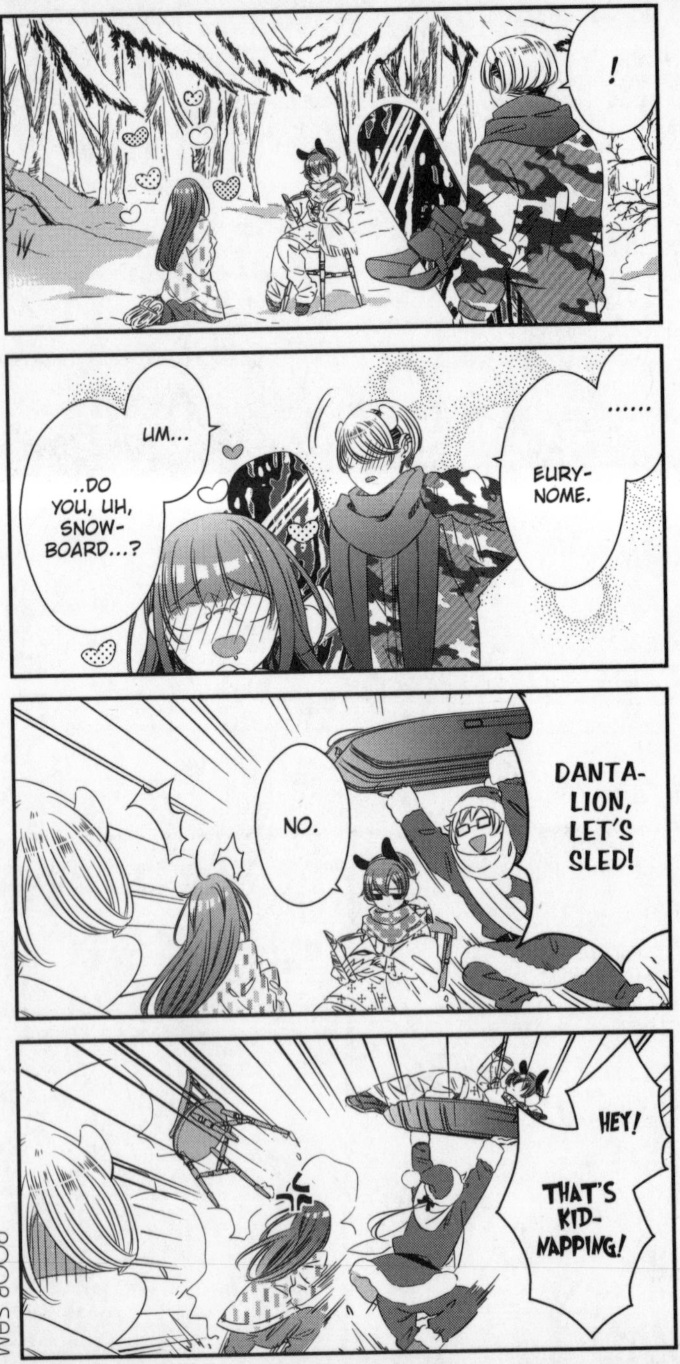
!
......
EURY-NOME.
UM...
..DO YOU, UH, SNOW-BOARD...?
DANTA-LION, LET'S SLED!
NO.
HEY!
THAT'S KID-NAPPING!

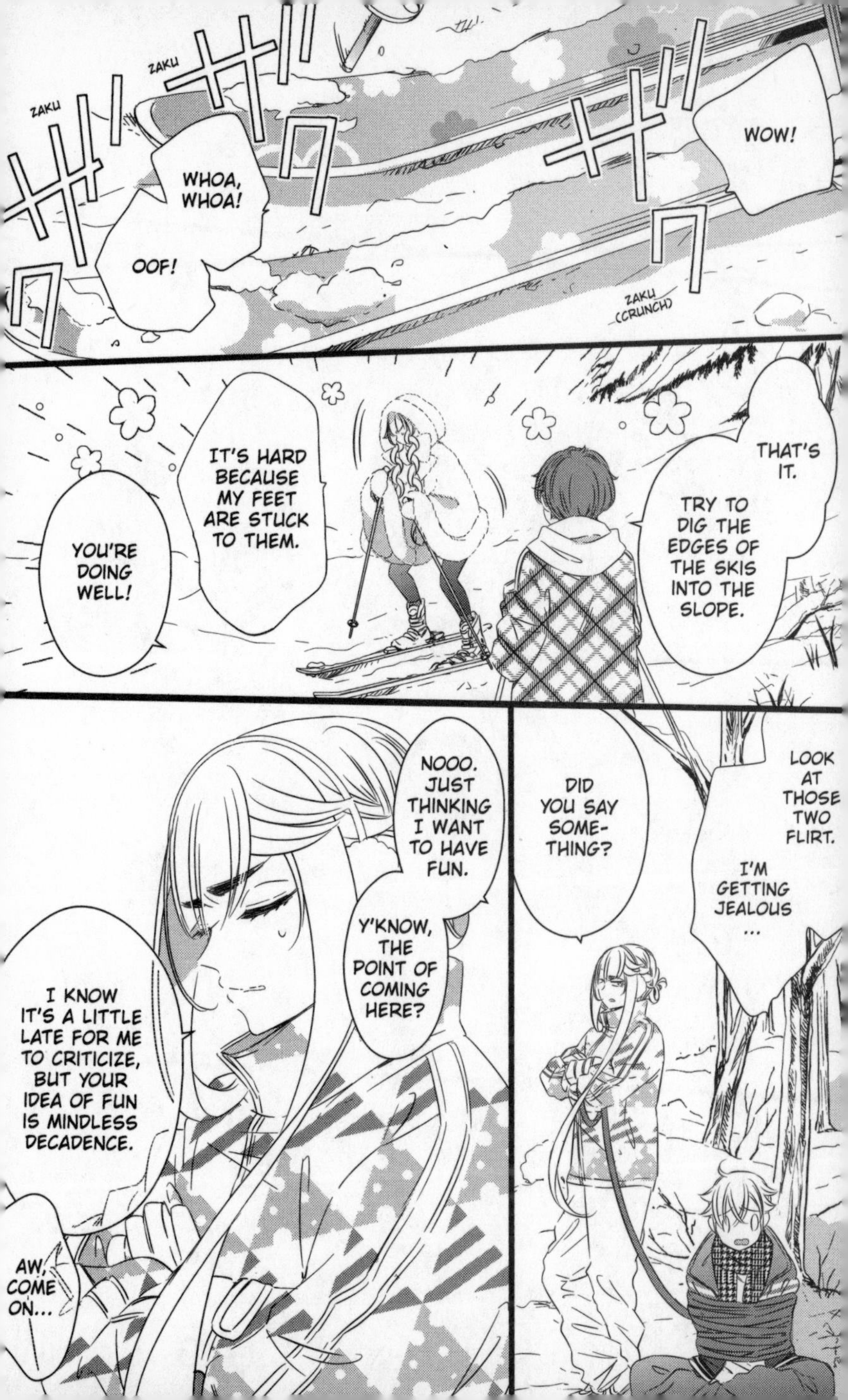
WOW!
ZAKU (CRUNCH)
ZAKU
ZAKU
WHOA, WHOA!
OOF!
THAT'S IT.
TRY TO DIG THE EDGES OF THE SKIS INTO THE SLOPE.
IT'S HARD BECAUSE MY FEET ARE STUCK TO THEM.
YOU'RE DOING WELL!
LOOK AT THOSE TWO FLIRT.
I'M GETTING JEALOUS...
DID YOU SAY SOME-THING?
NOOO. JUST THINKING I WANT TO HAVE FUN.
Y'KNOW, THE POINT OF COMING HERE?
I KNOW IT'S A LITTLE LATE FOR ME TO CRITICIZE, BUT YOUR IDEA OF FUN IS MINDLESS DECADENCE.
AW, COME ON...

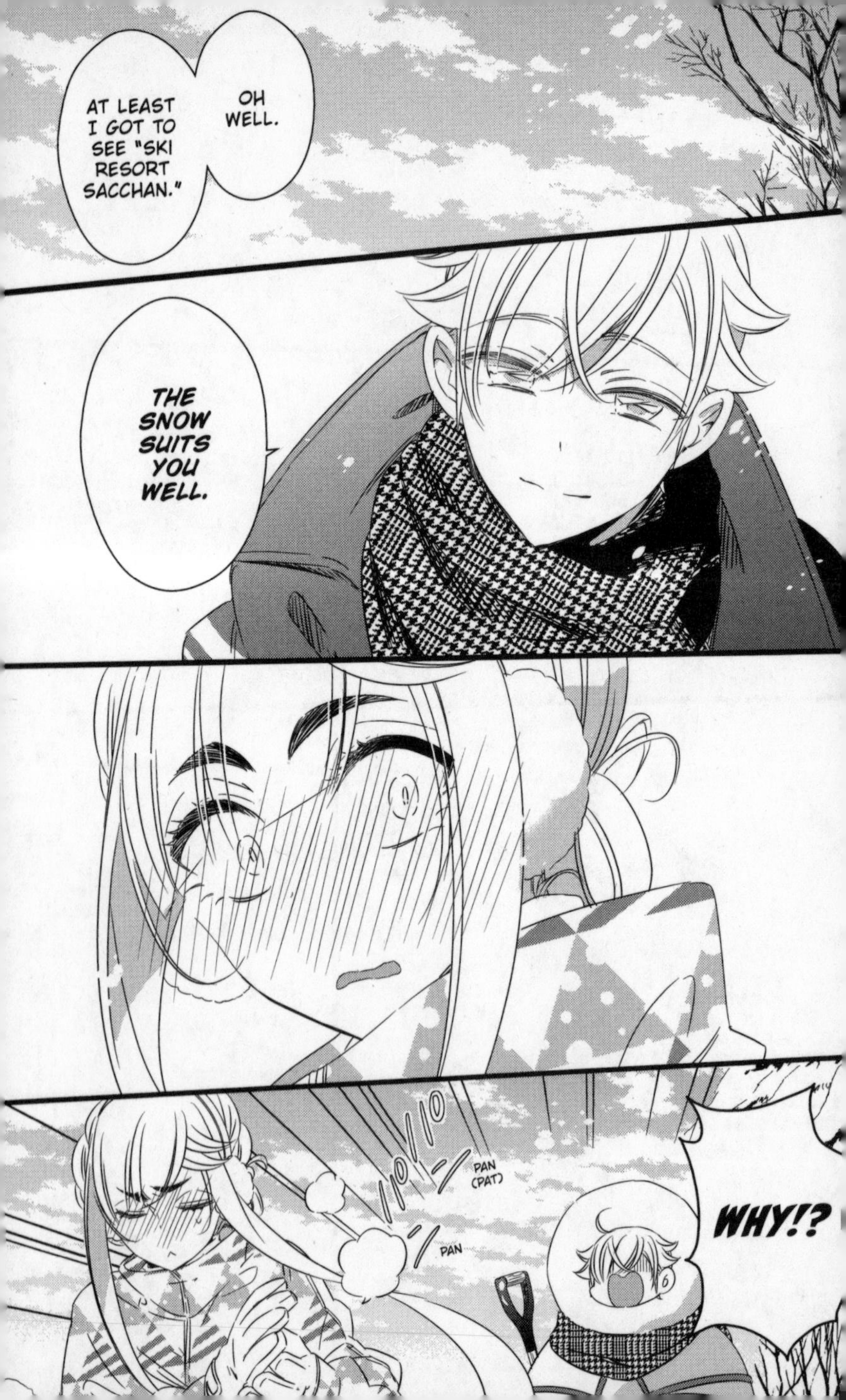
OH WELL.
AT LEAST I GOT TO SEE "SKI RESORT SACCHAN."
THE SNOW SUITS YOU WELL.
WHY!?
PAN (PAT)
PAN

NO WAY, NO HOW, NO DICE

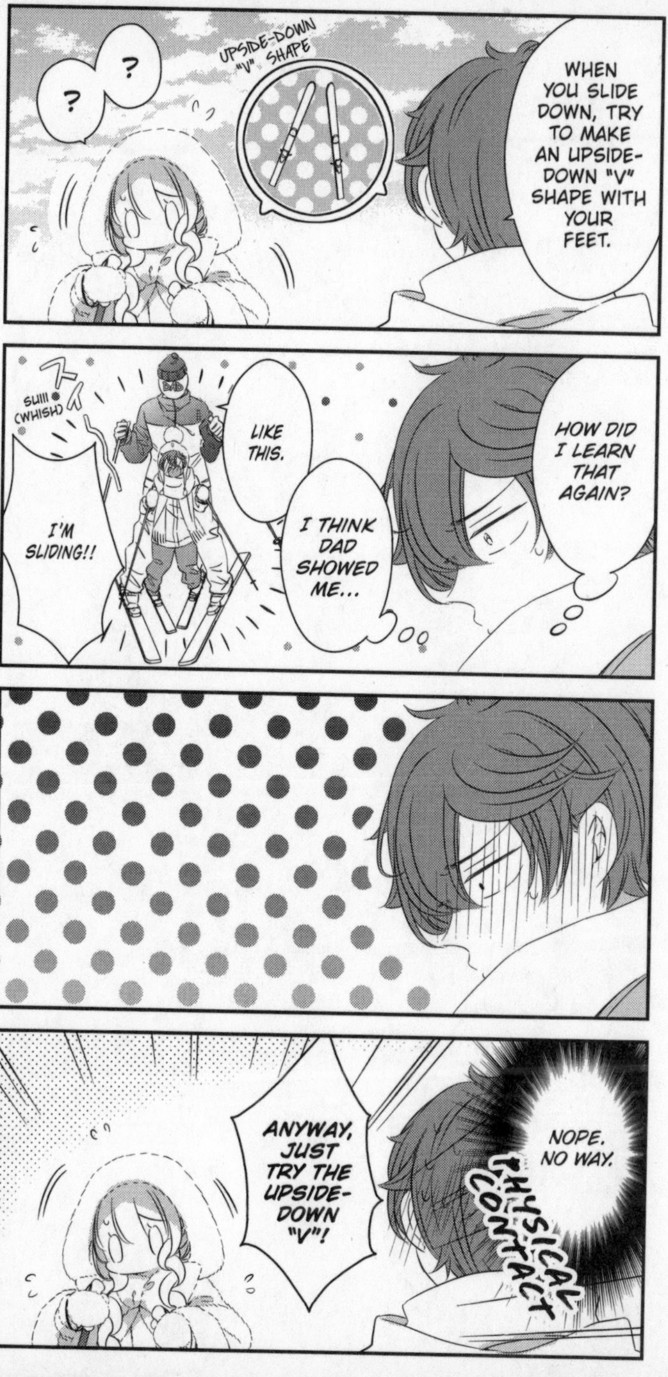
WHEN YOU SLIDE DOWN, TRY TO MAKE AN UPSIDE-DOWN "V" SHAPE WITH YOUR FEET.
UPSIDE-DOWN "V" SHAPE
? ?
HOW DID I LEARN THAT AGAIN?
I THINK DAD SHOWED ME...
LIKE THIS.
DAD
SUIII (WHISH)
I'M SLIDING!!
NOPE. NO WAY.
PHYSICAL CONTACT
ANYWAY, JUST TRY THE UPSIDE-DOWN "V"!

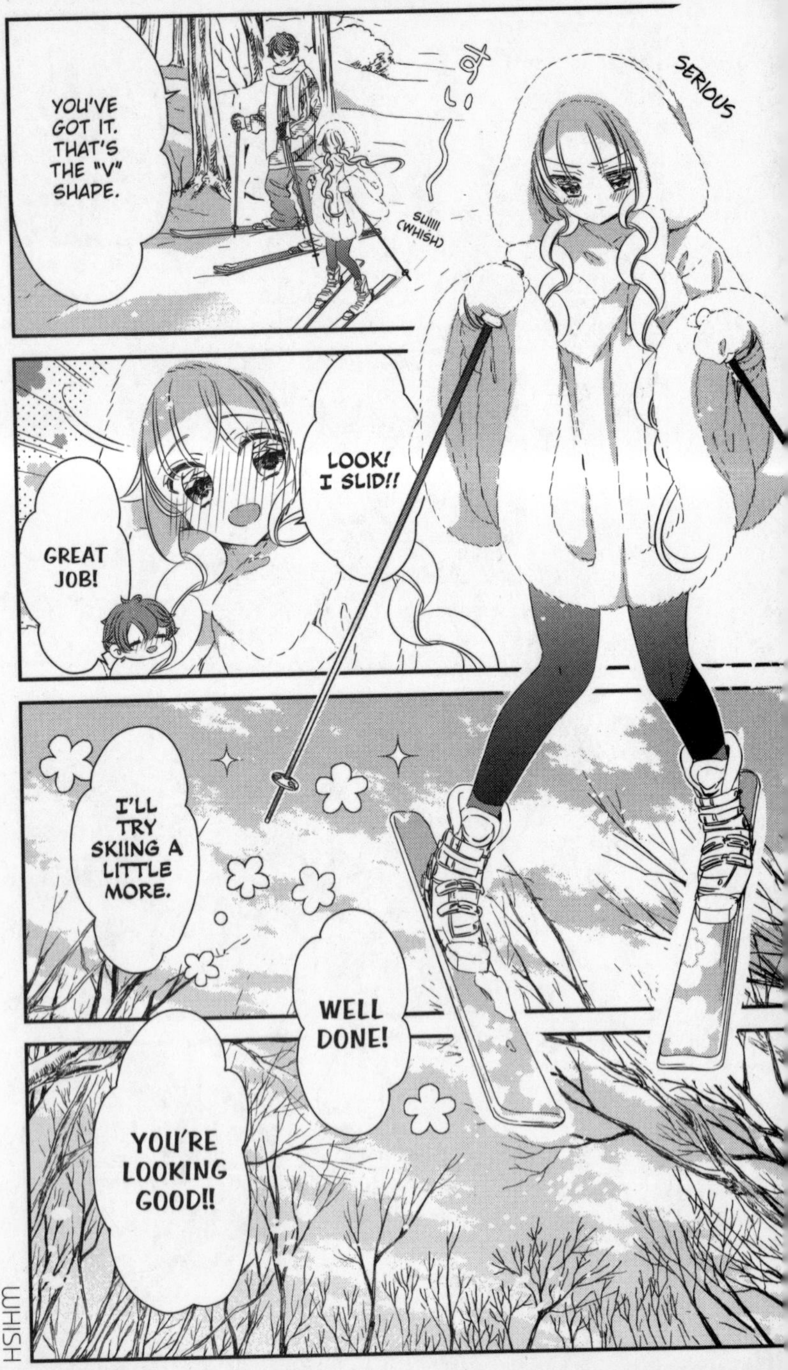
SERIOUS
すい〜
SUIIII (WHISH)
YOU'VE GOT IT. THAT'S THE "V" SHAPE.
LOOK! I SLID!!
GREAT JOB!
I'LL TRY SKIING A LITTLE MORE.
WELL DONE!
YOU'RE LOOKING GOOD!!
WHISH

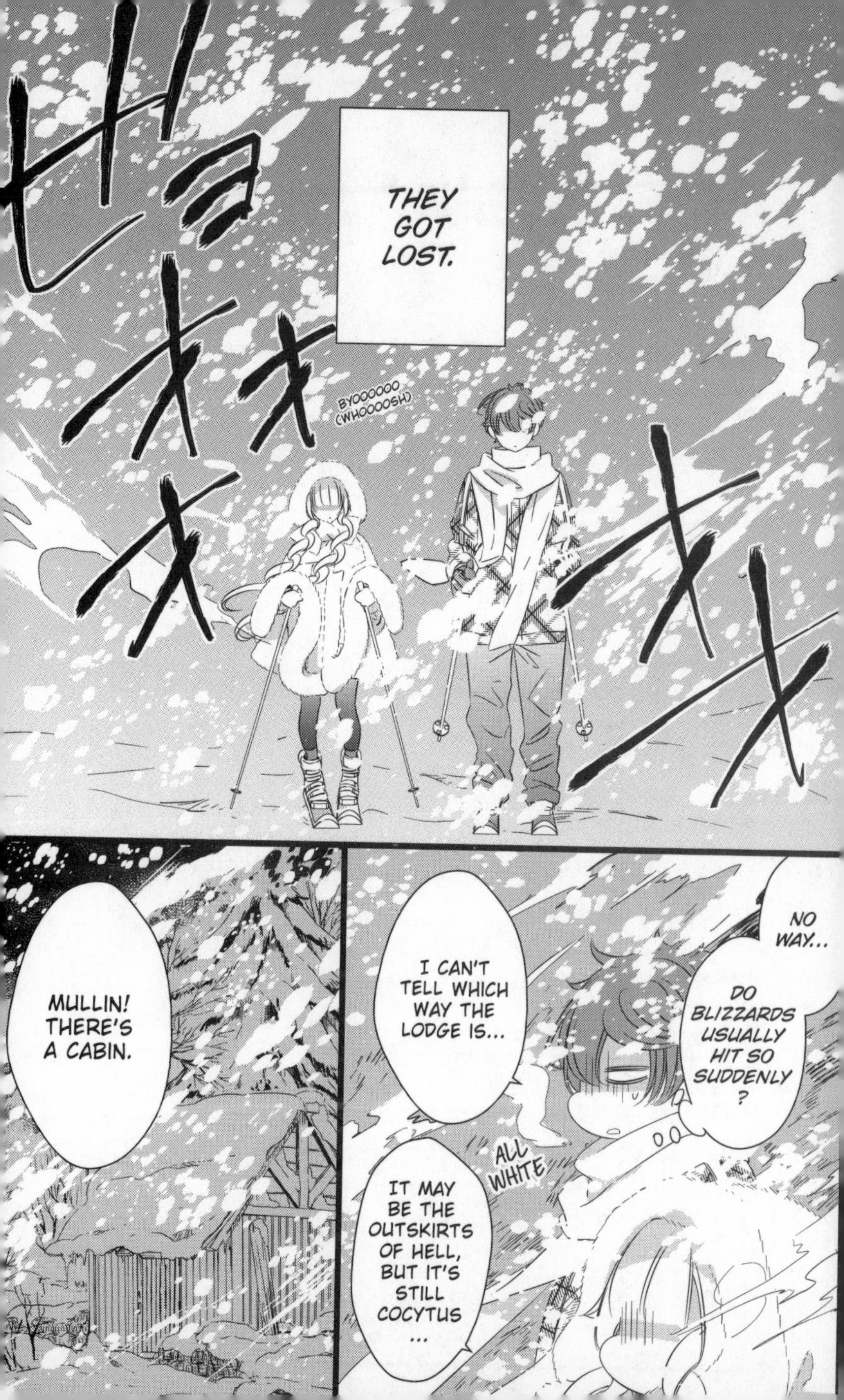
THEY GOT LOST.
BYOOOOOO (WHOOOOSH)
NO WAY...
DO BLIZZARDS USUALLY HIT SO SUDDENLY?
I CAN'T TELL WHICH WAY THE LODGE IS...
ALL WHITE
IT MAY BE THE OUTSKIRTS OF HELL, BUT IT'S STILL COCYTUS...
MULLIN! THERE'S A CABIN.

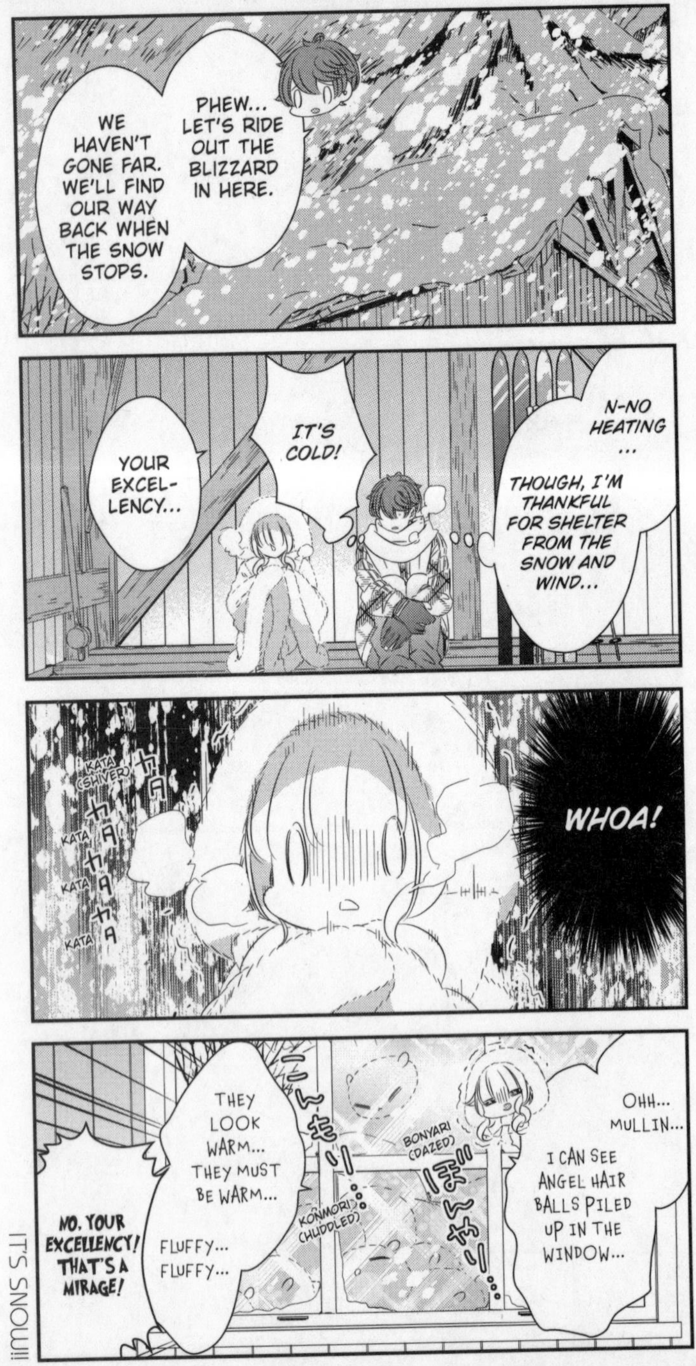
IT'S SNOW!!!
PHEW... LET'S RIDE OUT THE BLIZZARD IN HERE.
WE HAVEN'T GONE FAR. WE'LL FIND OUR WAY BACK WHEN THE SNOW STOPS.
N-NO HEATING... THOUGH, I'M THANKFUL FOR SHELTER FROM THE SNOW AND WIND...
IT'S COLD!
YOUR EXCELLENCY...
WHOA!
KATA (SHIVER)
KATA
KATA
KATA
OHH... MULLIN... I CAN SEE ANGEL HAIR BALLS PILED UP IN THE WINDOW...
BONYARI (DAZED)
KONMORI (HUDDLED)
THEY LOOK WARM... THEY MUST BE WARM... FLUFFY... FLUFFY...
NO, YOUR EXCELLENCY! THAT'S A MIRAGE!

OKAY, TOUGH GUY

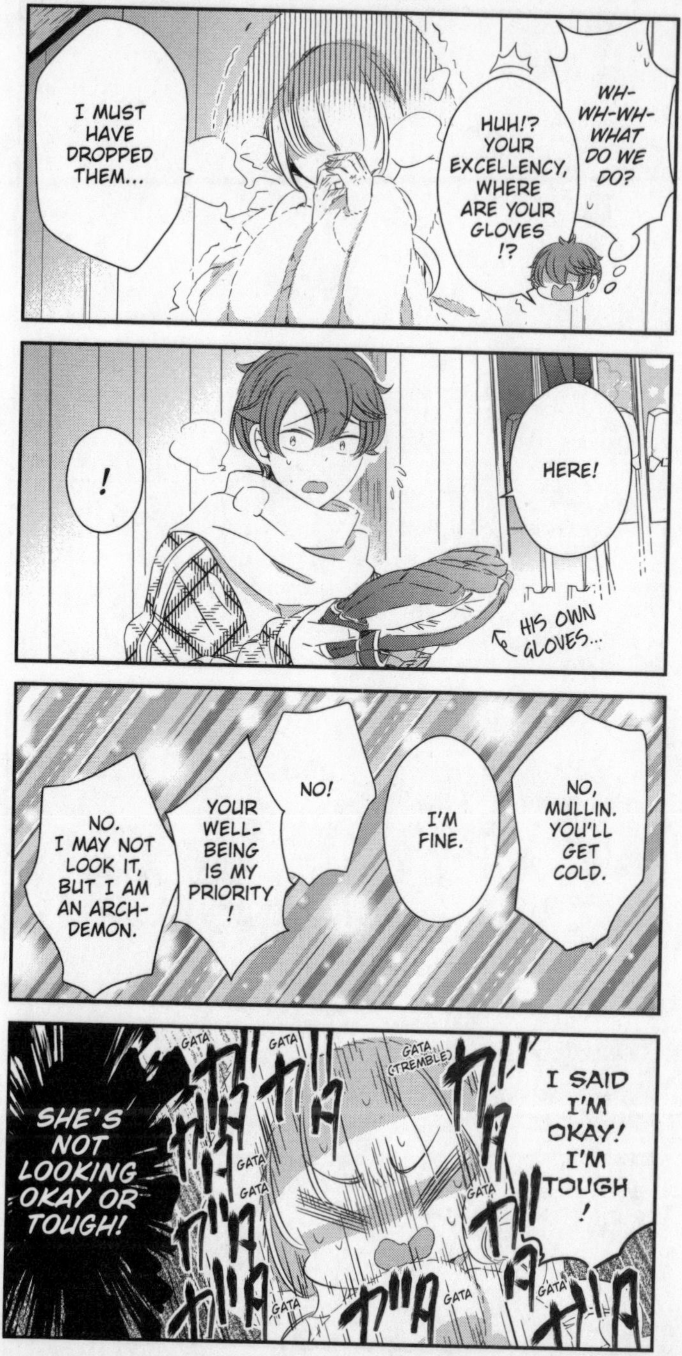

WH-WH-WH-WHAT DO WE DO?
HUH!? YOUR EXCELLENCY, WHERE ARE YOUR GLOVES!?
I MUST HAVE DROPPED THEM...
HERE!
HIS OWN GLOVES...
!
NO, MULLIN. YOU'LL GET COLD.
I'M FINE.
NO!
YOUR WELL-BEING IS MY PRIORITY!
NO. I MAY NOT LOOK IT, BUT I AM AN ARCH-DEMON.
I SAID I'M OKAY! I'M TOUGH!
GATA (TREMBLE)
GATA
GATA
GATA
GATA
GATA
GATA
GATA
GATA
SHE'S NOT LOOKING OKAY OR TOUGH!

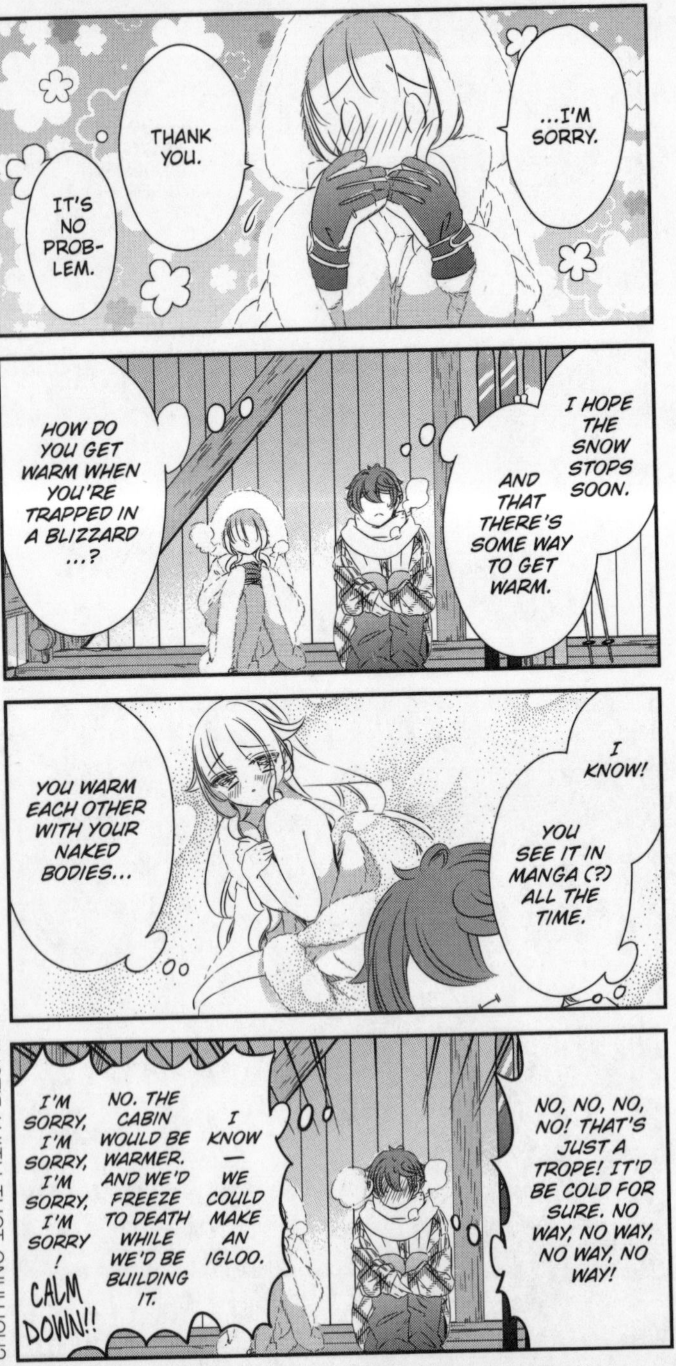
...I'M SORRY.
THANK YOU.
IT'S NO PROBLEM.
I HOPE THE SNOW STOPS SOON.
AND THAT THERE'S SOME WAY TO GET WARM.
HOW DO YOU GET WARM WHEN YOU'RE TRAPPED IN A BLIZZARD ...?
I KNOW!
YOU SEE IT IN MANGA (?) ALL THE TIME.
YOU WARM EACH OTHER WITH YOUR NAKED BODIES...
NO, NO, NO, NO! THAT'S JUST A TROPE! IT'D BE COLD FOR SURE. NO WAY, NO WAY, NO WAY, NO WAY!
I KNOW—WE COULD MAKE AN IGLOO.
NO. THE CABIN WOULD BE WARMER. AND WE'D FREEZE TO DEATH WHILE WE'D BE BUILDING IT.
I'M SORRY, I'M SORRY, I'M SORRY, I'M SORRY!
CALM DOWN!!

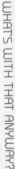

WHAT'S WITH THAT ANYWAY?

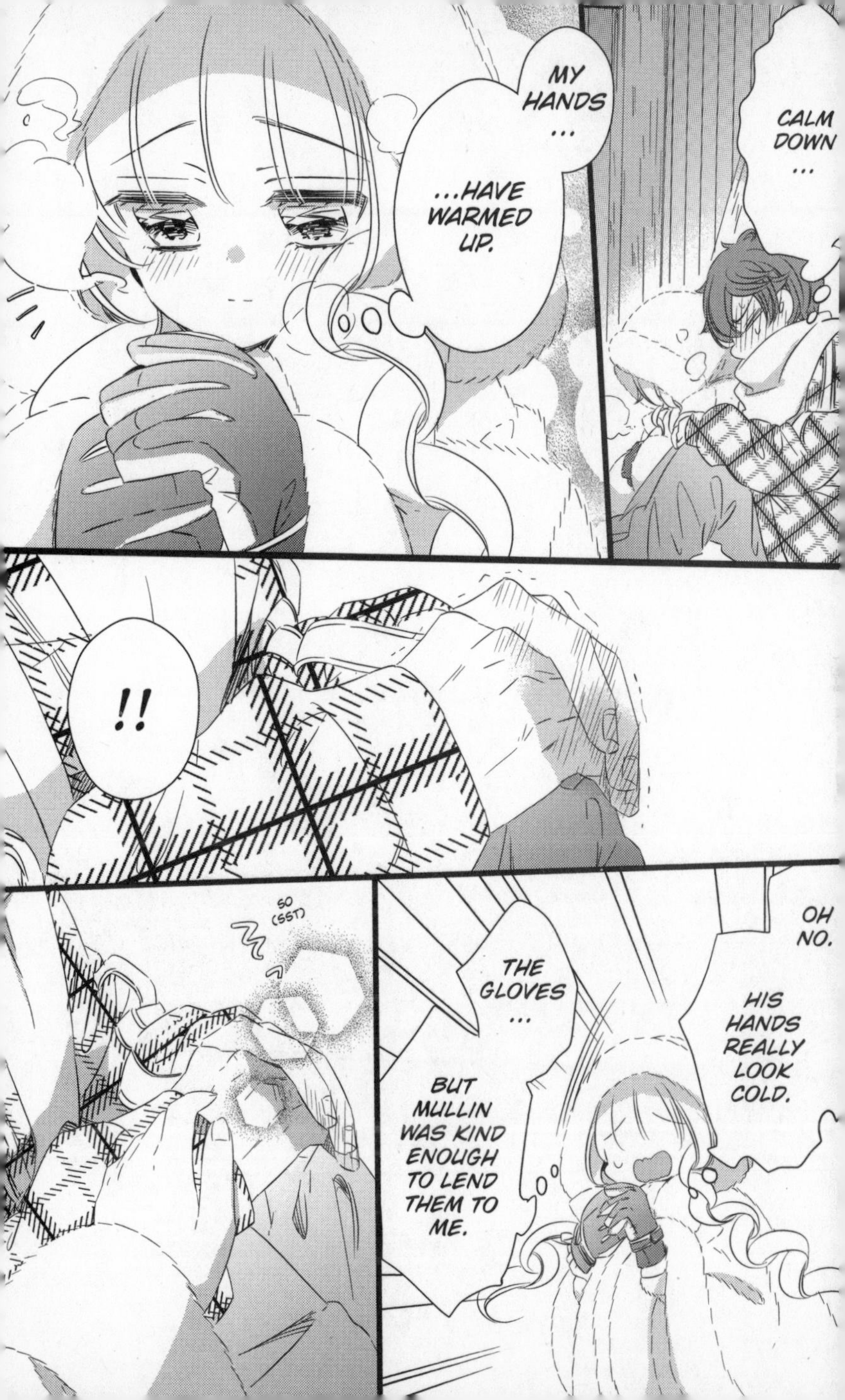
CALM DOWN ...
MY HANDS ...
...HAVE WARMED UP.
!!
OH NO.
HIS HANDS REALLY LOOK COLD.
THE GLOVES ...
BUT MULLIN WAS KIND ENOUGH TO LEND THEM TO ME.
SO (SST)

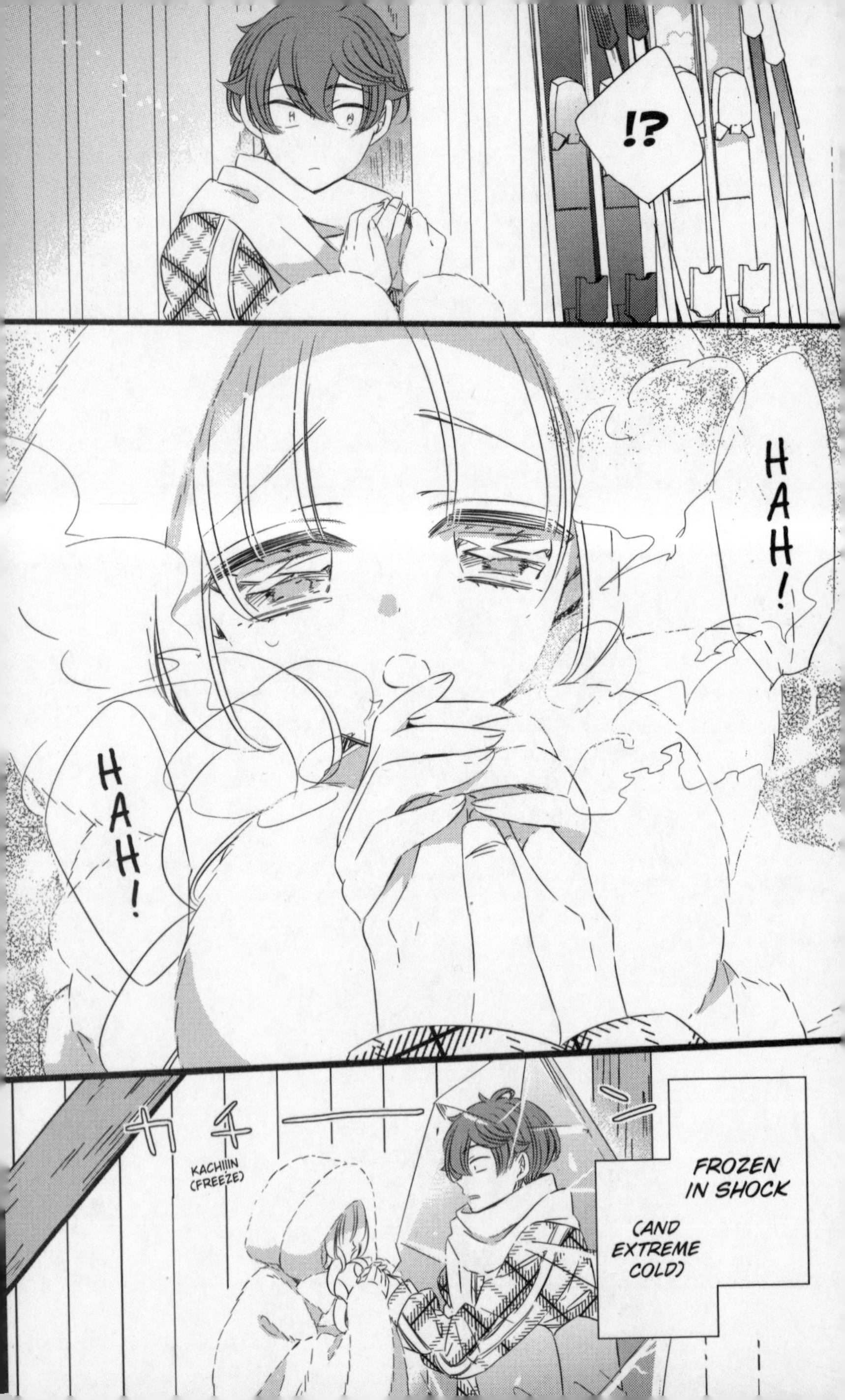
!?
HAH!
HAH!
FROZEN IN SHOCK
(AND EXTREME COLD)
KACHIIIN (FREEZE)

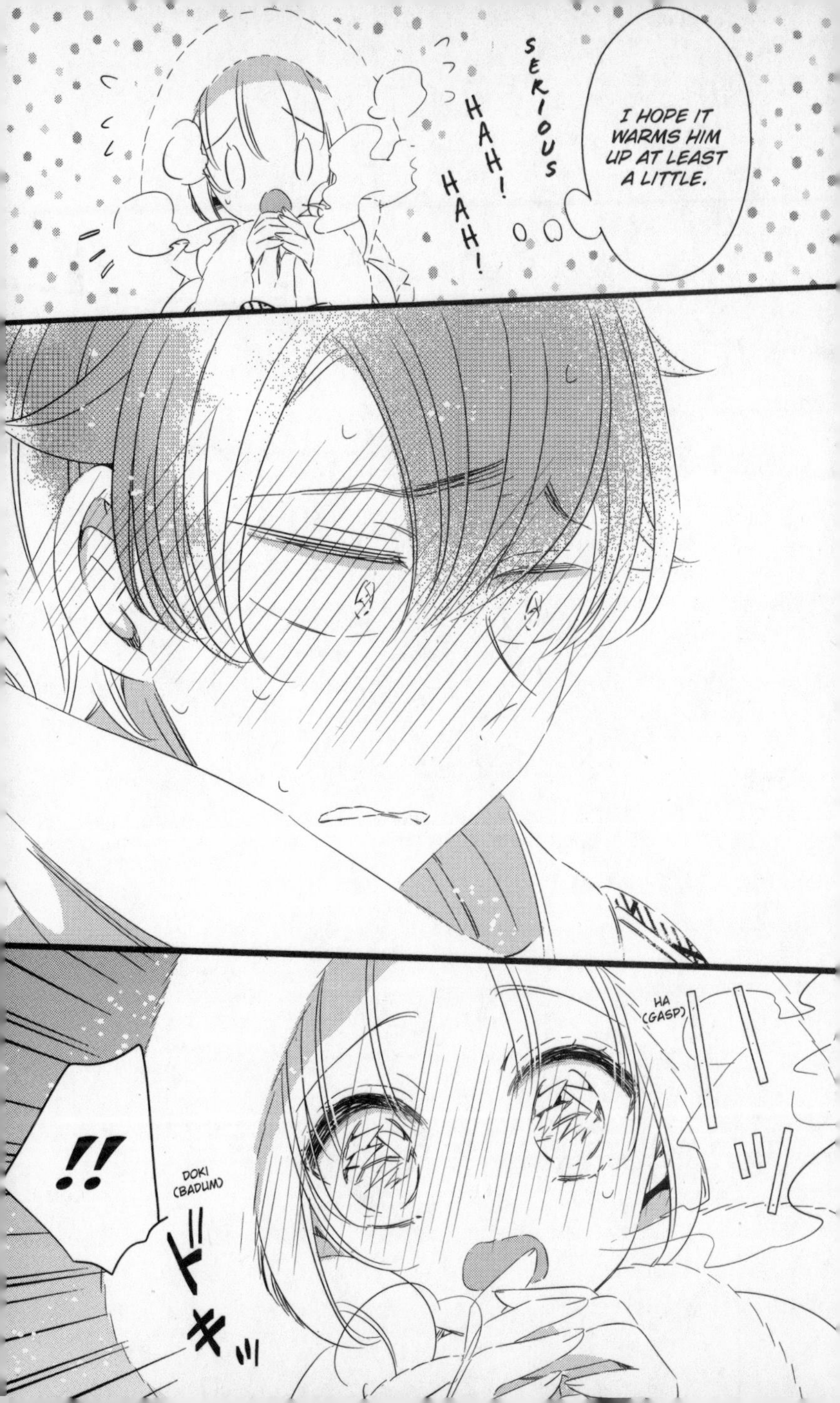

I HOPE IT WARMS HIM UP AT LEAST A LITTLE.
SERIOUS
HAH! HAH!
HA (GASP)
!!
DOKI (BADUM)

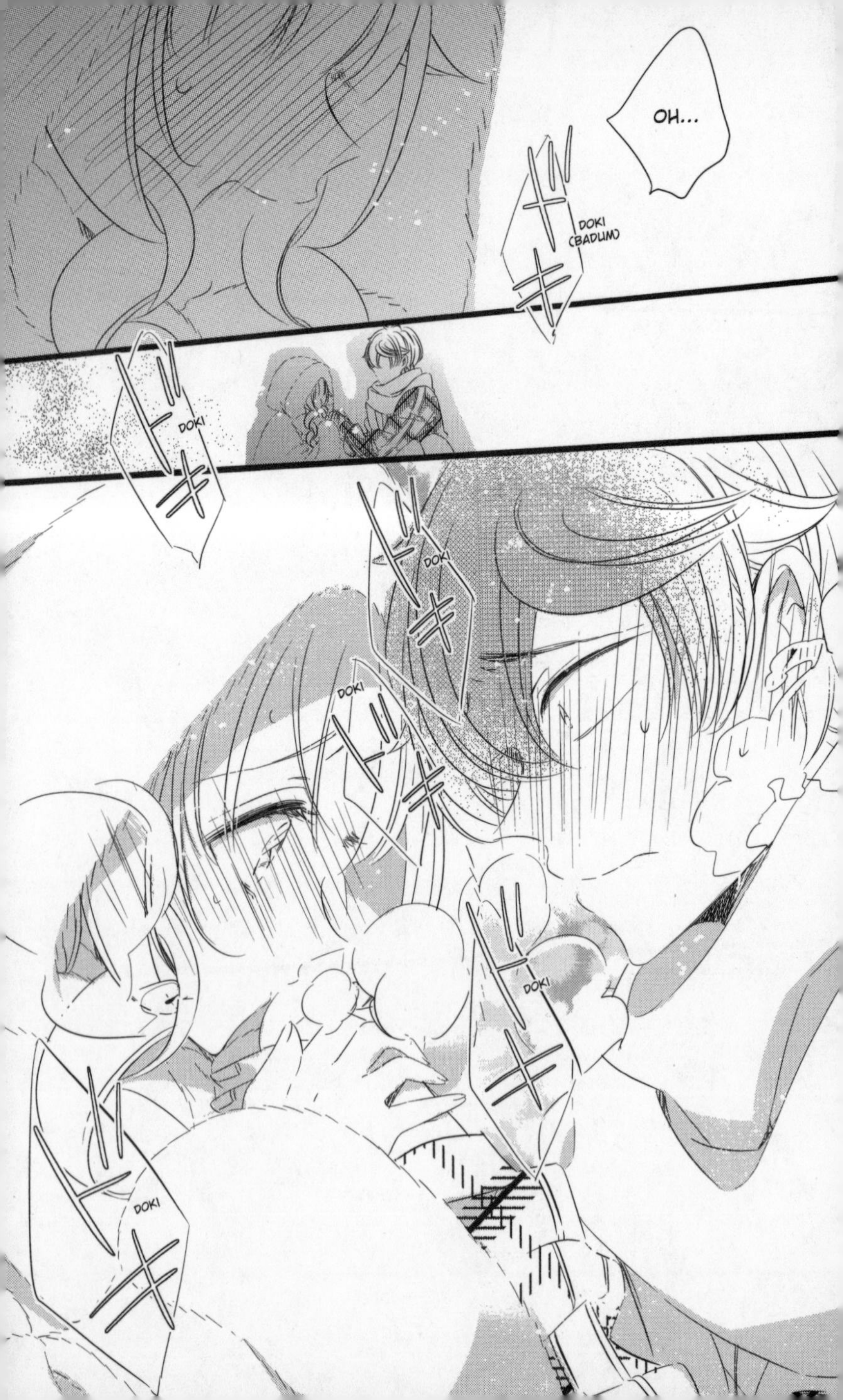
OH...
DOKI (BADUM)
DOKI
DOKI
DOKI
DOKI
DOKI

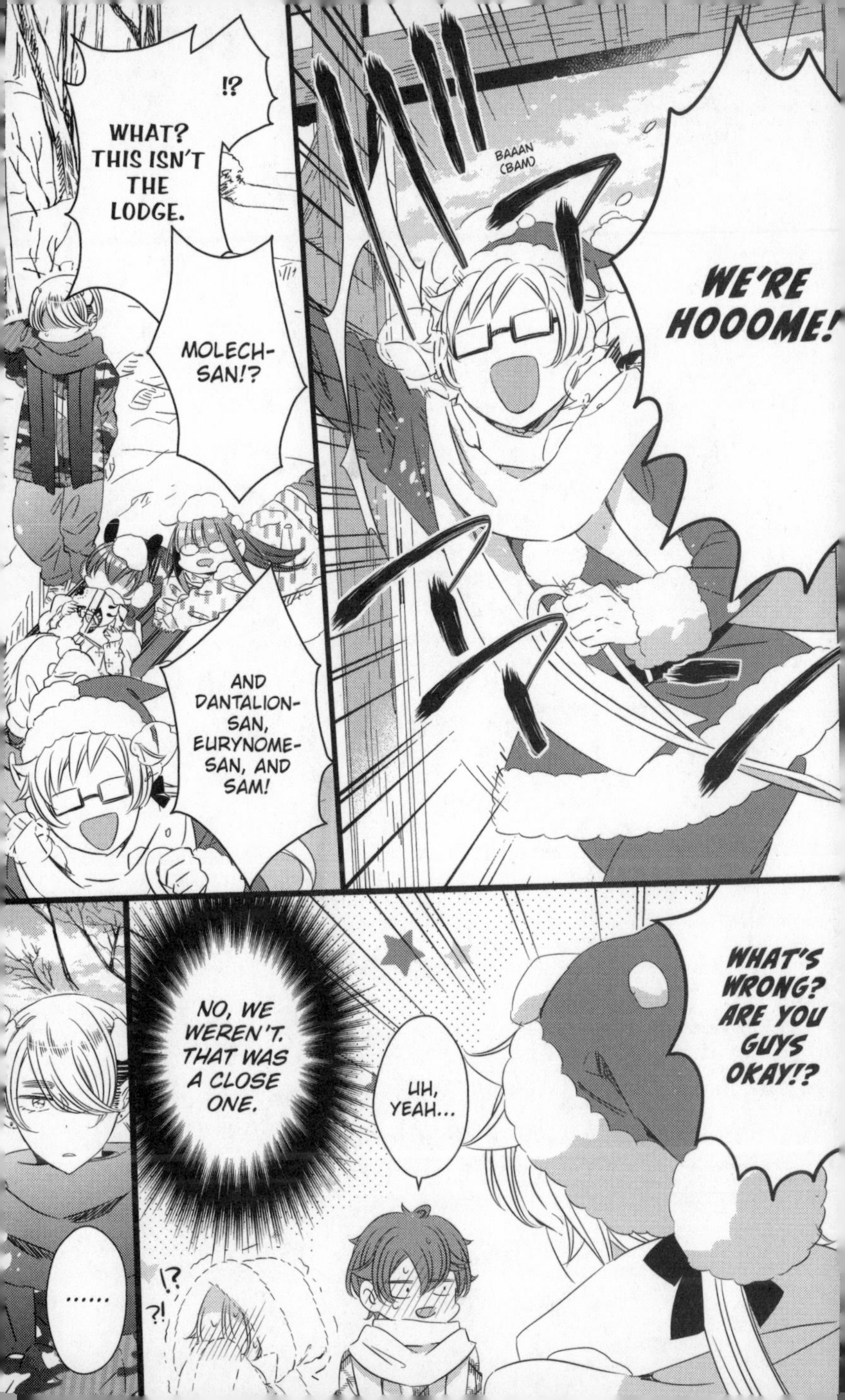
WE'RE HOOOME!
BAAAN (BAM)
!?
WHAT? THIS ISN'T THE LODGE.
MOLECH-SAN!?
AND DANTALION-SAN, EURYNOME-SAN, AND SAM!
WHAT'S WRONG? ARE YOU GUYS OKAY!?
UH, YEAH...
NO, WE WEREN'T. THAT WAS A CLOSE ONE.
!?
?!
......

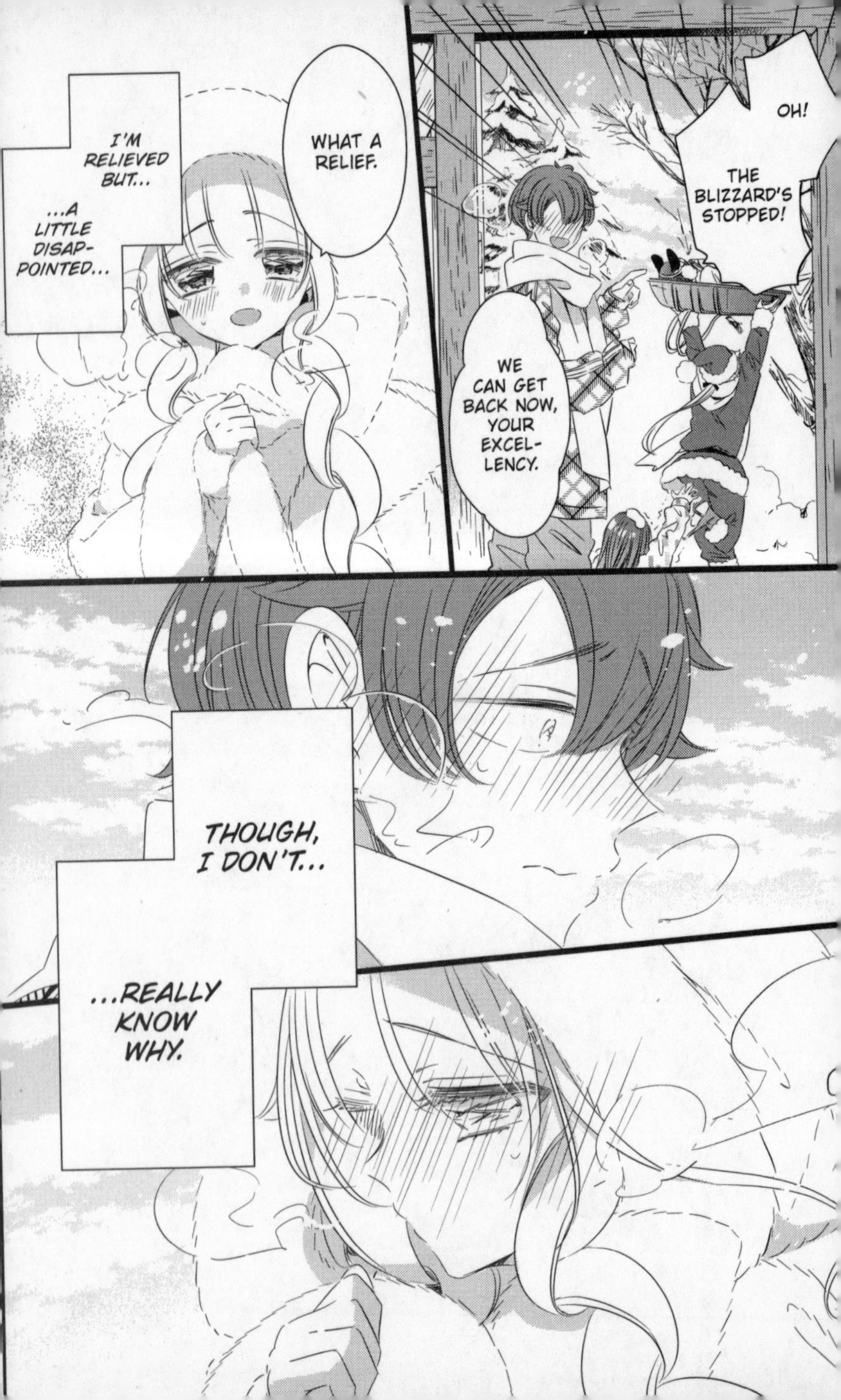
OH! THE BLIZZARD'S STOPPED!
WE CAN GET BACK NOW, YOUR EXCELLENCY.
WHAT A RELIEF.
I'M RELIEVED BUT...
...A LITTLE DISAPPOINTED...
THOUGH, I DON'T...
...REALLY KNOW WHY.

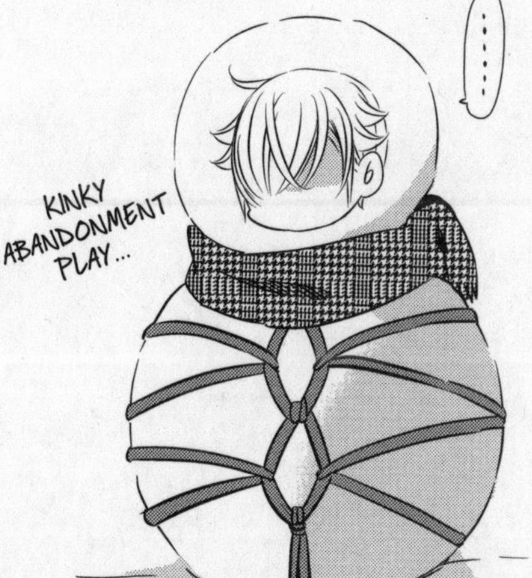
......
KINKY ABANDONMENT PLAY...

As Miss Beelzebub Likes

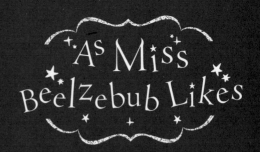

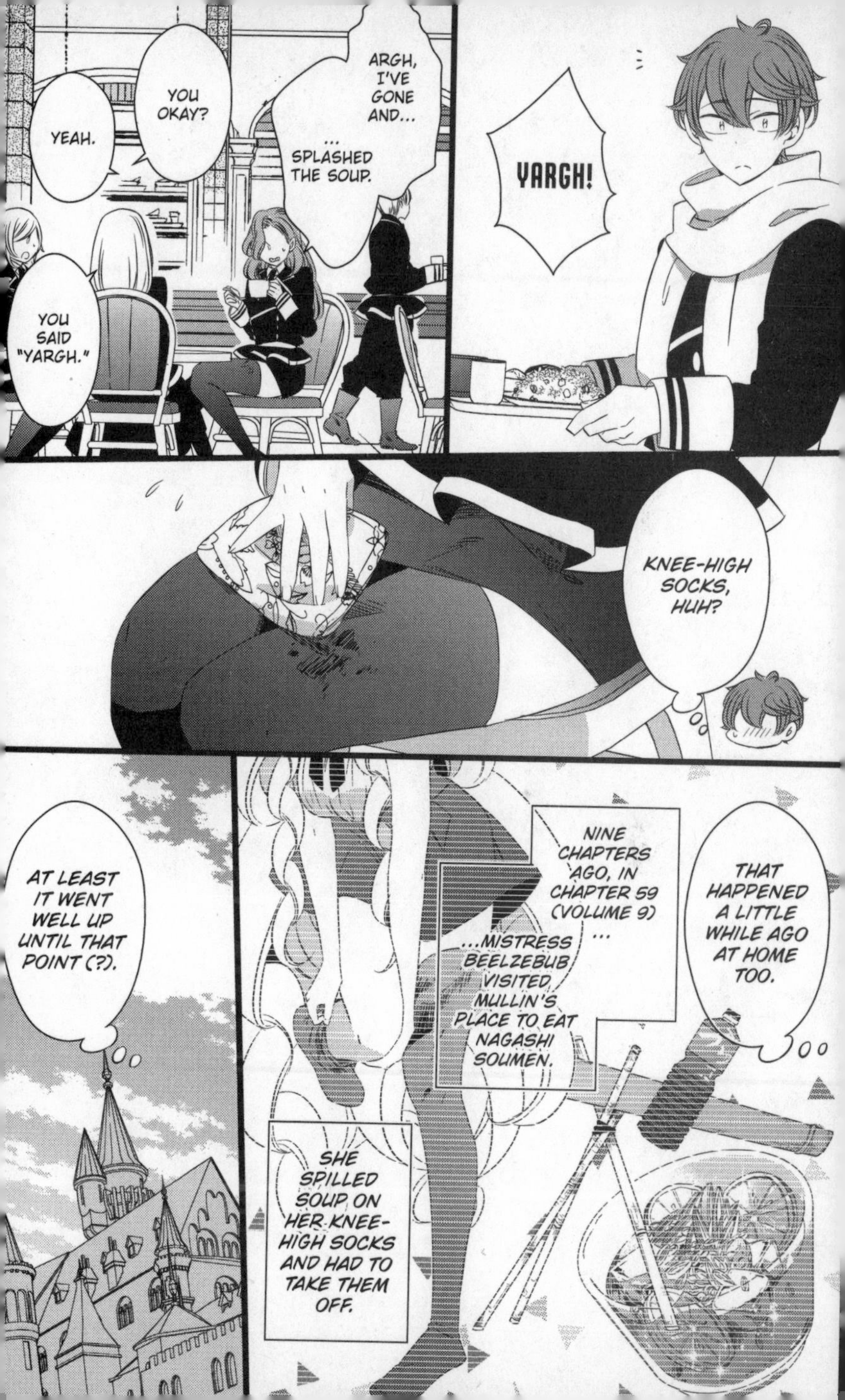
YARGH!
ARGH, I'VE GONE AND... ...SPLASHED THE SOUP.
YOU OKAY?
YEAH.
YOU SAID "YARGH."
KNEE-HIGH SOCKS, HUH?
THAT HAPPENED A LITTLE WHILE AGO AT HOME TOO.
NINE CHAPTERS AGO, IN CHAPTER 59 (VOLUME 9) ...
...MISTRESS BEELZEBUB VISITED MULLIN'S PLACE TO EAT NAGASHI SOUMEN.
SHE SPILLED SOUP ON HER KNEE-HIGH SOCKS AND HAD TO TAKE THEM OFF.
AT LEAST IT WENT WELL UP UNTIL THAT POINT (?).

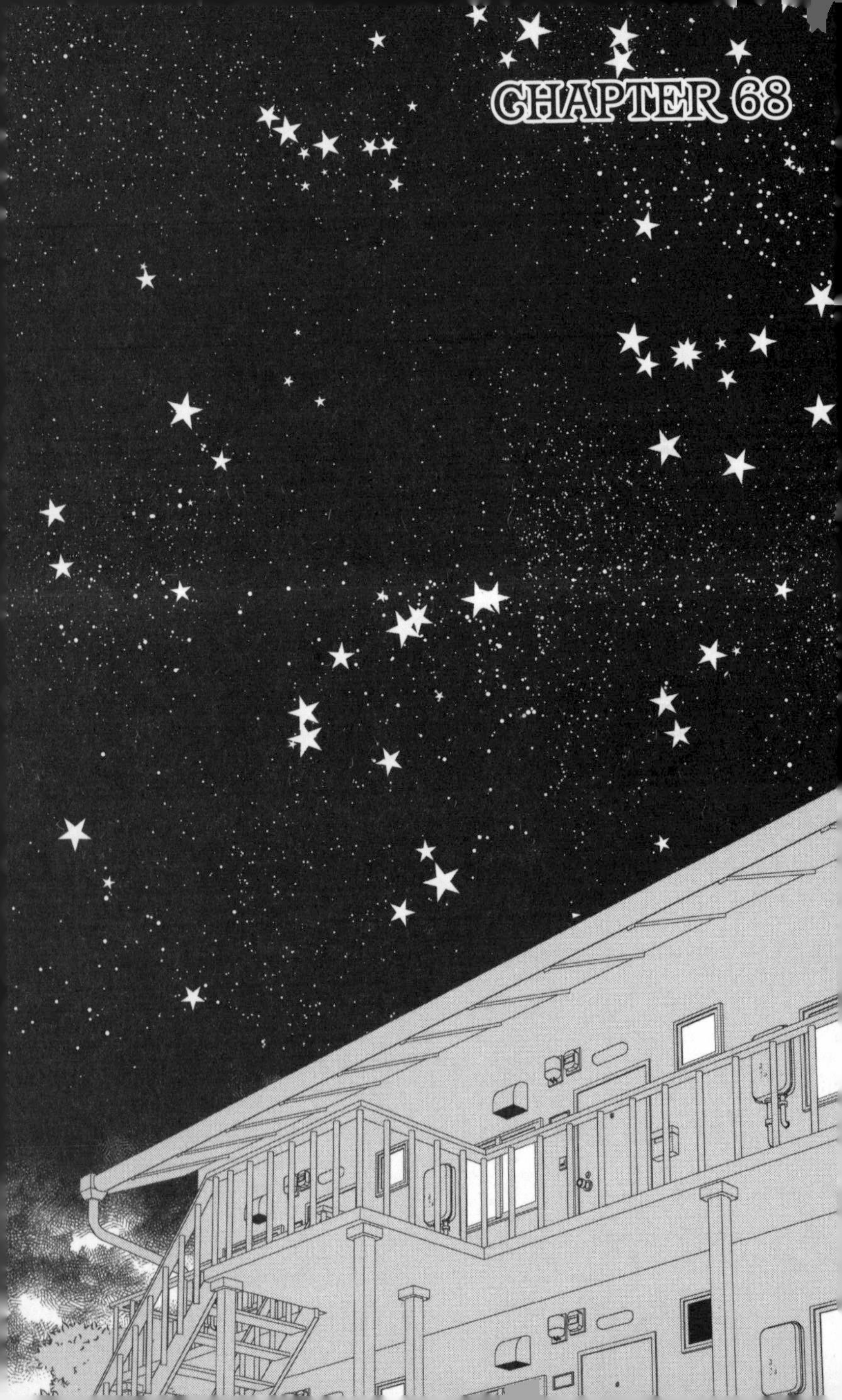
CHAPTER 68

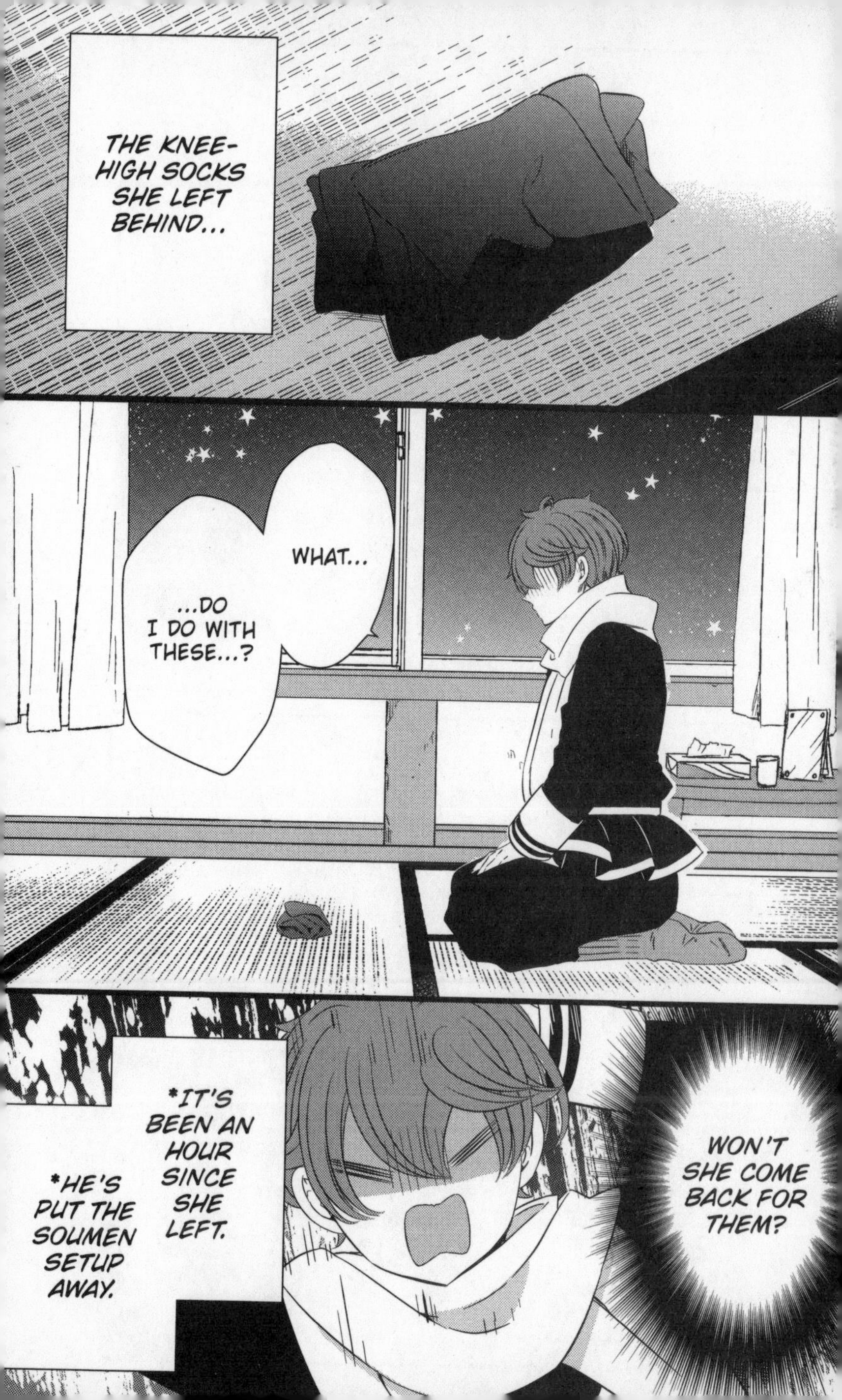
THE KNEE-HIGH SOCKS SHE LEFT BEHIND...
WHAT...
...DO I DO WITH THESE...?
WON'T SHE COME BACK FOR THEM?
*IT'S BEEN AN HOUR SINCE SHE LEFT.
*HE'S PUT THE SOUMEN SETUP AWAY.

IMPOUNDED PANTIES

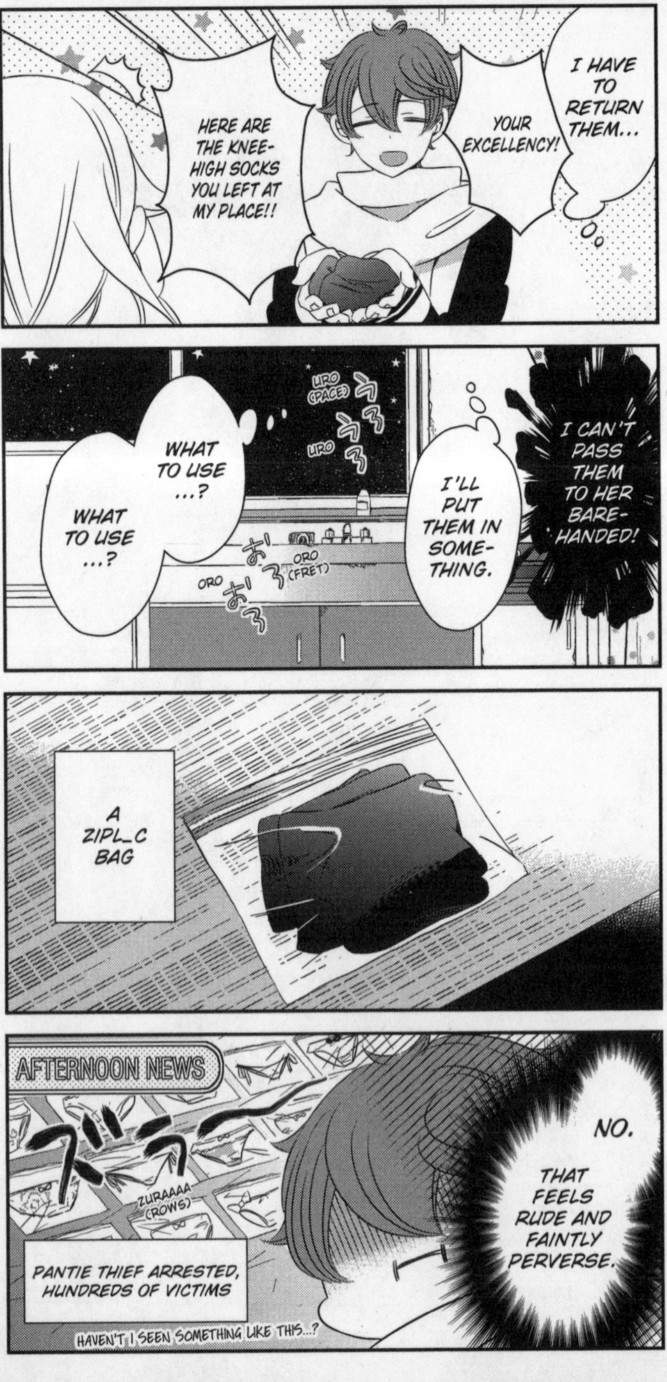
I HAVE TO RETURN THEM...
YOUR EXCELLENCY!
HERE ARE THE KNEE-HIGH SOCKS YOU LEFT AT MY PLACE!!
I CAN'T PASS THEM TO HER BARE-HANDED!
I'LL PUT THEM IN SOMETHING.
URO (PACE)
URO
WHAT TO USE ...?
WHAT TO USE ...?
ORO (FRET)
ORO
A ZIPL_C BAG
NO.
THAT FEELS RUDE AND FAINTLY PERVERSE.
AFTERNOON NEWS
ZURAAAA (ROWS)
PANTIE THIEF ARRESTED, HUNDREDS OF VICTIMS
HAVEN'T I SEEN SOMETHING LIKE THIS...?

MAKING A BAG

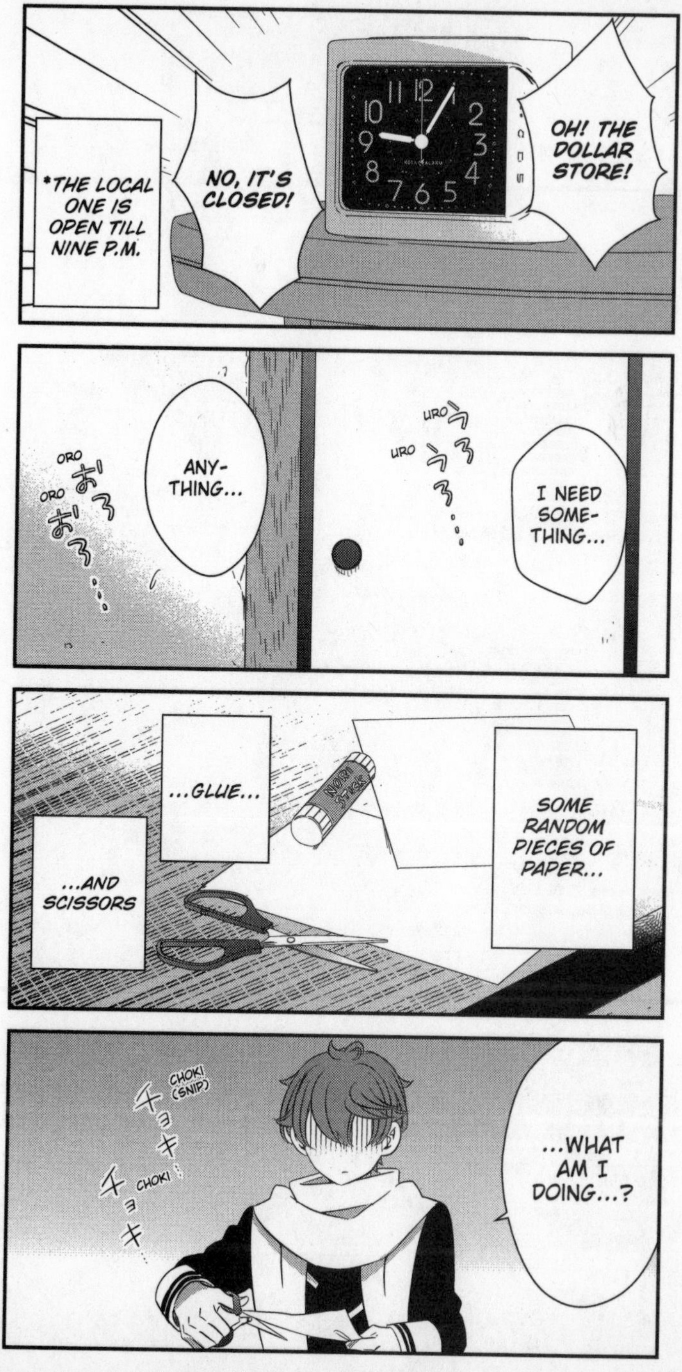
OH! THE DOLLAR STORE!
NO, IT'S CLOSED!
*THE LOCAL ONE IS OPEN TILL NINE P.M.
I NEED SOME-THING...
URO URO
うろうろ...
ANY-THING...
ORO ORO
おろおろ...
SOME RANDOM PIECES OF PAPER...
NORI STICK
...GLUE...
...AND SCISSORS
...WHAT AM I DOING...?
CHOKI (SNIP) CHOKI
チョキチョキ...

WORRYING

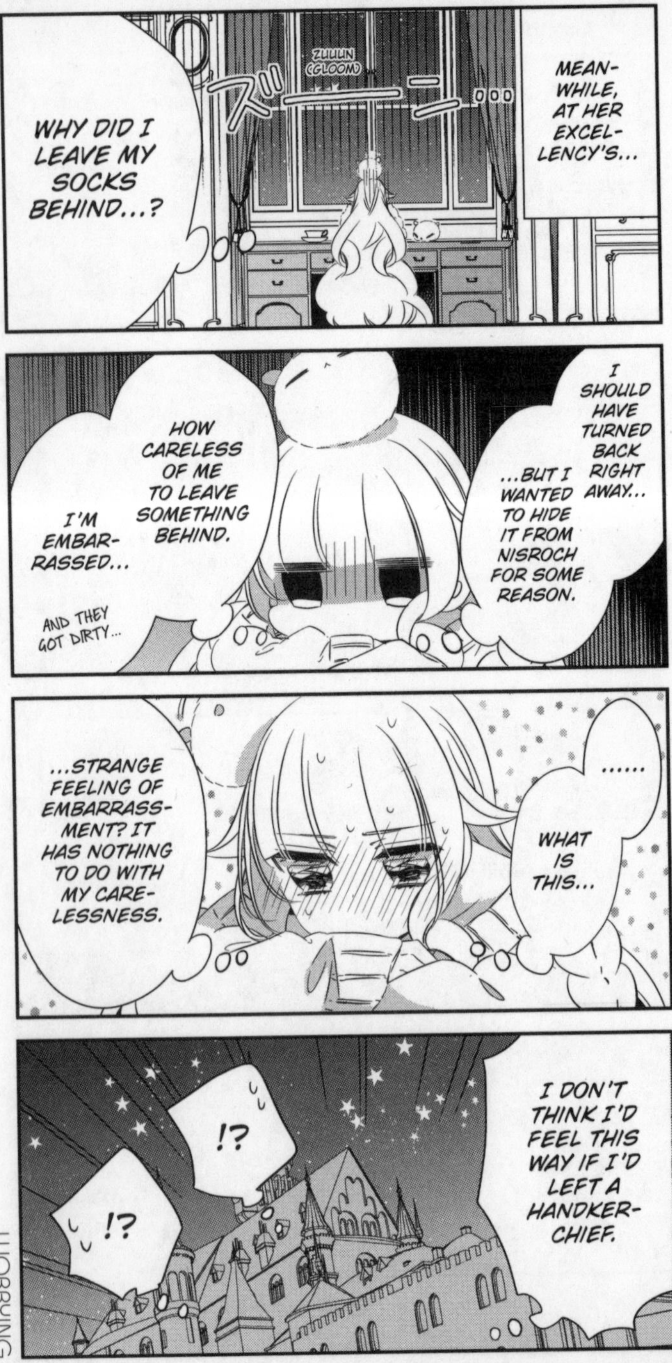
MEANWHILE, AT HER EXCELLENCY'S...
ZUUUN (GLOOM)
WHY DID I LEAVE MY SOCKS BEHIND...?
I SHOULD HAVE TURNED BACK RIGHT AWAY...
...BUT I WANTED TO HIDE IT FROM NISROCH FOR SOME REASON.
HOW CARELESS OF ME TO LEAVE SOMETHING BEHIND.
I'M EMBARRASSED...
AND THEY GOT DIRTY...
......
WHAT IS THIS...
...STRANGE FEELING OF EMBARRASSMENT? IT HAS NOTHING TO DO WITH MY CARELESSNESS.
I DON'T THINK I'D FEEL THIS WAY IF I'D LEFT A HANDKERCHIEF.
!?
!?

NO HOME WASHING MACHINE

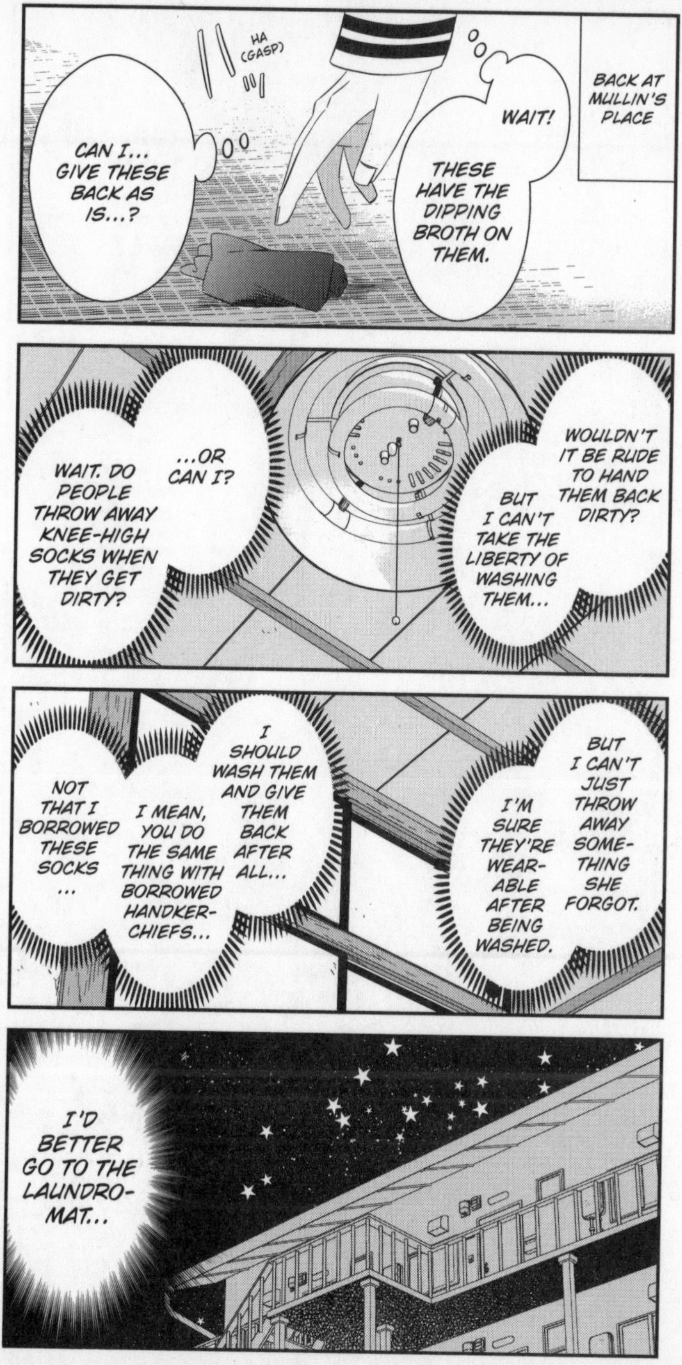
BACK AT MULLIN'S PLACE
WAIT!
THESE HAVE THE DIPPING BROTH ON THEM.
HA (GASP)
CAN I... GIVE THESE BACK AS IS...?
WOULDN'T IT BE RUDE TO HAND THEM BACK DIRTY?
BUT I CAN'T TAKE THE LIBERTY OF WASHING THEM...
...OR CAN I?
WAIT. DO PEOPLE THROW AWAY KNEE-HIGH SOCKS WHEN THEY GET DIRTY?
BUT I CAN'T JUST THROW AWAY SOME-THING SHE FORGOT.
I'M SURE THEY'RE WEAR-ABLE AFTER BEING WASHED.
I SHOULD WASH THEM AND GIVE THEM BACK AFTER ALL...
I MEAN, YOU DO THE SAME THING WITH BORROWED HANDKER-CHIEFS...
NOT THAT I BORROWED THESE SOCKS...
I'D BETTER GO TO THE LAUNDRO-MAT...

IN THE BATHROOM

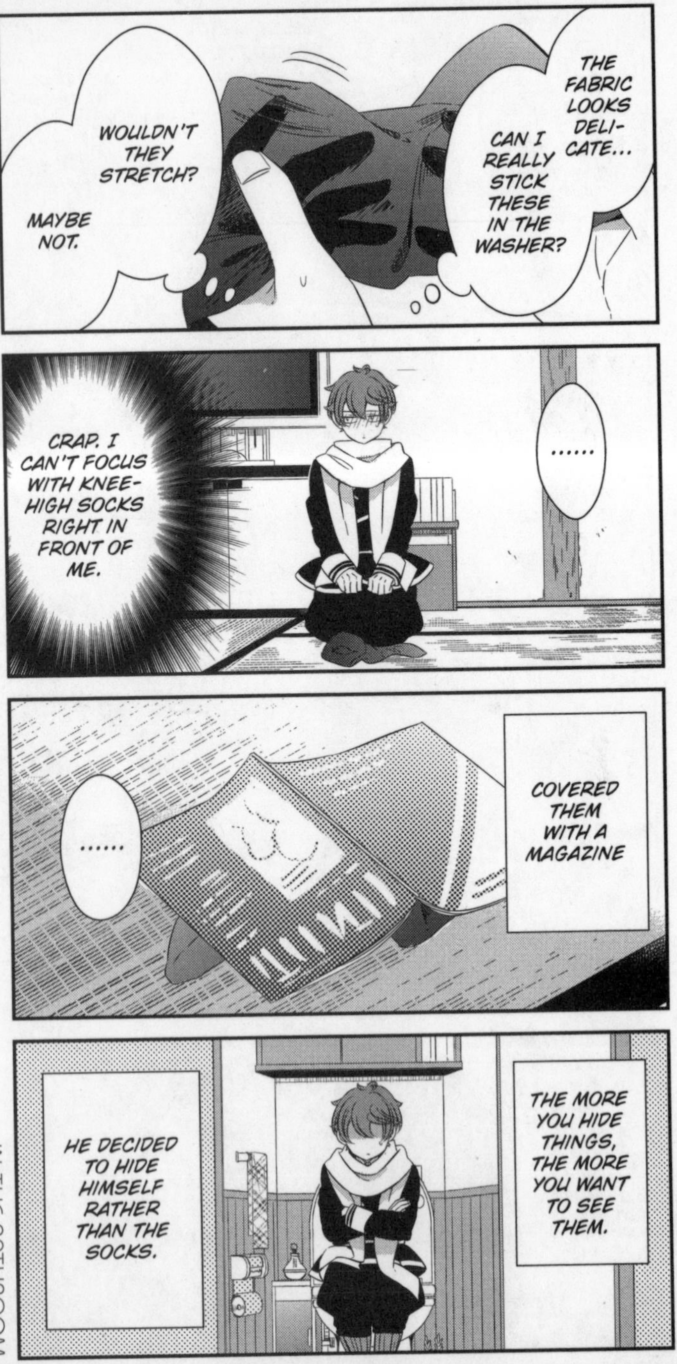
THE FABRIC LOOKS DELI-CATE...
CAN I REALLY STICK THESE IN THE WASHER?
WOULDN'T THEY STRETCH?
MAYBE NOT.
......
CRAP. I CAN'T FOCUS WITH KNEE-HIGH SOCKS RIGHT IN FRONT OF ME.
COVERED THEM WITH A MAGAZINE
......
THE MORE YOU HIDE THINGS, THE MORE YOU WANT TO SEE THEM.
HE DECIDED TO HIDE HIMSELF RATHER THAN THE SOCKS.

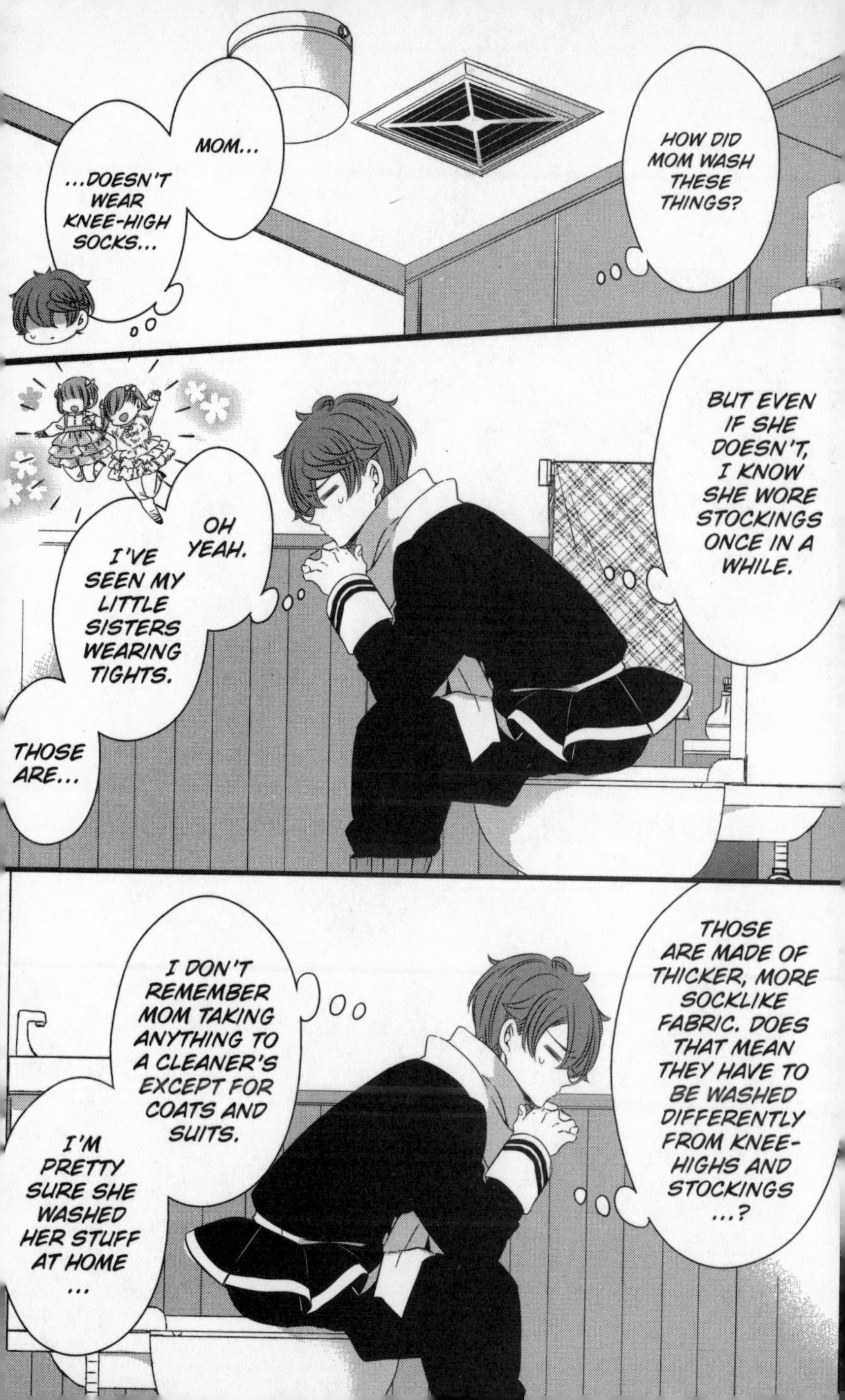
HOW DID MOM WASH THESE THINGS?
MOM... ...DOESN'T WEAR KNEE-HIGH SOCKS...
BUT EVEN IF SHE DOESN'T, I KNOW SHE WORE STOCKINGS ONCE IN A WHILE.
OH YEAH. I'VE SEEN MY LITTLE SISTERS WEARING TIGHTS.
THOSE ARE...
THOSE ARE MADE OF THICKER, MORE SOCKLIKE FABRIC. DOES THAT MEAN THEY HAVE TO BE WASHED DIFFERENTLY FROM KNEE-HIGHS AND STOCKINGS ...?
I DON'T REMEMBER MOM TAKING ANYTHING TO A CLEANER'S EXCEPT FOR COATS AND SUITS.
I'M PRETTY SURE SHE WASHED HER STUFF AT HOME ...

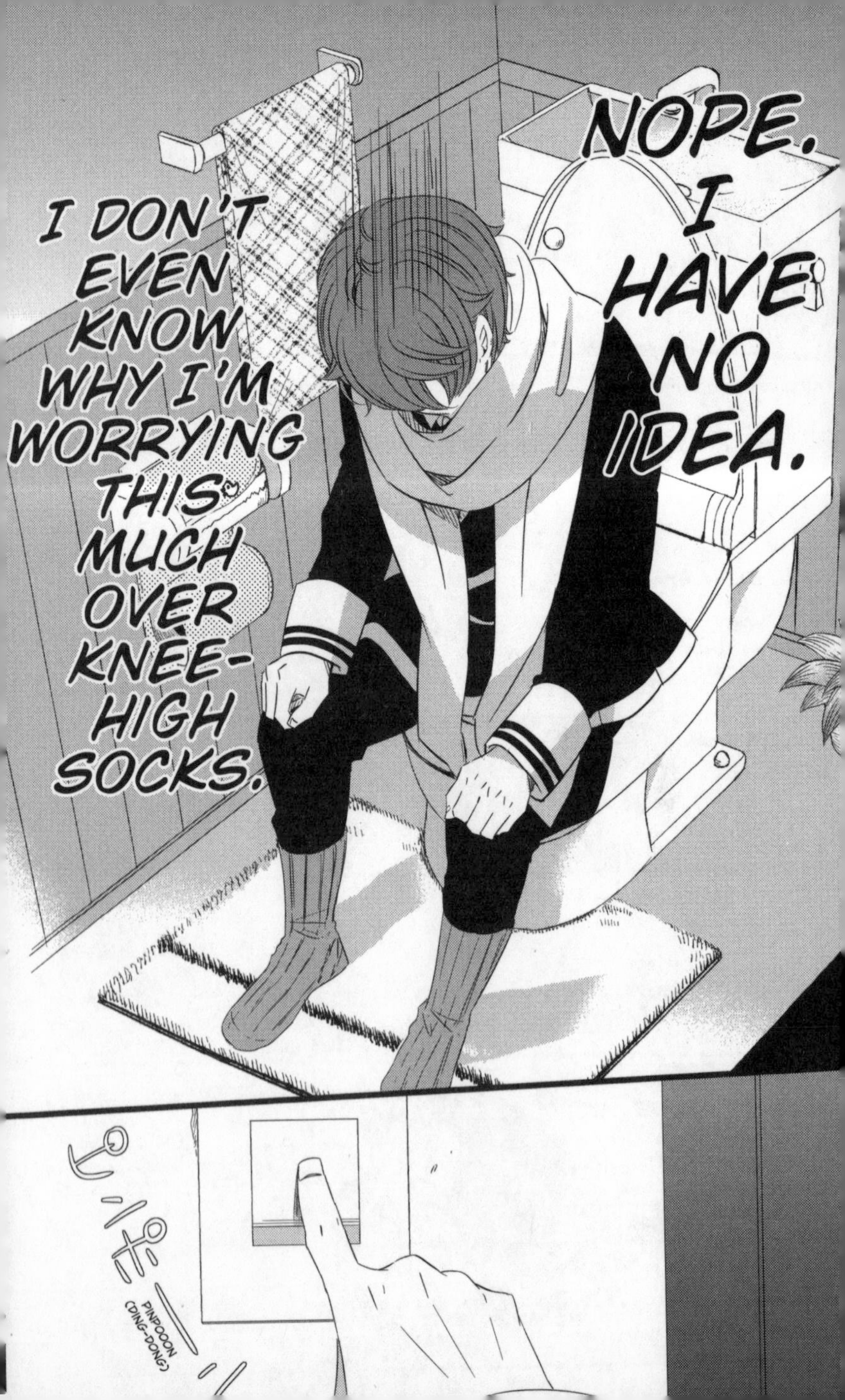
NOPE. I HAVE NO IDEA.
I DON'T EVEN KNOW WHY I'M WORRYING THIS MUCH OVER KNEE-HIGH SOCKS.
PINPOOON (DING-DONG)

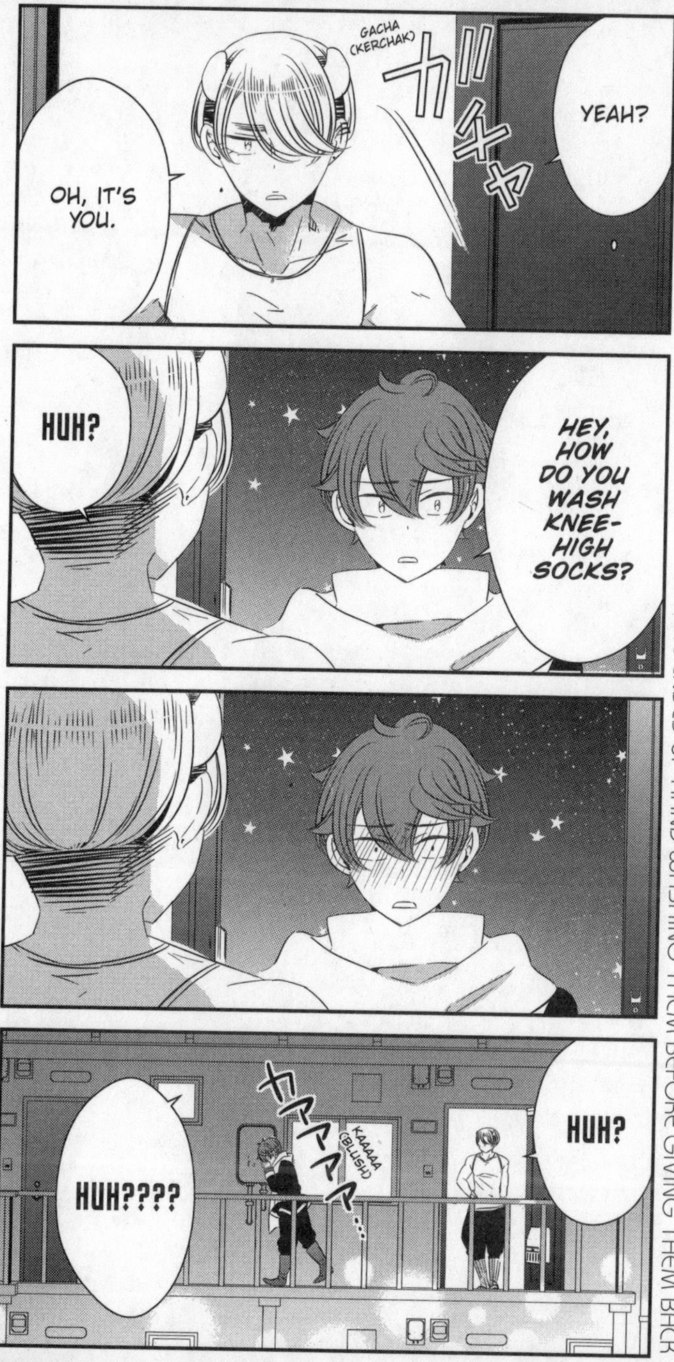
YEAH?
GACHA (KERCHAK)
OH, IT'S YOU.
HEY, HOW DO YOU WASH KNEE-HIGH SOCKS?
HUH?
HUH?
KAAAAA (BLUSH)
HUH????

HE ENDED UP HAND-WASHING THEM BEFORE GIVING THEM BACK

AS MISS BEELZEBUB LIKES VOLUME 10 END

As Miss Beelzebub Likes

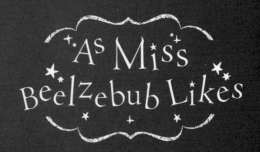

SOFT AND FLUFFY TO THE VERY END...A DEMONIC BONUS MANGA

ANSWER ME, MULLIN-KUN!

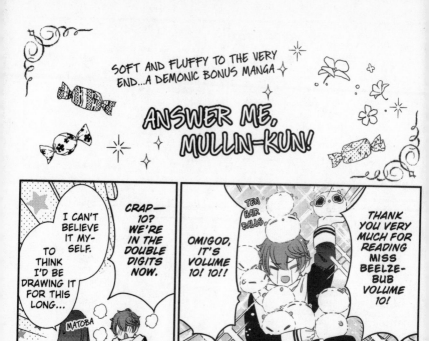

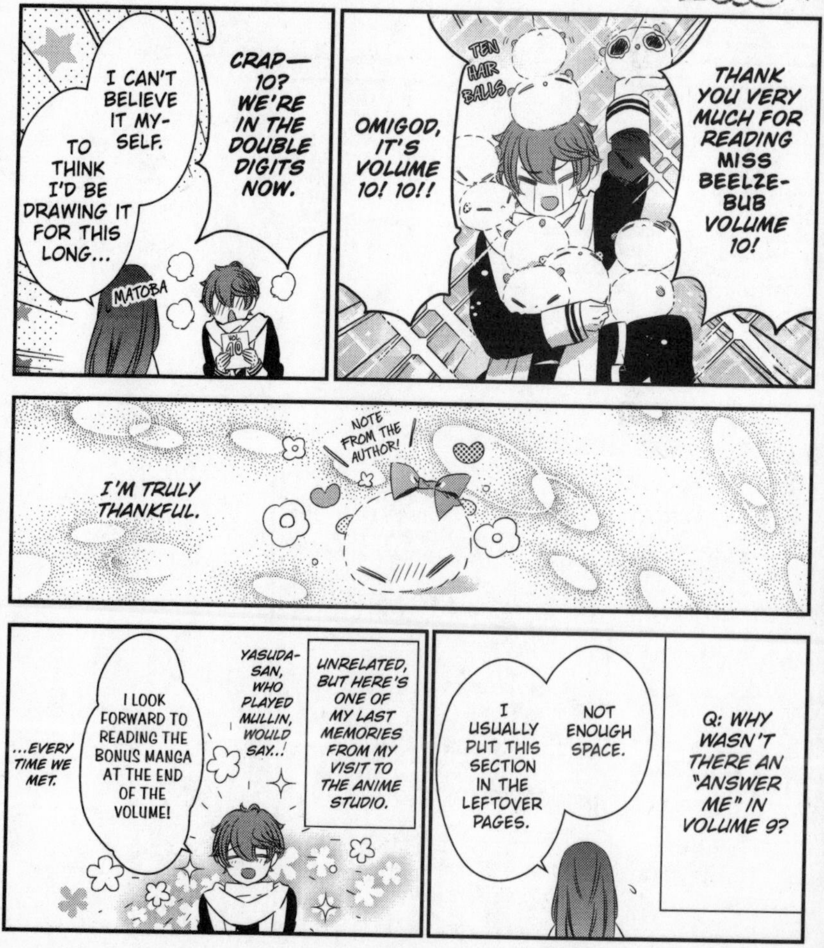
THANK YOU VERY MUCH FOR READING MISS BEELZEBUB VOLUME 10!
TEN HAIR BALLS
OMIGOD, IT'S VOLUME 10! 10!!
CRAP— 10? WE'RE IN THE DOUBLE DIGITS NOW.
I CAN'T BELIEVE IT MYSELF.
TO THINK I'D BE DRAWING IT FOR THIS LONG...
MATOBA
VOL 10
NOTE FROM THE AUTHOR!
I'M TRULY THANKFUL.
Q: WHY WASN'T THERE AN "ANSWER ME" IN VOLUME 9?
NOT ENOUGH SPACE.
I USUALLY PUT THIS SECTION IN THE LEFTOVER PAGES.
UNRELATED, BUT HERE'S ONE OF MY LAST MEMORIES FROM MY VISIT TO THE ANIME STUDIO.
YASUDA-SAN, WHO PLAYED MULLIN, WOULD SAY...!
I LOOK FORWARD TO READING THE BONUS MANGA AT THE END OF THE VOLUME!
...EVERY TIME WE MET.

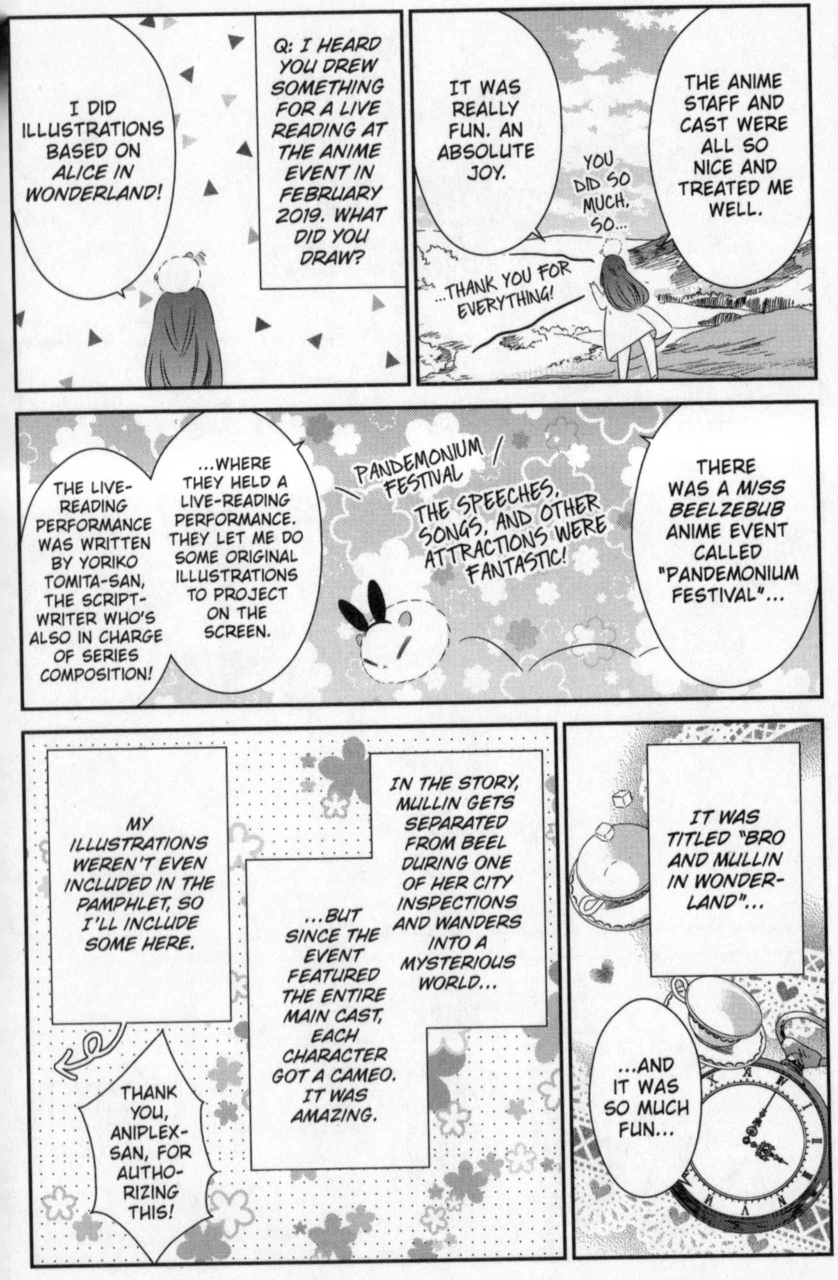
THE ANIME STAFF AND CAST WERE ALL SO NICE AND TREATED ME WELL.
IT WAS REALLY FUN. AN ABSOLUTE JOY.
YOU DID SO MUCH, SO...
...THANK YOU FOR EVERYTHING!
Q: I HEARD YOU DREW SOMETHING FOR A LIVE READING AT THE ANIME EVENT IN FEBRUARY 2019. WHAT DID YOU DRAW?
I DID ILLUSTRATIONS BASED ON *ALICE IN WONDERLAND*!
THERE WAS A *MISS BEELZEBUB* ANIME EVENT CALLED "PANDEMONIUM FESTIVAL"...
PANDEMONIUM FESTIVAL
THE SPEECHES, SONGS, AND OTHER ATTRACTIONS WERE FANTASTIC!
...WHERE THEY HELD A LIVE-READING PERFORMANCE. THEY LET ME DO SOME ORIGINAL ILLUSTRATIONS TO PROJECT ON THE SCREEN.
THE LIVE-READING PERFORMANCE WAS WRITTEN BY YORIKO TOMITA-SAN, THE SCRIPT-WRITER WHO'S ALSO IN CHARGE OF SERIES COMPOSITION!
IT WAS TITLED "BRO AND MULLIN IN WONDER-LAND"...
...AND IT WAS SO MUCH FUN...
IN THE STORY, MULLIN GETS SEPARATED FROM BEEL DURING ONE OF HER CITY INSPECTIONS AND WANDERS INTO A MYSTERIOUS WORLD...
...BUT SINCE THE EVENT FEATURED THE ENTIRE MAIN CAST, EACH CHARACTER GOT A CAMEO. IT WAS AMAZING.
MY ILLUSTRATIONS WEREN'T EVEN INCLUDED IN THE PAMPHLET, SO I'LL INCLUDE SOME HERE.
THANK YOU, ANIPLEX-SAN, FOR AUTHO-RIZING THIS!

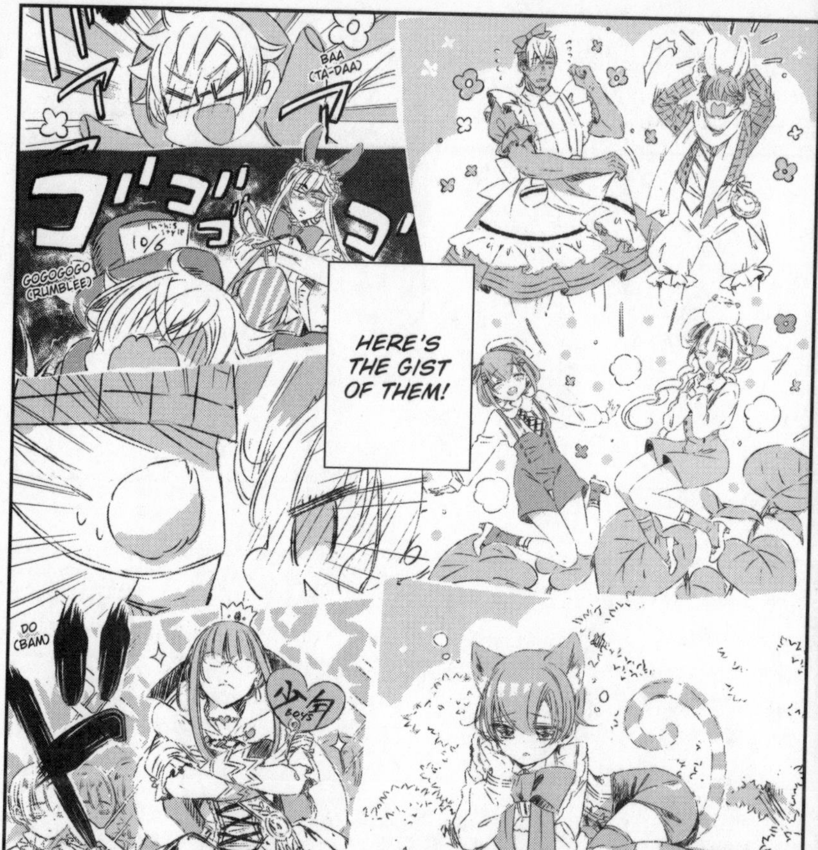
BAA (TA-DAA)
GOGOGOGO (RUMBLEE)
10/6
HERE'S THE GIST OF THEM!
DO (BAM)
BOYS

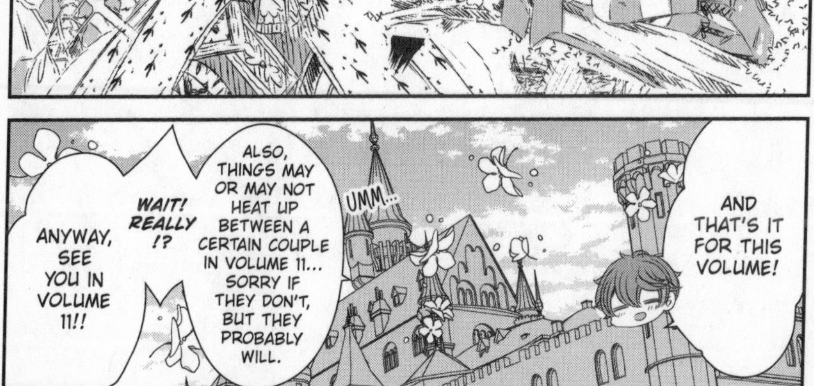
AND THAT'S IT FOR THIS VOLUME!
UMM...
ALSO, THINGS MAY OR MAY NOT HEAT UP BETWEEN A CERTAIN COUPLE IN VOLUME 11... SORRY IF THEY DON'T, BUT THEY PROBABLY WILL.
WAIT! REALLY!?
ANYWAY, SEE YOU IN VOLUME 11!!

A SNEAK PEEK INTO VOLUME 11 ☆

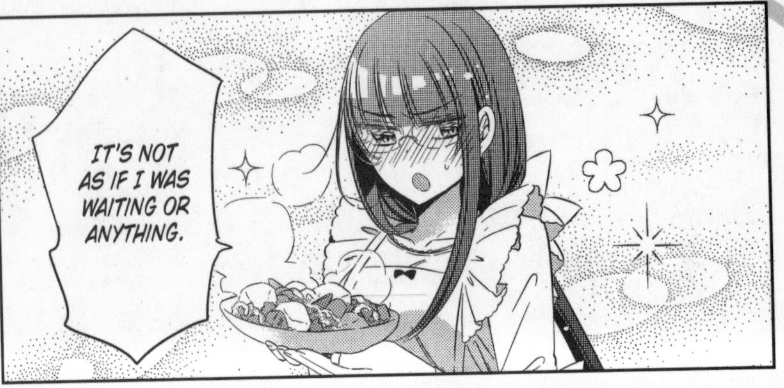
IT'S NOT AS IF I WAS WAITING OR ANYTHING.

Samyaza, a man who can cook.
What will tonight's side dish be?

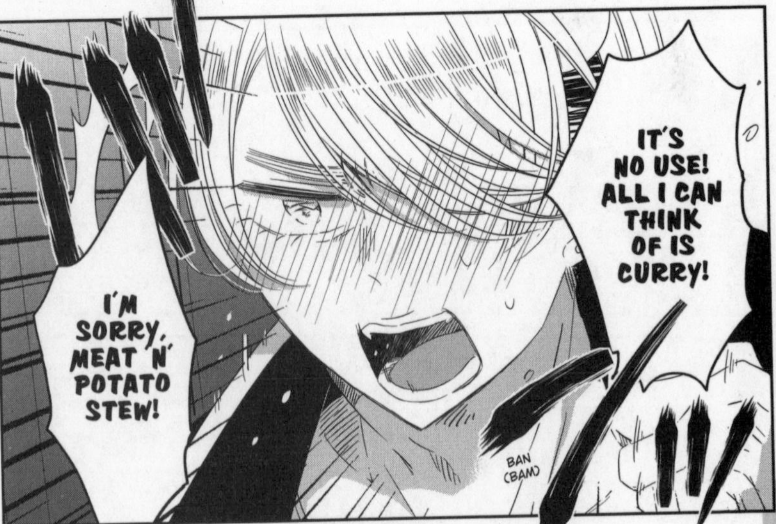
IT'S NO USE! ALL I CAN THINK OF IS CURRY!
I'M SORRY, MEAT 'N' POTATO STEW!
BAN (BAM)

SET FOR FALL 2020!!

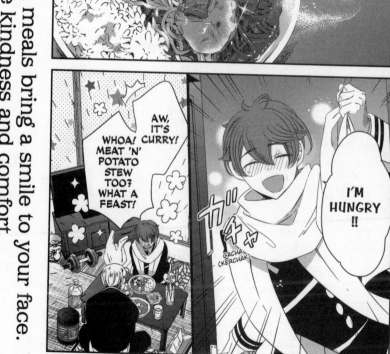

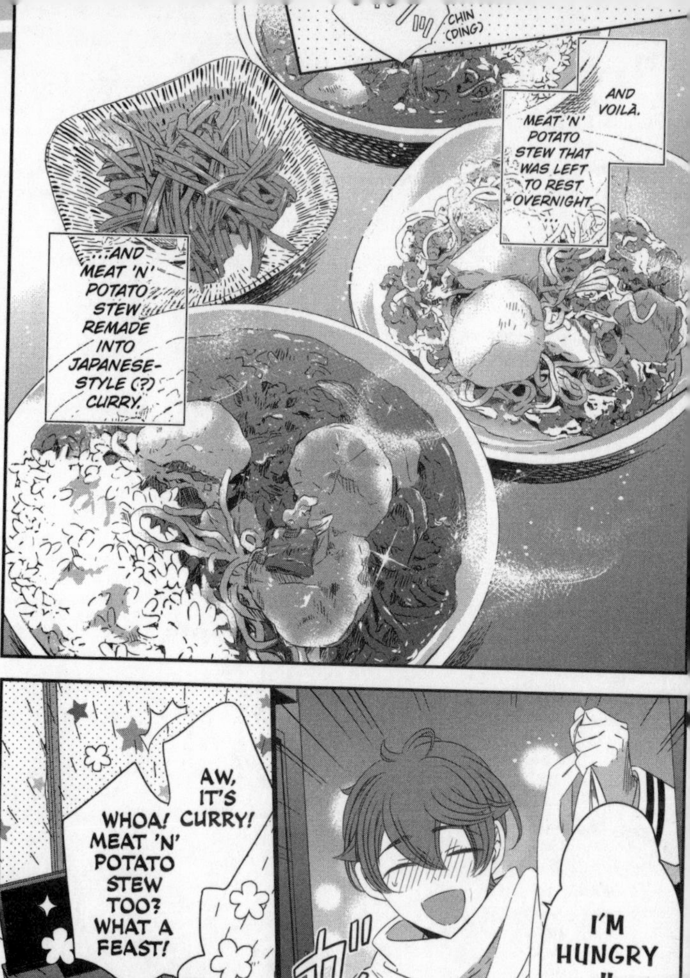
CHIN (DING)
AND VOILÀ.
MEAT 'N' POTATO STEW THAT WAS LEFT TO REST OVERNIGHT...
...AND MEAT 'N' POTATO STEW REMADE INTO JAPANESE-STYLE (?) CURRY.
I'M HUNGRY!!
GACHA (KERCHAK)
AW, IT'S CURRY!
WHOA! MEAT 'N' POTATO STEW TOO? WHAT A FEAST!

Home-cooked meals bring a smile to your face.
It must be the kindness and comfort...

AS MISS BEELZEBUB LIKES VOL. 11

Translation Notes

COMMON HONORIFICS

no honorific: Indicates familiarity or closeness; if used without permission or reason, addressing someone in this manner would constitute an insult.

-san: The Japanese equivalent of Mr./Mrs./Miss. If a situation calls for politeness, this is the fail-safe honorific.

-sama: Conveys great respect; may also indicate that the social status of the speaker is lower than that of the addressee.

-shi: An impersonal honorific used in formal speech or writing, e.g. legal documents.

-dono: Roughly equivalent to "master" or "milord."

-kun: Used most often when referring to boys, this indicates affection or familiarity. Occasionally used by older men among their peers, but it may also be used by anyone referring to a person of lower standing.

-chan: An affectionate honorific indicating familiarity used mostly in reference to girls; also used in reference to cute persons or animals of either gender.

-tan: A cutesy version of *-chan*.

-(o)nii/(o)nee: Meaning "big brother"/"big sister," it can also refer to those older but relatively close in age to the speaker. It is typically followed by *-san*, *-chan*, or *-sama*.

-senpai: An honorific for one's senior classmate, colleague, etc., although not as senior or respected as a *sensei* ("teacher").

100 yen = approximately 1 USD.

PAGE 19
"I mustn't run away...I mustn't run away...!" is a famous quote from Shinji Ikari, the main character of the anime *Neon Genesis Evangelion*, used when he tries to convince himself not to follow his cowardly instincts.

PAGE 20
Fist of the N___h Star is the action manga *Fist of the North Star*. Its hero, Kenshiro, has a characteristic rapid-fire yell when he fights. In Japanese, Belphegor is trying to say the word *watashimasu* ("hand over"), but her stuttering turns it into "watatatatatatatatata."

PAGE 32
The word **"Grigori,"** as it appears on the banner, is written using Japanese *kanji*. However, while *kanji* are generally used such that the specific characters have inherent meaning, in this case, they're purely phonetic (*Gu-Ri-Go-Ri*) and don't really make sense together (literally "Foolish-Advantage-Protection-Advantage"). Azazel and Samyaza are both part of the Grigori Corps.

PAGE 33
Ya__uza is *yakuza*—the Japanese mafia. The word is often censored in Japanese entertainment or at least replaced with alternative terms or euphemisms, so that decision is replicated here. Even the original Japanese term for **"Japanese mob movie,"** *ninkyou eiga* ("chivalrous movie"), is based on the *yakuza's* own euphemism for themselves: *ninkyou dantai*, or "chivalrous organization."

PAGE 34
Oden is a Japanese pot dish consisting of soy-flavored broth and various ingredients such as *daikon* radish, *konjak*, fish cakes, and boiled eggs.

PAGE 35
The use of **soak** and **soaked** was originally a wordplay joke based on the word *shimiru*. It can mean both "That hit the spot!" (Mullin's intent) and "to soak up" (Samyaza's intent).

In Japan, **convenience stores** typically sell *oden* by the front counter, where you can pick and choose your ingredients. Convenience-store *oden* may also come with sachets of **miso sauce** (fermented soybean paste) for flavoring. *Shirataki* are translucent noodles made from the konjac yam.

F__ilyMart and **7-El__en** are FamilyMart and 7-Eleven, two nationwide convenience stores found in Japan. While 7-Eleven was first established in the United States, it's so successful in Japan, the country has more of the stores than any other country in the world.

PAGE 36

While bathing is practiced the world over, being able to take piping hot baths is practically a cultural institution in Japan. However, they are primarily used for relaxation, and bathers are supposed to wash themselves off beforehand to keep the bathwater clean.

PAGE 43

UnderworldWalker is a reference to *TokyoWalker*, a magazine that contains information about events and other goings-on in the city.

PAGE 54

Signature Confection Miyoko is a parody of Tokyo Hiyoko, a brand of chick-shaped sweet buns that is commonly bought as souvenirs by those traveling back from Tokyo.

PAGE 73

Adding *o* as a prefix to certain words in Japanese conveys a sense of reverence or respect. *Osashimi* basically means "honored sliced raw fish," though, in the context of the **Osashimi-chan** shirt, it's just a cutesy naming motif.

PAGE 80

Daifuku is a ball of *mochi* (pounded rice) with filling.

PAGE 88

"Out of the Azure" in Japanese was "*Yabu kara* Stick," a reference to the idiom *yabu kara bou ni*—literally "a stick coming out from a bush" but meaning "out of the blue."

PAGE 108

-Kyun is a cutesy mangling of the honorific *-kun*.

PAGE 117

In Japanese, **"okay"** and **"tough"** are very similar-sounding words with common origins: *daijoubu* and *joubu*.

PAGE 127

Soumen is a type of thin wheat-flour noodle. **Nagashi soumen** is served by sending the noodles in icy water down a bamboo chute.

PAGE 142

Meat 'n' potato stew (translated in previous volumes as "Japanese meat 'n' potatoes") is *nikujaga*, a Japanese take on Western-style beef stew that also incorporates onion stewed in soy sauce.

As Miss Beelzebub Likes

matoba

volume 10

Translation: Lisa Coffman
Lettering: Lorina Mapa

BEELZEBUB-JO NO OKINIMESU MAMA. Vol. 10
©2019 matoba/SQUARE ENIX CO., LTD.
First published in Japan in 2019 by SQUARE ENIX CO., LTD. English translation rights arranged with SQUARE ENIX CO., LTD. and Yen Press, LLC through Tuttle-Mori Agency, Inc., Tokyo.

English translation ©2020 by SQUARE ENIX CO., LTD.

Yen Press
150 West 30th Street, 19th Floor
New York, NY 10001

Visit us at yenpress.com
facebook.com/yenpress
twitter.com/yenpress
★ yenpress.tumblr.com
instagram.com/yenpress

First Yen Press Edition: August 2020

Yen Press is an imprint of Yen Press, LLC.
The Yen Press name and logo are trademarks of Yen Press, LLC.

The publisher is not responsible for websites (or their content) that are not owned by the publisher.

Library of Congress Control Number: 2017963582

ISBNs: 978-1-9753-0931-2 (paperback)
978-1-9753-0930-5 (ebook)

10 9 8 7 6 5 4 3 2 1